Resumes
for the
Rest of Us

Secrets From the Pros for Job Seekers
With Unconventional Career Paths

Arnold Boldt

CAREER
PRESS

Franklin Lakes, NJ

RESUMES FOR THE REST OF US
EDITED BY KIRSTEN DALLEY
TYPESET BY MICHAEL FITZGIBBON
Cover design by Design Concept
Printed in the U.S.A. by Book-mart Press

To order this title, please call toll-free 1-800-CAREER-1 (NJ and Canada: 201-848-0310) to order using VISA or MasterCard, or for further information on books from Career Press.

The Career Press, Inc., 3 Tice Road, PO Box 687,
Franklin Lakes, NJ 07417
www.careerpress.com

Library of Congress Cataloging-in-Publication Data
Boldt, Arnold G.
    Resumes for the rest of us : secrets from the pros for job seekers with unconventional career paths / by Arnold Boldt.
        p. cm.
    Includes index.
    ISBN-13: 978-1-56414-983-1
    ISBN-10: 1-56414-983-8
        1. Resumes (Employment) 2. Job hunting. I. Title

HF5383.B54 2008
658.14′2—dc22

2007041477

Dedication

To my late mother, who encouraged me to believe in my dreams;
to my father, who taught me the value of hard work;
and to my wife and muse, who inspires me to be creative and challenges me to
pursue excellence in all my endeavors.

Acknowledgments

In February of 2007, Career Press contacted me with an idea that one of their editors, Kirsten Dalley, had suggested for a new book: "What about a resume book for the rest of us—a book that covers resume writing for people with unconventional career paths?" Of course, as you saw when you picked up this book, these two phrases almost instantly became the title and subtitle for the book. Thanks to Kirsten and to Senior Acquisitions Editor, Michael Pye, for presenting me with this concept.

During the fall of 2005, Wendy Enelow, an esteemed colleague and careers industry leader, called me and asked if I'd be interested in collaborating with her on two new titles, *No-Nonsense Resumes* and *No-Nonsense Cover Letters*. Considering that Wendy has authored more than 20 books on job-search topics, I couldn't ask for a better mentor and coach as I embarked on my first endeavor as an author. Both of these titles are currently available from Career Press. Thanks to Wendy for setting me on the path to becoming a published author.

In 1998, David Noble, PhD, a noted author and editor, was seeking sample resumes for a new book, *Professional Resumes for Tax and Accounting Professionals*. New to the business, I was apprehensive about submitting my work, but finally decided to send in everything I could pull together. Months later, I was astonished when the book was released and a total of 12 examples of my work had been included. Similarly, a few years later, best-selling author Martin Yate was kind enough to include some of my sample resumes and letters in his acclaimed *Knock 'em Dead* series. This led to further contributions to more than 30 books and helped build my reputation as a careers professional. Thanks to Martin and Dr. Noble for validating the quality of my work.

Without these business relationships and this series of events spread over the past 14 years, I doubt that I would be where I am today or that this book would be a reality.

On a more personal note, I would be remiss if I didn't publicly thank Norma R. Smith, my assistant, who has proofread manuscripts for this and other books I have written before they were sent off to the publisher. Without her devotion and diligence, this work would not be possible. My wife and business partner, Gail Smith Boldt, has also been an essential part of creating this book, functioning as a sounding board for ideas and my own advance copy editor, reviewing and suggesting changes to the manuscript while it was still a work in progress.

And, of course, I must acknowledge the efforts of the Career Press staff. Much work has gone into creating this book, and, as the author, I have relied upon the expertise of these dedicated professionals for such critical aspects as cover design, formatting, and final editing. Without them, you would not have the book you are holding in your hands.

Lastly, special thanks to the 47 colleagues who contributed more than 100 examples of their work to this book. Some are seasoned veterans, and some are newcomers to the careers field, but their diverse approaches enhance this work, and their dedication to helping job seekers achieve career success makes them a tremendous asset to our industry. They are listed by name in Appendix C at the end of this volume.

Contents

Introduction

On a cold and snowy February day in 1994, my manager at a company at which I had worked for nine years invited me into his office to explain that they were making some "organizational changes" and that my job had been eliminated. This shocking news sent me on a journey that has become all too familiar to many workers in the United States during the past 15 years or so. Through much self-examination, research, and consultation with trusted confidants, and with the help of my loving and devoted spouse, I founded a business offering resume services to job seekers who found themselves in circumstances similar to those I had experienced. This also put me on a new career path that can only be described as unconventional, giving me even more in common with the job seekers this book is written for.

There are mountains of resume books that focus on traditional careers and conventional career paths, including at least one other which I authored with an esteemed colleague. But the reality of today's job market is that fewer people than ever before have what anyone would call a traditional or conventional career path. The average worker changes jobs every two or three years, and will have three or more distinctly different careers during his or her working life. These may include stints as an entrepreneur or business owner, detours into different industries or job functions, or truly unusual jobs. As an "unconventional" who is married to another "unconventional," I can relate to many of the issues such job candidates face when they sit down to write a resume.

This book tackles these resume-writing challenges, breaking down what may, at first, seem like insurmountable obstacles into manageable steps. Chapters 1 through 3

discuss the fundamentals of organizing your personal information; developing a winning strategy for preparing your resume; and writing and designing a resume that
targets the specific audience you wish to reach. Chapter 4 addresses the steps necessary to create a resume that is compatible with today's technology, whether e-mailing
documents to a prospective employer or dealing with an online application.

Chapters 5 through 15 offer specific advice to job seekers in several different
categories. You may find that you fit into more than one of these categories and
can benefit from the advice outlined in each of several chapters. For example, you
may be self-employed, but also a manager without a degree. You could be a recent
immigrant or a return-to-work mom or dad. In any event, these chapters provide
relevant tips to help you "express forward" your skills and accomplishments toward your next targeted job. The sample resumes included in these chapters have
been prepared by professionals and illustrate a variety of approaches to different
scenarios within each category.

By following the advice in the opening chapters and reviewing the sample resumes with an eye toward how they compare to your own circumstances, you should
be able to develop a resume that attracts attention, earns you job interviews, and
sets you on your desired career path, no matter how unconventional it may be.

Let's begin!

Chapter 1

The Right Stuff—Gathering the Correct Information

Professionals in the careers industry agree that if you have an unconventional career path, developing a winning resume for yourself may be a considerable challenge, indeed. As a credentialed professional resume writer and career coach who has written literally hundreds of successful resumes for folks across a wide spectrum of occupations and professions, I have found that there are plenty of great books out in the marketplace to guide you through the resume-writing process. In fact, I have been invited to contribute samples of my own work to many of these, and have happily done so. However, it's less common to find practical advice specifically designed to assist people with nontraditional career paths who face unique issues when the time comes to create a winning resume. This is precisely the value you'll discover in these pages.

Right at the outset, you should know that my career path could easily be characterized as unconventional at best. For example, just when I had reached the pinnacle of my career (up until that point), I was unexpectedly downsized. Summarily dismissed. Fired. *"Incredible!"* I thought at the time. *"This can't be happening to me! I was a great employee."* What's more, having previously pursued numerous promising opportunities, both as an employee as well as an entrepreneur across several different disciplines, I quickly learned how some prospective employers react to what may at first appear to be an unconventional work history: "Run for your life!"

The good news is that we unconventionals are no longer alone. Research shows that the average worker will have at least two or three significant career changes during the course of his or her working life—these include both voluntary and

11

involuntary changes, or, more likely, both. Moving into a new job every two to three years has become the typical pattern.

Still, those of us with uniquely nontraditional work histories face exceptional challenges when it's time to create a winning resume—whether we dared to pursue our dreams, followed our passions, or even if we embarked on what we fully intended at the outset would be a traditional, conventional, "straight line" career and have instead endured more than a surprise or two along the way. Developing a document that expresses who we are and the value we bring to a new work situation can present formidable hurdles that may seem insurmountable at first.

I believe (and I'm sure my colleagues would agree) that a resume is one vitally important step along the path to your next opportunity. As such, a winning resume must be much more than a simple list of work experiences and educational credentials. In fact, the primary goal of creating a resume is to open the door to your next job opportunity—that is, to get the interview.

I'm writing to share professional career insider secrets, activities, and strategies that will help you write a powerful, targeted, and polished resume—even if your path has been uniquely unconventional—and to help you navigate the path leading to where I hope you want to be: thriving in a career that you love.

Determining Your Objective:
Who Are You and What Do You Really Want?

Because I consider myself to be a person endowed with a great deal of common sense, I used to look down my nose at such questions and scornfully reply (silently to myself, of course), *"Obviously, I want a good job! Anyone with even half a brain should be able to discern that I'm a good person who is very qualified for many things, including this job!"* Perhaps. And yet, if your goal is to persuade a prospective employer that you deserve to be interviewed for your ideal job because your skills and experience can add value to the organization, then how you express who you are can make all the difference in the world. How do you want to be perceived by recruiters and prospective employers?

To best express who you are in the context of your resume, it's extremely helpful to have an understanding of what you are looking for in your next job. Please note that this is not what you would settle for, or what you believe you would be willing to tolerate, but rather what you truly wish to do in your next position. You may already have identified all of your strongest capabilities and have a target job objective in mind, or at least a sense of the types of positions you'd like to pursue. Great! If you're at all uncertain about the next step along your career path, please consider investing the time and energy to explore your core competencies, your demonstrated skills, what you most enjoy, and what inspires you.

The following are a few surveys designed to help you meaningfully review your work history and clarify your career goals. Feel free to skip to the next section if you already feel perfectly clear about this. I encourage you to complete the first worksheet in any case, though, as it will prove helpful as we move through process of developing your resume.

Survey 1: Work history summary

List each job you have held, beginning with your very first one. Don't be concerned at this point about whether you think it's wise for each of these to appear on your resume or whether you're proud of your time with a particular employer; ultimately, not every job will appear on your final resume document. And don't be distracted by any gaps between positions at this time. Let's not get too far ahead of ourselves; those issues will be evaluated further along in the process.

Remember to include volunteer commitments, too. Whether compensation takes the form of conventional payroll or other personal fulfillment, volunteering your expertise in any capacity requires certain skills and abilities that may well prove to be transferable to your next position, may be appealing to your next employer, and can be powerful demonstrations of the value you bring to the table.

Survey 1	
Job Title	
Dates (From/To)	
Employer's Name	
City, State	
Responsibilities	

Training Received	
Recognition Awards or Other Honors	

Survey 2: Victories at work

Using the material you have written in the previous exercise as a foundation, think back to your very first job. Review your responsibilities and the specific tasks you carried out to fulfill them. Whatever the job, at some point there likely was a moment—or two, or maybe even more!—when you felt triumphant as a result of something you achieved, even if that sense of victory lasted only for an instant. Perhaps you discovered a new supplier for heavily used materials that resulted in cost savings; maybe you reorganized a set of files that everyone had been carelessly abusing, and your new system saved everyone time; perhaps you applied your foreign language skills in translating a complex document for a coworker; or maybe you were required to plan a social event and developed a theme that turned out to be hugely popular with the guests. Recall each job you have held, and list your victories and accomplishments in the spaces provided. Feel free to use your own private shorthand to scribble brief notes to yourself; you're the only one who will see this worksheet. Write just enough to trigger your memory of each episode.

As you write, place a mark for each of your victories in either the "savor" or the "dread" column. There is little magic in this: Apply your very own honest judgment. Although your actions may have worked out for the best at the time and genuinely qualify as a victory, it's quite possible that you may never want to repeat the experience, and, in fact, may even shrink from the very notion of engaging in that particular activity—hence the "dread" column. It's not uncommon to be really good at something and simply not enjoy it for a variety of reasons. On the other hand, if the experience is one that you thoroughly enjoyed and you still savor the memory, good for you!

Survey 2		
Victories at Work	**Savor**	**Dread**
Example: Set up electronic schedule for tracking conference room reservations.	✓	
Reconfigured all the office computers to accommodate updated software.		✓

Survey 3: Your core competencies and transferable skills (activities you wish to pursue)

Now that you have traveled back through your own personal time tunnel again, reviewing each of your jobs (including volunteer commitments) and identifying and listing each of your victories—large, small, and everything in between—it's time to delve a layer or two more deeply into your experiences. The purpose of this exercise is to closely scrutinize each of your victories to determine the skills that lie beneath and support your success.

Earlier, I stated that for a resume to be truly winning, the document must be more than a simple list of experiences and credentials. Here's where we conjure a little magic, finally. This exercise will guide you through the process of building the case that your natural abilities and learned skills have perfectly equipped you to meet the needs of and solve the challenges facing your next employer in spite of your unique unconventionality. In other words, this will help you to identify your **transferable skills**.

Beginning with those that you savor, examine each victory listed in Survey 2. Consider the situation leading up to your action(s). Then think about what personal characteristics or acquired skills equipped you so well for this particular challenge that a victory resulted. What sets you apart from other job candidates? What is it about you that made it possible for you to perform better than the average person might have in a similar situation? Then, describe more fully how you actions benefited the company or organization. What you write here will form the basis of your **success stories**, which will be discussed more fully later.

Again, although each item will not necessarily find its way onto your resume, it is vital for you to be familiar and conversant with this information while developing your resume, as it will also prove infinitely helpful in preparing for your interview after your resume has opened that door.

I humbly encourage you to take your time with these surveys. Relax and allow your mind to wander just a bit as you recall your various experiences. Many different phenomena may occur as you work through these exercises. Please excuse and accept my indulgence in a little poetic drama here. It's possible that you may experience one or more "Aha!" moments as you reflect on a victory or accomplishment that made you feel truly alive, made time fly by, or actually made your heart sing. What are the stakes here? Well, all that hangs in the balance is the next phase of your working life; and yet, it's possible to have fun with this.

For example, perhaps you figured out a more efficient method of effectively keeping track of orders and developed your own version of the "just-in-time" inventory approach without even realizing it at the time. So, perhaps now you may be motivated to target a new position in supply chain management. If your research indicates it's necessary, consider pursuing further education or training in this area. Maybe you identified the people at city hall who could expedite building permits or site inspections, and successfully shaved precious days from a tight project schedule. Perhaps other such contacts you have cultivated and nurtured together with your networking abilities would be valuable to construction project management

Survey 3			
Challenge	**Action(s) Leading to Victory**	**Abilities/Skills Characteristics Demonstrated**	**Benefits**
Example: Chaos—outside sales reps independently scheduling client meetings without realizing conference rooms not available (already in use, etc.) creating unfavorable impression of company and sales staff as well as loss of productivity	Recognized problem Sought and gained management approval Developed electronic scheduler to track appointments requiring conference room use Coordinated with IT dept. to ensure remote online access	Initiative; highly motivated Computer skills: Microsoft Office applications, including Scheduler Equally at ease working independently or as valued team member Comfortable working across various disciplines and departments to achieve agreed-upon objectives	Enhanced professional image of company and sales reps Provided reliable access to facilities for private client consultations Developed organized process out of chaos

firms. Or perhaps you can identify opportunities in other environments such as manufacturing, where expediting and slicing through red tape are also highly valued. What if you found a way to make a real connection with a potential customer over the phone, and discovered that you're really good at "cold calling" (a.k.a. telesales)? There are numerous other arenas in which people possessing such skills, and who genuinely enjoy applying them, are keenly sought. We'll discuss the importance of research more fully later.

Survey 4: Your optimal work environment

Refer to Survey 1, and for each position, list aspects of your work environment that you value highly. For example, on my list, "flexible work schedule" might appear in the first column, whereas "many daily internal committee meetings" would appear in the second column. Other aspects to consider may include the following: working in isolation or as a member of one or more teams; level of decision-making authority and responsibility; many tight, challenging deadlines vs. longer-term projects; level of personal interaction that is internal or external to the organization; level of telephone contact; extent of computer usage (all day at a computer screen?); extent of local and/or out-of-town travel required; and so on.

Survey 4	
Aspects of Work Environment:	
Desired	**Potential Deal-Breakers**
Example: Flexible work schedule	Daily schedules loaded with many

It's equally important to be aware of items in both columns as you explore future opportunities. For example, if you are offered a position that seems at first to be your dream come true, and later learn that it includes a large dose of entries in the "potential deal-breakers" column, then at least you have the self-awareness to help you make an informed decision.

Once you have identified the skills and abilities that you truly enjoy, considered how they might be applicable to future positions, discovered one or more success stories, and thought about the kind of work environment that you prefer and wish to pursue, you're much better equipped to develop a resume that demonstrates to a potential employer the value you bring to the table. That is to say, you have gathered the right stuff.

If, after spending time and effort working with the surveys in this chapter, you're still decidedly uncertain about the direction your career should take, let me recommend that you consult with an experienced career coach or career counselor. These pros can offer more comprehensive career assessment services than is possible within these pages. Following are some resources that may guide you in locating a qualified career professional to further assist you in your quest:

- □ *www.CertifiedCareerCoaches.com*
- □ The Career Management Alliance: *www.careermanagementalliance.com*
- □ International Coaching Federation: *www.coachingfederation.org/ICF*
- □ National Career Development Association: *www.ncda.org*

Mining for Job Seekers' Gold: Research, Research, Research

So far, your work has been all about you, as it should be. To write a truly effective resume, however, it must be written with your target position in mind. Therefore, the more information you have about your target industry, field, or position, the better and stronger the case you can make that you have the right stuff to succeed.

Happily, the Internet has made such research somewhat more convenient; however, it's best to use other approaches as often as you can. Your local public library can be an invaluable resource during your job search. Remember to ask for assistance from librarians, as they can guide you to reliable online sources and help you identify other resources, too. Keep in mind that your personal and professional networking contacts may be vital to your research. Perhaps your uncle's next-door neighbor is a hiring authority in a similar organization to your target. Or perhaps a former coworker's spouse actually works at your target company and can share valuable insights into the culture of the organization. There's nothing quite like "soft" personal information combined with hard facts to help you learn about your target.

Depending upon the nature of your job target, often one very valuable document to the resume-writing process is the position description itself. If it's not possible to obtain the position description for the job you seek, then perhaps you can find analogous or at least somewhat similar job postings to help give you a sense of what prospective employers in your target industry are seeking. For example, many chambers of commerce in communities across the country have Websites containing extremely valuable information for job seekers. Many corporations and nonprofit organizations also maintain Websites that can be mined for job seekers' gold. Even if these sites are not directly applicable to your situation, you can gather numerous clues to what employers in your chosen field are seeking, which can then contribute to your developing a resume that will positively resonate with them and open the door to your next career step. The information you gather will also prove to be invaluable to your further preparation for the interview. But let's not leap too far forward—yet!

Chapter 2
Developing a
"Write" Strategy

It's vital to create a resume that strategically positions you for your next target position. Your resume has to reveal absolutely the best you for consideration by prospective employers. To accomplish this, each component of your resume must be crafted to optimally show how you are the best candidate for your target job. Professional resume writers employ a variety of techniques and adapt them to each unique situation—all based upon what you bring to the table and how that fits the requirements of your job target. For those of us with nontraditional career paths, it's even more essential to understand and effectively apply these approaches to our advantage.

5 Keys to Building a Successful Resume

- Know yourself and understand what you have to offer prospective employers (see surveys 1, 2, and 3 in Chapter 1).
- Identify what you're looking for in your next job (see Survey 4 in Chapter 1).
- Write your resume in terms that are "expressed forward."
- Demonstrate, don't merely narrate.
- Use keywords relevant to your target field.

Gaining mastery of what these key concepts mean and how to optimally apply them to your own particular situation will help you write a strong and effective resume that will open doors and generate interviews. If you have taken your time in completing the surveys contained in Chapter 1, you should have a clearer sense of who you are and what you bring to the table. If not, there's still time. Go back!

Now, let's explore each of the next three keys in more depth as we begin to examine the components of an effective resume.

⚷ Expressing Forward

A dangerous yet commonly held belief is that writing your resume is all about documenting your past. The truth is that anyone who builds a resume based on this assumption risks total failure. How can this be? Presumably you're reading this book because you're ready for the next step in your career; you wish to explore your options, and you're ready to discover or create new opportunities to build a prosperous future. Yes! There's that vitally strategic word: *future*. To be optimally successful, your resume must be "expressed forward"—that is, it must be written with your job goal and target audience held uppermost in your mind.

This approach is especially important for unconventionals, or, "the rest of us" who, for whatever reason, have not followed a traditional career path directly from point A to point B. Keep in mind that many prospective employers, recruiters, and human resources representatives may have followed a much more traditional, straight-line career path than those of us with unconventional work histories. It's simply human nature for people to feel more confidence in and have a greater affinity for others who appear to be similar to themselves and who share analogous backgrounds. Therefore, one important goal of your resume is to clearly communicate and effectively demonstrate that you do, in fact, have "the right stuff" they are looking for in a candidate, in spite of your dissimilar backgrounds. In fact, I'm convinced that it is precisely because of our nontraditional work histories that we unconventionals (of any age) have acquired unique insight and wisdom beyond our years—characteristics that may not be easily recognized or appreciated by those with more traditional work histories, but which can be extremely advantageous to employers. They need us on board because we are uniquely equipped to help them achieve their goals.

The distinction between a straightforward recap of your work history and expressing it forward may seem unimportant or too subtle to you now. Still, don't ever underestimate the transformational power of an expressed-forward resume to paint a compelling picture of you, set you apart from other job candidates, and position you to win opportunities to show that you have the right stuff.

Let's examine this concept in action in the resume of someone who wishes to make a significant career change. Rosalyn Woodson is a librarian who wishes to move into the world of book publishing. After carefully considering her options, she determined that she would delight in the role of acquisitions editor for a publishing house that has a strong fiction presence. Clearly, to demonstrate her transferable capabilities, it was first vital to understand the expectations and requirements of the new target job (research!). Next, by working through the survey worksheets presented in Chapter 1, Rosalyn identified the many areas in which she excelled as a public librarian that actually prepared her for a successful transition into publishing.

Rosalyn's unique combination of transferable proficiencies and successes are highlighted both in the summary as well as in the descriptions of her activities in each of her previously held positions. These proficiencies and successes include: knowledge and understanding of literature; familiarity with current and emerging trends in the reading public; facility for making excellent networking connections; demonstrated ability to interact with authors and persuade them to participate in special events; state-of-the art research capabilities; and terrific people skills. Rosalyn's majors in college are identified in the resume to further strengthen the notion that she is a Renaissance person with a high degree of natural curiosity, a strong intellect, and genuinely wide-ranging aptitudes and interests—characteristics that are shared by many prominent, successful publishing professionals.

Rosalyn Lee Woodson

1058 Cranberry Court ● Branfield Junction, NY 14687

RosLeeWood@yahoo.com

315.737.4182 (C) / 315.281.4182 (H)

LIBRARY DIRECTOR
● *Literature Collection Development* ● *Author Programming Initiatives* ●

Accomplished library leader with extensive education and professional expertise in building literature collections and developing innovative programs featuring noted authors. Established numerous, popular book clubs, each focusing on a variety of genres and topics such as: current political biographies; recent foreign translations; current celebrities; murder mysteries (cozies/police procedurals/classics); and intrigue/espionage. Exceptional ability to foster relationships with diverse constituencies, including community stakeholders at all levels; cultural and neighborhood organizations; state and municipal government leaders; reading aficionados; as well as the general public. Expertise establishing mutually beneficial collaborations among diverse individuals and organizations. Proven success in these key areas:

● Selecting New Releases Popular with the Public	● Establishing & Advancing Strategic Vision
● Influencing Decision-Makers at All Levels	● Developing & Implementing Major Policies
● Building & Motivating Teams	● Networking with Diverse Audiences
● Sophisticated Problem-Solving Capabilities	● Advocating for Programs & Resources

PROFESSIONAL EXPERIENCE:

BRANFIELD PUBLIC LIBRARY; Branfield Junction, New York
Director   **2000 – Present**

Recruited to fulfill executive leadership role on an interim basis for this dynamic public library with $5.4 million budget and annual circulation of 1.2 million items; appointed to permanent position in 2001.

KEY INITIATIVES:

➤ *Expanded program offerings to include special events featuring noted authors. Encouraged senior management team to identify and pursue special interests with a focus on establishing a wide variety of book clubs designed to appeal to diverse readers at all levels. Personally contacted publishers and individual authors, extending special invitations to attend events uniquely designed to delight attendees, grow readership, and enhance community awareness of library programming*

➤ *In recognition of significant need to provide meaningful programming and resources designed to meet the needs and expectations of teens, developed leading-edge teen center incorporating latest technology and design elements to appeal to this audience. Secured funding from multiple sources to supplement traditional operating budget.*

➤ *Developed and implemented with senior management team the reconfiguration of public services. Provided telephone headsets to reference staff in order to enhance efficiency. Significantly reduced patrons' waiting time for circulation and reference services.*

➤ *Pioneered the design and construction of state-of-the-art, in-library café in response to strong public interest to provide enhanced library experience for visitors and further increasing the library's appeal as a "destination."*

Previous experience comprises a range of library leadership roles, including Director of Library Development at the state level (PA); Executive Director of a regional cooperative (CT); Director of a county-wide library system with 25 members including a central urban library with 15 urban branches (NJ); Library Director of a multi-branch suburban library (NY); and Department Head within a large urban library (NY).

EDUCATION:

Master of Arts, New York University; New York, NY
> *(Double major: Contemporary American Literature; English Literature)*

Master of Library Science, School of Library & Information Science - SUNY Geneseo; Geneseo, NY

Bachelor of Science, Cornell University: Ithaca, NY
> *(Triple major: Modern American Literature; Physics; Chinese)*

- -

Notice how Rosalyn's earlier resume, written when she was targeting the position at Branfield (a conventional progression in the same field) significantly differs, although it is still expressed forward. In the following example, her library-related leadership accomplishments and library-specific abilities are emphasized in order to illustrate that she is fully prepared to take on the role of director at Branfield while remaining in the public library field.

Rosalyn Lee Woodson

1058 Cranberry Court ● Branfield Junction, NY 14687

RosLeeWood@yahoo.com

315.737.4182 (C) / 315.281.4182 (H)

LIBRARY DIRECTOR
● *Innovative Manager* ● *Author Programming Initiatives* ●

Accomplished library leader with extensive education and professional expertise in integrating leading-edge technology into the public library; developing innovative programs; and building collections. Exceptional ability to foster strong relationships with diverse constituencies, including community stakeholders at all levels; cultural and neighborhood organizations; state and municipal government leaders; as well as the general public. Demonstrated expertise in managing budgets and capital projects to strengthen library's financial stability. Successful track record of securing grants to enhance library's offerings even during fiscally constrained conditions; and establishing mutually beneficial collaborations among diverse individuals and organizations. Proven success in these key areas:

- Establishing & Advancing Strategic Vision
- Developing & Implementing Major Policies
- Networking with Diverse Audiences
- Advocating for Programs & Resources

- Influencing Decision-Makers at All Levels
- Building & Motivating Teams
- Shaping & Managing Budgets
- Sophisticated Problem-Solving Capabilities

PROFESSIONAL EXPERIENCE:

BRANFIELD PUBLIC LIBRARY; Branfield Junction, New York
Director 2000 – Present

Recruited to fulfill executive leadership role on an interim basis for this dynamic public library with $5.4 million budget and annual circulation of 1.2 M items; appointed to permanent position in 2001.

KEY INITIATIVES:

➢ *Developed and implemented with senior management team the reconfiguration of public services. Provided telephone headsets to reference staff in order to enhance efficiency. Significantly reduced patrons' waiting time for circulation and reference services.*

➢ *In recognition of significant need to provide meaningful programming and resources designed to meet the needs and expectations of teens, developed leading-edge teen center incorporating latest technology and design elements to appeal to this audience. Secured funding from multiple sources to supplement traditional operating budget.*

➢ *Pioneered the design and construction of state-of-the-art, in-library café in response to strong public interest to provide enhanced library experience for visitors and further increasing the library's appeal as a "destination."*

➢ *Expanded program offerings to include special events featuring noted authors. Encouraged senior management team to identify and pursue special interests with a focus on establishing a wide variety of book clubs designed to appeal to diverse readers at all levels. Personally contacted publishers and individual authors, extending special invitations to attend events uniquely designed to delight attendees, grow readership, and enhance community awareness of library programming.*

Rosalyn Lee Woodson

RosLeeWood@yahoo.com

Résumé – Page Two   315.737.4182 (C) / 315.281.4182 (H)

PENNSYLVANIA STATE LIBRARY; Harrisburg, Pennsylvania

Director, Department of Library Development 1996 - 2000

Reported directly to State Librarian, with accountability for organizing, planning, and directing Library Development Department, which provided consulting services and technical assistance in creating and/or enhancing statewide library services. Managed $27 million in state and federal grant funds.

- Developed statewide library service plan and contributed to team forming state-wide policies.
- Reviewed new and existing state and federal legislation to understand impact on public libraries.
- Directed planning efforts encompassing the State Library, Pennsylvania Library Network and other statewide as well as regional organizations.
- Negotiated with vendors to procure products and services with favorable terms for the Pennsylvania Library Network.
- Promoted cooperation between and among various statewide organizations and their constituencies

Key Accomplishments

➢ *Championed the concept and managed the implementation of new web portal to statewide library services. Selected vendor and negotiated contract to create website. Directed testing and authentication of website prior to launch.*

➢ *Wrote statewide strategic plan. Managed introduction and implementation of new strategy, coordinating efforts of many constituencies and outside consultants to achieve statewide goals.*

➢ *Restructured organization and created new Youth Services Coordinator position to better address library needs of young adults.*

➢ *Managed the selection, purchase, and implementation of new statewide interlibrary loan and virtual union catalog. Developed highly innovative funding solution, engendering cooperation and support of library systems throughout the state. Directed the launch, including local staff training across the state. Program selected as model benchmark by National Library Association.*

EDUCATION:

    Master of Arts, New York University; New York, NY

    Master of Library Science, School of Library & Information Science - SUNY Geneseo; Geneseo, NY

    Bachelor of Science, Cornell University: Ithaca, NY

Other resume examples illustrating the concept of expressing forward may be found in Chapter 3 (Aurelio Diaz) and throughout Chapters 5 through 15.

⚷ Demonstrate! Illustrate! (Don't Merely Narrate!)

One important goal of your resume is to illustrate in a meaningful way what you have done that supports what you say you are capable of doing. In effect, you need to paint a compelling picture with words. Which of the following two excerpts is more appealing to you? Which one paints a more compelling picture of what the candidate actually accomplished, and is therefore capable of achieving in a new target job?

Narrated: Responsible for clothing store management. Accountabilities include personnel, merchandising, and profitability.

Demonstrated: Manage upscale men's retail sportswear shop.
- Recruit, train, and supervise employees.
- Select and order leading-edge merchandise.
- Create innovative and appealing window and in-store displays.
- Increased year-to-date profits by 12% from last year's.
- Reduced employee turnover by 70% in past two years.

The simple truth is that people are much more likely to read a document they find genuinely interesting—or, dare I say, more compelling or even exciting than one that, well, to be perfectly candid, bores them beyond caring. Again, it's human nature. Although this book refers to "prospective employers," "recruiters," and "human resources representatives," remember that these are human beings with emotions and interests (as difficult as that may be to acknowledge at times during a job search!). Let's use this understanding to our advantage and focus on building documents that, at their best, will result in the reader exclaiming, "I've really got to meet this person!"

One common technique that you may have already heard of is to begin each statement with an action verb, particularly when listing responsibilities and tasks. It is possible to overdo this, however. Taking this advice to extremes can result in statements that are contrived, silly, or downright embarrassing. As with any pearl of wisdom, be sure to combine this technique with a large dose of common sense. Hopefully, as you work through this process, you'll develop a stronger sense of what sounds good and feels right to you. Pay attention to that seventh sense! Ideally, have a trusted friend review what you write, and ask for an honest critique.

Notice also in the demonstrated excerpt how powerful it is to include quantified accomplishments, as found in the last two bullets. Even if the candidate is not targeting another retail clothing store management position, he or she is demonstrating strong capabilities that may be transferable to other fields. Look at your

Surveys 2 and 3 from Chapter 1 and identify a few especially significant victories that are most relevant to your next job target; these are strong contenders to appear on your resume. It's best to quantify such accomplishments as often as you can. Clearly, not everything in this world is truly quantifiable; however, if it's a valid, significant, and verifiable accomplishment, consider including it on your resume—provided, of course, that it is directly relevant in some way to your new target job. Following are several examples of non-quantified accomplishments from a cross section of disciplines:

- Awarded Perfect Attendance bonuses for three consecutive years.
- Selected to participate in Corporate Staff Exchange Program.
- Recognized for excellent customer service with two Service Beyond Measure awards.
- Recommended, won approval for, and implemented new Employee Incentive Award program to promote enhanced workplace safety.
- Updated and revised company's records retention policies; received A++ rating from State accreditation agency.
- Built strong client network through honest approach and providing reliable service and sound recommendations to meet client's objectives.
- Developed and implemented new office filing system to better organize in formation and improve file retrieval efficiency.

Keywords

There is great power in choosing the optimal language for a particular purpose and for a specific audience. We've discussed how prospective employers and recruiters are, in fact, human beings who will respond more favorably to a document that is well-written and genuinely captures their interest. These people are also most likely highly knowledgeable in their respective fields of endeavor, and you'll create a much more positive impression and strengthen your credibility if you write in their language—that is, the language of your target job, or **keywords**.

Just about anyone who has conducted any kind of search on the Internet has most likely encountered and is familiar with the concept of keywords. Keywords encapsulate the essential skills, knowledge, and expertise that distinguish experienced candidates in a particular profession or trade. Prospective employers, recruiters, and their agents use many tools, both internally and externally, to search for candidates whose resumes contain keywords that are especially relevant to positions they seek to fill. Imagine you're in the human resources department of a large manufacturing company. A department manager has requested the resumes of recent applicants, and, based upon your conversation with him or her, you enter the following search terms to scan your database: "project management," "lean manufacturing," "Six Sigma Black Belt." This should result in candidates who have project management experience in lean manufacturing environments and possess the Six Sigma Black Belt. Frequently, results will be ranked in sequence based upon the number of times the search engine identifies the requested keywords in each candidate's resume.

The challenge for those of us with unconventional career paths is to successfully translate our workplace achievements into language that potential employers will be familiar and comfortable with. Ultimately, your proper use of keywords will contribute to the impression that you have credibility in your new target field and are capable of meeting new challenges.

If you're an observant reader, you may have noticed that many field-specific keywords have been used already. You will see that this will continue throughout the remaining pages. Review your own proficiencies and achievements identified during your work in Chapter 1, and circle any keywords you may have already used that are applicable in your new target job. Keep these worksheets handy as we move through building the components of a successful resume.

As you review the sample resumes in Chapters 5 through 15, take note of how the savvy use of targeted, field-specific keywords subtly promotes the credibility of the candidates and their ability to excel in their prospective endeavors. In Appendix B, look for more tips on the correct and judicious use of keywords, and advice on discovering the most up-to-date and relevant language for your chosen field.

Chapter 3
Building Your Resume—
The Key Components

Let's examine the components of a resume and see how the 5 Keys in action can transform an ordinary document that simply records your employment history into a dynamic instrument that will open doors to your next career opportunity.

Resume Components:

- ☐ Contact information
- ☐ Summary or profile
- ☐ Work history
- ☐ Educational background
- ☐ Training, technical skills, and other qualifications
- ☐ Other relevant information, including honors, awards, relevant hobbies, and volunteer experience
- ☐ Formatting and design

Contact Information

Although this very first section may seem to be the simplest of all, extreme care is required to ensure that every element of your contact information is accurate and up-to-date. It's vitally important to consider the questions listed on the following pages as you collect this information. After all, these are the means by which prospective employers will identify and contact you. Let's work through each piece of the contact maze, and you'll see what I mean.

Your name

Are you or have you ever been known by another name, due to marriage or divorce or simply a nickname? For example:

- ☐ Johanna (Svensen) Rivera
- ☐ R. Peter Ostrowski ➜ R. Peter "Rich" Ostrowski

Is your name especially difficult to pronounce? Do you use a "call" name? For example:

- ☐ Ulhas Aastuv Gumasti ➜ "Yulie" Gumasti
- ☐ Somvimane Ranguswami Thouapha➜ Somvimane "Ragu" Thouapha

Do you have a gender-neutral name? There are some first names that don't indicate a gender, and some people may still be uncertain how to handle these encounters. Prospective employers may be reluctant or uncomfortable about contacting you if it's unclear how to address you, or they simply may be more anxious when doing so. Why not first win the interview, and then decide how you feel about the prospective employer—in other words, don't give them a reason to screen you out this early in the process. Consider using a title, for example:

- ☐ Ms. Kelley O'Rorke
- ☐ Mr. Gale Figueroa
- ☐ Ms. Junko Hilo

Your e-mail address

Do you have a personal e-mail account? Even if you're the last person on your block to establish one, it's not too late! Many employers and recruiters prefer to make initial contact via e-mail, and electronic communication can often expedite things on both sides. It's completely inappropriate and not advisable to use your work e-mail account for your job search. Rather, it's better to establish a personal account with one of the free resources (Yahoo!, AOL, and so on), if you do not have one offered through your Internet provider at home.

Take special care when setting up your account; humor is a very individualized art, and what may strike you as innocently funny may be offensive or otherwise off-putting to others. Your goal should be a professional-sounding screen name, ideally one that is easily identifiable as you—for example, Arnold.Boldt@aol.com—rather than something like DarlingAngelbelle@resumesos.com.

Your address

Are you relocating? Do you have a temporary address? If you're planning to relocate and have a temporary address in the new market or are a graduating college student, be very clear about which is most current:

George Arnold
GeorgeA@ResumeSOS.com

Current Address:	*After June 1, 2008:*
625 Panorama Trail, North	816 Rockwell Street
Nathaniel, New York 14688	Richmond, Maine 04912
585.333.0535 (Cellular)	207.388.5913 (Home)

Telephone number

Which contact number should you use? It's preferable to list only your home telephone and/or your personal cellular telephone number. Even if you have a direct telephone extension at work, can you absolutely ensure that you'll be alone when a prospective employer calls? Why risk awkwardness or embarrassment—or worse!

Be mindful that if you hold a conventional day job that makes it impractical or impossible to have your cell phone turned on, it's important to check for messages throughout the day if possible, or at least once during business hours, so that you may return any calls promptly. This also holds true for checking your home voice mail regularly, if that is the primary contact number you have provided. Therefore, it's essential that you take a fresh listen to your voice mail message(s). Take care that your recorded message is professional, articulate, and in good taste.

There are many acceptable formats and styles for use in the contact section. A variety may be found in Chapters 5 through 15, and several others follow here. Find the most appropriate one for you from among these examples to use as a guide when developing the contact section of your own resume.

Anna Maria (Martelli) Rasmussen

1018 Townsend's Crossing ◆ Maryville, NY 12865 ◆ 518.290.6322 ◆ AnnaMaria@gmail.com

Aleksander Nureyev

Aleks@earthlink.net

1812 Snowden Place
Medford, Massachusetts 02199
617.264.3301 (H) / 617.710.4155 (C)

Marisol Diaz-Garcia

96 Summer Sky Drive
Stockton, California 92012

Marisol.Diaz-Garcia@msn.com

(Home) 415-298-0456
(Cell) 510-311-8491

The Summary or Profile

One very powerful technique that can set the forward tone of the resume right from start is to begin with the profile or summary section, usually placed immediately following your name and contact information at the very top. The summary is often an excellent opening section for many job seekers, although not appropriate in every instance. This section gives you the opportunity to highlight those skills and abilities you most want your readers to notice. Imagine that the readers of your resume may spend only a matter of seconds scanning its contents. What do you want them to focus on? The skills and abilities they're seeking, and which you possess! What will draw their attention and arouse their interest enough to prompt them to read further? A compelling summary statement of what you offer and have demonstrated that you can achieve.

Let's get to the bottom line: the purpose of the summary section is to concisely communicate the value you bring to the prospective employer. It can be one or two carefully worded sentences, a paragraph, or a bullet list of items with a brief introductory sentence or two. Notice that the summary is not explicitly written as an expression of what you are seeking from an employer in a new job. Rather, the most effective summary is written to facilitate the reader, recognizing the value that you have to offer to the employer by stating the many benefits the prospective employer will gain by hiring you.

To illustrate the concept of expressing forward, let's examine the summary sections of two resumes that were written for the same individual, but were developed for two very different job objectives. Our candidate, Serena Montoya, has a bachelor's degree and a long work history that includes positions in management as well as extensive experience in administrative support. Having worked extensively in both nonprofit and corporate environments, she felt she possessed a keen understanding of both, yet risked being rejected by both worlds because she had moved back and forth several times. She remarked once that she had "never really settled on what she wanted to do when she grew up." Does this sound at all familiar?

At one point in her career, Serena left a position as manager of a nonprofit agency to start her own business. After two years of excruciatingly hard work and tremendous investment of human capital, it failed. Following a great deal of soul-searching and prioritization of her life goals, she decided to reenter the conventional job market in an administrative assistant position, and identified a specific job opportunity she wished to pursue. Because Serena had worked as an executive secretary earlier in her career, she needed a resume that would emphasize her proven abilities and success in this area.

She perceived this as a double-edged sword; although she did have extremely relevant work experience, it was not acquired in her most recent position. Worse yet, she worried that prospective employers seeking administrative support personnel would be apprehensive about hiring her for yet another reason: Because administrative support positions tend to attract people who are comfortable with taking frequent direction from superiors and agreeable about filling a supporting role, Serena was concerned that her entrepreneurial experience would identify her in an employer's eyes as someone unprepared to play a supporting role. Although you should be wary of such broad generalizations, when developing your resume an effort should be made to anticipate how prospective employers may react to the information you include.

By working through exercises similar to those outlined in Chapter 1, Serena identified strengths and skills that were transferable from the "other worlds" in which she had worked (nonprofit, corporate, and entrepreneurial) and that would be highly appealing to a prospective employer (in this case, the president of a large organization) who was seeking an accomplished administrative assistant. Choosing from among these, she began to see patterns and strengths that would apply to the target position.

Serena's research into the organization turned up the fact that, in addition to reporting directly to the president, there was a "dotted line," or indirect, reporting relationship to the public relations director. Take note of how her expertise in this area is introduced in the very opening section of the resume, thus subtly setting the tone from the top that this is a person who has the "right stuff." Even though she had not held a position that could be technically categorized as being in the public relations field, she had actually performed many of the relevant functions, including writing press releases and dealing with media contacts, in several other jobs.

Through her networking contacts, Serena also learned that the organization was in transition, and the president was therefore in the midst of managing a number of complex personnel challenges. Hence, she included her relevant personality traits such as tact, discretion, and her ease in dealing with individuals at all levels.

Notice how the bullet points listed in the summary are all directly relevant to the responsibilities of Serena's target position; this is expressing forward that she already possesses personal attributes and abilities required for success in the new position. At the same time, notice that several other perfectly worthy skills and experiences, ones which are not directly relevant to her new job target, are *not* highlighted in the summary—for example, her extremely successful and innovative agency management expertise; her college degree; her specialized training; her foreign language fluency; and other valuable experiences. In fact, those same areas are downplayed throughout this version of her resume. This technique is known as re-weighting: that is, shifting emphasis from one area of expertise to another in order to support your current career objectives and portray yourself as the superb candidate that you are.

When expressing forward, it is perfectly acceptable to carefully select which qualifications and experiences to accentuate and to provide more detail about these, including victories and success stories. It is not necessary to state any falsehoods—indeed, it is unacceptable under any circumstances.

Serena S. Montoya

6211 Admiral's Crossing ● Seaport, New York 10029 ● 212.863.2918 ● Serena@msn.com

ADMINISTRATIVE ASSISTANT / EXECUTIVE SECRETARY
SUMMARY

Highly organized and motivated office professional with capabilities in a broad array of key functional areas:

- **Extraordinary people skills: tact, diplomacy, and discretion. Ability to comfortably interact with individuals at all levels.**
- **Excellent project-management skills, encompassing planning, organization, team leadership, and budget accountability.**
- **Innovative problem-solver with ability to develop unique solutions to complex challenges.**
- **Superior verbal and written communication skills, with experience writing press releases, preparing marketing and promotional collaterals, and dealing with print and electronic media representatives.**
- **Proficient in all current Microsoft Office Suite applications; Publisher; DreamWeaver.**

At just about the same time, Serena wished to pursue a lead on an opening for a personal assistant. The prospective employer was an author and illustrator who, although officially retired, remained extremely active in a variety of pursuits. With a young family based in northern Pennsylvania, homes in Hawaii and Colorado, and an estate in the Hamptons, the employer needed a candidate who could demonstrate multiple areas of expertise combined with a healthy dose of initiative. For example, the position called for someone who was equally at ease planning social events ranging from small, intimate dinner parties at home, as they were arranging catered galas hosting hundreds of invited guests, including the news media. The newly created job description encompassed many other varied responsibilities, including coordinating the employer's schedule, managing contractors, hiring the children's nannies, maintaining high-level written correspondence, and serving as the employer's personal media representative. This prospective employer, although only recently retired, was an admitted technophobe. Although he was neither familiar nor comfortable with cutting-edge technology, he recognized its importance and sought someone with expertise in this area, as well.

Believing that her varied experience across several disciplines (including her entrepreneurial experience) was actually an asset in this instance—finally!—Serena felt fully equipped to exceed expectations in this position, too. However, to optimize her chances of being considered, she decided that her resume needed to be re-weighted.

With the job posting in hand, Serena again consulted her list of skills and abilities, identified competencies she believed would transfer well to this personal assistant role, and developed a new summary with a very different tone. If you read carefully, you can still recognize Serena. Although some of the same facts are contained in both summaries, they are tailored to fit the requirements of each position. Plus, she added back in some of the attributes and capabilities that were simply not relevant to the administrative support position. Because this version is more comprehensive, and includes more of her background and abilities, she decided to call this section her profile. In short, this version also truthfully describes Serena, but she has successfully positioned herself in such a way that each prospective employer cannot help but conclude that she is fully prepared to exceed expectations in the role she is interviewing for.

Serena S. Montoya

6211 Admiral's Crossing • Seaport, New York 10029 • 212.863.2918 • Serena@msn.com

PROFILE
Highly versatile, motivated individual with demonstrated, creative capabilities in diverse areas:

- **Superior verbal and written communication skills, with successful track record of public speaking; writing press releases; and dealing with representatives of print and electronic media.**

- **Extraordinary people skills: tact, diplomacy, and discretion. Ability to quickly develop positive rapport and comfortably interact with individuals at all levels, of all ages. Warm and professional telephone personality.**

- **Excellent project management skills, encompassing planning, organization, implementation, team leadership, and budget accountability.**

- **Innovative problem-solver with ability to develop unique solutions to complex challenges.**

- **Expertise in a wide range of arts and crafts; creative sense of style; accomplished amateur musician.**

- **Proficient in all MS Office Suite (including Word, PowerPoint, Excel and Access).**

- **Comfortable with Internet applications including e-mail; various search engines; and Web design (DreamWeaver and Front Page).**

- **Fluent in Spanish, Italian, and French.**

The summary or profile has actually replaced the "career objective" that was commonly used at the top of resumes for many years. In general, objectives have fallen out of favor because they tend to be too limiting and too specific, and inappropriately eliminate candidates from consideration:

OBJECTIVE:

Research Assistant in the law department of a Fortune 100 Corporation

Or else an objective is often way too vague and broad, with the end result sounding ultimately meaningless and embarrassing:

Objective: A professional position that will utilize my skills and abilities with opportunities for advancement and growth.

Here's one of the very few instances where including an explicit career objective instead of a summary is recommended. If you completely and absolutely lack any experience whatsoever in your target field, even when you consider every job you've held and every volunteer position you've worked in, it may be best to express your new objective right up front. This is also a method of including relevant keywords early and speaking the language of your new field right at the start:

OBJECTIVE: An entry-level opportunity with a leading freight or passenger rail company.

This candidate, in his 40s, was eager to become an engineer for a railroad. A lifelong buff, he decided the time was now to finally pursue his dream. He knew he would have to take any job he could get to break into the industry. His functional resume supported his candidacy, as did an impassioned cover letter that outlined his experience with a local railroad museum as well as his heavy equipment operator experience.

Here are several optional headings for the summary section:

➤ **Profile**	➤ **Career Profile**	➤ **Professional Profile**
➤ **Executive Profile**	➤ **Summary**	➤ **Skills Summary**
➤ **Career Summary**	➤ **Qualifacations Summary**	

A trend that's been growing in popularity during the past several years is to write a headline for your resume instead of using one of the titles in the previous list. This can be a short, two-line list of the job titles for which you're qualified and/or are targeting, plus the industries in which you either have experience or wish to work. You'll find numerous examples of this approach among the sample resumes in the later chapters, but here are a few to give you an idea how it might look:

CHIEF FINANCIAL OFFICER / CONTROLLER
Manufacturing • Pharmaceuticals • Food & Beverage Industry

DIRECTOR OF BUSINESS DEVELOPMENT/SENIOR SALES EXECUTIVE
Paper Products • Printing / Graphic Arts • Transportation

JOURNEYMAN TOOL & DIE MAKER / MAINTENANCE MECHANIC
Injection Molding • Metal Stamping • High-Volume Manufacturing • Robotics

ADMINISTRATIVE ASSISTANT / OFFICE MANAGER / EXECUTIVE SECRETARY
Not-For-Profit Agencies • Financial Services • Marketing / Media Sales

If you're fortunate and clever, you have saved performance appraisals and reviews from your prior jobs. Retrieve them from your archives and take a fresh look at them. Are there any statements from previous supervisors that speak to your strengths that are transferable to your job target? Have you received any letters of commendation? How about any letters from clients or customers praising you for some special achievement or for being a great help to them in some way?

Depending upon its level of relevance to your new job target, consider including a particularly compelling quotation on your resume. It may be a quotation that transcends your field—for example, speaking of your high ethical standards or commitment to quality customer service. Alternatively, the quotation may be more field-specific, in which case consider including it only if it is directly relevant to your target job. Often, the best location for this is immediately following the summary section. There are several samples of effective use of quotations in Chapter 15. Following are two more examples:

> *"Maria is extraordinarily gifted in anticipating and preparing in advance for many contingencies. She has a remarkable ability to maintain her composure along with the utmost quality standards in high-pressure circumstances under the tightest deadlines."*

> **—Walter Smith, Former Supervisor**

> *"Jonah's uncanny negotiating skills have saved this company many thousands of dollars through the years. I'd always want him on my side of the table in any parley. He adheres to the highest ethical standards and would be an asset to any organization."*

> **—Glenn James, Director of Sales, Bind-O-Corp, LLC**

Work History

Clearly, prospective employers justifiably expect to see your work history on your resume, however spotty, incongruous, or otherwise unattractive or challenging it may appear to be at this point. Keeping in mind the overall strategy of portraying yourself as prepared to succeed in your next job target, careful consideration must be invested in precisely how to include your work history on your resume.

Typically, presentation of your work history will follow the summary section which includes your strongest skills and qualifications that uniquely combine to equip you for your target position. The presentation of your work history needs to clearly support those skills and qualifications you have already highlighted. One exception to this sequence is if you have recently acquired education or training that is highly relevant to your job target. In this case, it's a good idea to place this information nearer the top, immediately following the summary.

Professional resume writers use a variety of formats in order to make as direct a connection as possible between your work experience, the skills and abilities you possess, and the requirements of your target job. Three of these approaches to presenting your work history on your resume are (1) chronological, (2) functional, and (3) a combination of the first two.

1. The chronological format—or more precisely stated, the reverse-chronological format—calls for a listing of your jobs in sequence from most recent to oldest. Beware! How similar is your target job to the last job you held? (My own? Not at all!) Are you seeking to change fields? Are there gaps in your employment history? Remember your overarching goal of appealing to prospective employers based on your readiness for your target job. For those of you with unconventional career paths, a straightforward listing of your previous jobs in chronological order often proves to be singularly unhelpful in convincing a conventional prospective employer that you're the right candidate for the job—that is, if such a listing were the first and/or only information presented.

2. The functional format can be a powerful tool to support re-weighting and truthfully demonstrate how you actually do possess the qualifications and abilities required to succeed in your target job. As the name implies, the focus is on function; categories of skills and/or accomplishments that span your entire work history are presented without any dates attached to them. This approach affords you optimal flexibility to emphasize those very abilities and qualifications you believe will best position you to capture the attention of the prospective employer and, ultimately, to secure your target job.

Not surprisingly, the functional format has suffered a great deal of criticism, some of which has been well-deserved. When used exclusively, without including specific employment dates, job titles, and duties, many readers suspect that the writer of such a document is trying to hide something.

3. The combination format, which combines the functional format with a subsequent reverse-chronological listing of your work history, may be the best option to both support your overall strategy and provide assurance that you are not, in fact, hiding anything. The rationale is that by leading off with the functional presentation (which more strongly demonstrates your value to the prospective employer), you stand a better chance of capturing the reader's interest. Then, with the subsequent reverse-chronological work history, you show that you're not trying to hide anything. The 100-plus sample resumes included later in this book cover an array of approaches; find examples that best correspond with your own circumstances to adapt to your own unique situation.

As you review the sample resumes, notice that the functional format provides the opportunity to present first those skill sets and capabilities with the most relevance to your target job. Of course, your research into the target discipline, organization, or job will be invaluable in prioritizing your material here. As you work through this section, constantly ask yourself, "Which of my capabilities will be most important to this prospective employer? Which of my skills will I need the most in order to succeed in this target position?"

What to include?

The good news is that you've already finished much of the heavy lifting if you took your time with Surveys 1, 2, and 3 in Chapter 1. Now, it's time to review that information and make some more important decisions. Do you need to include every job you have ever held? Not necessarily. The answer to that question will depend on a number of factors that need to be considered, weighed, and prioritized, and even then, often there are some tough decisions. As a colleague of mine is fond of remarking, the first rule of resume writing is that there are no hard-and-fast rules (except to be honest and truthful at all times)! Although that truth may provide ultimate flexibility, it can also be daunting. Here are some criteria for you to consider when deciding what to include in this section:

Aspects of your age

- How recently did you acquire the skills or areas of expertise required for your target position?
- How recently have you received any advanced training in your target field?
- How recently did you work in a job or volunteer position utilizing this expertise?

Relevance

- How relevant is your most-recent paid or unpaid position to your target job?
- Are there certain aspects of your most-recent job responsibilities that can be shown to directly relate to your target job requirements?

□   If you do not have any work history directly related to your next job target, have you taken any courses or received any training along the way? Do you volunteer or are you active in a hobby that contains ele ments of your target job responsibilities and requirements? The functional format provides you with the flexibility to list skills and accomplishments from paid or unpaid work experiences early in your resume.

If you determine that the chronological format is best for you, then you'll want to include these three aspects for each position:

1. Your job responsibilities (the challenge: what you were supposed to do).
2. The skills necessary to carry out those responsibilities (your actions: how you did it).
3. Specific accomplishments (the stellar results of your efforts).

Look at your completed Survey 3 and consider whether the primary contributing factor to each victory you have listed was a wide array of skills, or a *depth* of expertise and skills. If these skills are transferable to your target job, then perhaps a skills-focused summary would be most effective for you. Alternatively, perhaps you have listed many significant victories and accomplishments that are relevant to your target job. If so, then perhaps an achievement-focused approach would be most effective for you. Carefully examine the following examples.

Conventional Job Entry:

Vice President of Production (1999-2007)
LIGHT MANUFACTURING, LLC, Elkhart, IN
Senior Executive responsible for eight manufacturing facilities generating $235 million in annual revenues. Managed transition to low-cost provider status, improving efficiencies and enhancing profitability. Implemented measures of performance, established operating goals, defined re-alignment initiatives, and championed cost reduction programs that consistently increased output, enhanced quality, and improved customer satisfaction.

Accomplishments:
● Led cross-functional team that developed and drove cost-reduction initiatives, delivering $33 million in savings during a 30-month period by implementation of process automation.
● Reduced fixed spending by 13% ($19 million) and overhead spending by 18% through re-allocation of existing resources and implementing cost-reduction initiatives.
● Cut workers' compensation claims by 30% ($550K annually) by implementing innovative health and safety plans, management accountability, and equipment safeguards.

- Reduced manufacturing scrap by 29%, saving $1.3 million in raw materials cost by optimizing production processes.
- Enhanced customer service satisfaction 6% annually over most recent 24 months (measured by order fill accuracy and on-time delivery) through effective supply chain management and flexible manufacturing practices.

Skills-Focused Job Entry:

THE SOMMERS GROUP, Elmira, NY   1995 to 2008
    Senior Accountant (2003 to 2008)
    Staff Accountant (1998 to 2003)
    Accounting Clerk (1995 to 1998)
    Promoted through positions of advancing responsibility based on consistently strong job performance. Accomplishments included:

Accounting/Auditing

- Managed Payables/Disbursements totaling more than $2.1 million annually, Receivables exceeding $2.8 million per year, and over $750K in capital assets.
- Maintained General Ledger system. Developed and implemented accounting policies and procedures.
- Instituted internal controls, including expense account reconciliations for premium collections, reducing write-offs by $57K annually.

Financial Analysis & Reporting

- Coordinated and prepared financial statements in accordance with industry and governmental regulations for jurisdictions in all 50 states.
- Prepared financial statements in accordance with GAAP for the Board of Directors and shareholders, and managed SEC filings for portfolios totaling $900 million in assets.
- Coordinated audits with internal/external audit and regulatory agencies. Compiled financial data for auditors. Prepared internal audit reports.

Cash Management/Budgeting

- Performed cash-management functions to meet investment objectives and prepared timely corporate cash-flow forecasts.
- Developed and implemented banking policies for accounting, premiums, commissions, and benefits.
- Coordinated $35 million budget preparation process for all departments within the business unit.

Project-Focused Job Entry:

CONTINENTAL LIQUORS & WINES, INC.   **1997 to Present**

EAST COAST BRAND INNOVATION GROUP — BOSTON, MA

Product Innovation Senior Technologist (10/05 to 5/08)

Worked closely with Marketing and Sales on branding and product positioning. Networked with worldwide suppliers and served as manufacturing liaison to ensure efficient commercialization according to product specifications.

SELECTED PROJECTS & HIGHLIGHTS

- Established product research and testing labs in US and Asia, from planning and design to start-up and launch, that fully supported product development and met state-of-the-art equipment and process standards.
- Championed the development and introduction of new beverage line that achieved Top Ten status in its category, plus another product which won a Diamond Goblet Award in the Galaxy Spirits competition (Melbourne, Australia – 2006).
- Honored by company CEO for the "Best Innovation Project" and awarded the Brand Group's Gold Medallion for "Best Product Launch" of a successful product line.
- Managed the product development of innovative new carbonated and non-carbonated products, from concept to commercialization in several key markets (Asia, Europe, and Latin America).

Achievement-Focused Job Entry:

Carraba's   2000 to Present

General Manager–New England

- Excelling in company's training program, immediately took on general manager role in under-performing New Haven, CT location. Assembled and motivated strong management team that stabilized operations **while growing profits by 33%.**
- **Slashed employee turnover from 150% to 40%** by providing hands-on leadership that fostered loyalty and built esprit de corps.
- Championed facility upgrades that enhanced customer experiences, and **internally financed $1 million** in renovations through effective budgeting and cost management.
- Managed successful Grand Opening of new Hartford, CT store, **achieving $2.5 million in sales during first 18-months.**
- **Recognized for achieving the highest customer satisfaction ratings** in "mystery-shopper" program within 30-unit regional franchise group that ranked second in the nation.
- Assumed leadership role at Worcester, MA location, a facility with low profitability. Implemented costs controls that **doubled profitability** within one year to achieve Top Ten ranking for the region.

The age question

Let's be honest: For better or worse, in the world of work even today, age does still matter somewhat. Age discrimination is still perpetrated and it's not fair. However, based on my own experience working with many clients, I believe that a compelling, well-written resume can overcome virtually anything and everything—*if* it accomplishes the goal of portraying you as a candidate who possesses the abilities and qualifications needed to succeed in the target position.

All of that said, if you're going to call upon skills that you honed in positions held, say, 40 years ago and have not used since, your approach and the format of your resume may be quite different from those of someone who may have a very long work history but whose job target requires skills and abilities demonstrated in more recently held jobs. This is a clear example of the power of the functional format. Even if a particular skill set was acquired and used long ago, if it applies directly to your new job target, definitely include it in the functional portion of your resume. Alternatively, if your work history is quite long, and your early jobs are not directly relevant to your target, then it is acceptable to summarize the early work experiences as shown in later examples.

Following is a sample profile (summary) written for a retiring executive secretary who most recently had held various positions in a large commercial bank, positions which were not directly related to her job target. As someone who genuinely enjoys interacting with all kinds of people, Mary targeted a part-time telephone receptionist position for the next phase of her work life, when she hoped to have more energy and time to smell the roses.

It turned out that that the business she had targeted was a career consulting practice, which meant that the callers often would be highly stressed due to recent downsizings, and would come from widely diverse backgrounds with a variety of needs and expectations. She therefore determined that communicating to the prospective employer her successful dealings with people at all levels within the bank, as well as with external customers, would serve her particularly well in dealing with clients and prospective clients via telephone in this new role.

By visiting the Website and talking to friends who had used the service, she learned that the business was very small, with only two principals, and that there was the potential to be given more substantive assignments, including the proofreading of resumes and other job-search documents. Happily, this was fine with her. There was also a possibility that she could work from her home, so she wanted to portray herself as detail oriented, self-motivated, and capable of working without close supervision, as she had performed well under analogous circumstances in the past. Here is Mary's profile for the telephone receptionist target position:

PROFILE: Accomplished executive assistant with extraordinary communication skills
and keen attention to detail. Excellent capacity to work independently
without direct supervision or as productive and supportive team member.
Demonstrated track record of exceeding expectations; willing to enthusiastically volunteer for challenging assignments and consistently recognize
total customer satisfaction as the highest priority. Highly personable;
gifted in developing quick, warm, productive rapport with individuals at all
levels. Superb telephone personality; accustomed to working with highly
confidential information, exercising highest levels of discretion, tact and
diplomacy. Highly skilled in Microsoft Office Suite applications.

Next, let's look at Mary's resume prepared in the conventional, reverse-
chronological format. Notice how every effort was clearly made to emphasize skills
and abilities most relevant to her target position. Each responsibility and duty was
carefully considered in the context of how relevant it would be to the target position.
Note also how the summary really sets the tone and lays the foundation: she states
her strengths, then shows how her experience proves that she possesses the skills
highlighted. Because the target position required interacting with a wide variety of
people at all levels and from different fields, she wanted to demonstrate the depth
of her own experience, so she felt comfortable including more than reception-
related duties. Nicely done, to be sure.

However, also notice how a quick glance at this document could result in her
being dismissed as a candidate for a more typical part-time receptionist position. In
addition to her solid history in full-time employment, her most recent position would
most likely be perceived as well beyond the scope of reception work; in other words,
she risks being categorized as overqualified for her target position. In this particular instance, because the target employer was actually seeking an accomplished,
seasoned administrative support professional, the resume was right on target.

Mary Frances Rowley

1018 Crystal Valley Overlook • Honeoye Falls, New York 14472 • (585) 624-7579 • MaryR@yahoo.com

PROFILE:

Accomplished executive assistant with extraordinary communication skills and keen attention to detail. Excellent capacity to work independently without direct supervision or as productive and supportive team member. Demonstrated track record of exceeding expectations; willing to enthusiastically volunteer for challenging assignments and consistently recognize total customer satisfaction as the highest priority. Highly personable; gifted in developing quick, warm, productive rapport with individuals at all levels. Superb telephone personality; accustomed to working with highly confidential information, exercising highest levels of discretion, tact and diplomacy. Highly skilled in Microsoft Office Suite applications.

RELEVANT PROFESSIONAL EXPERIENCE

BANK OF AMERICA; Rochester, New York

Executive Assistant   (3.02 – 6.08)

Accountable for a range of support functions, including managing the schedules of the Vice-President/Trust and Estate Planning; handling confidential client information; providing secretarial support on ad hoc basis for team of five Certified Financial Planners; greeting high-net-worth clients; and maintaining office equipment and supplies for the unit.

➢ Selected to serve as mentor to recently recruited administrative support personnel.

➢ Chosen to participate as member of team developing new employee orientation programs.

➢ *Received President's Award for Exceptional Customer Satisfaction based on results of client survey conducted over 18-month period.*

Administrative Secretary (2.95 – 3.02)

Provided confidential secretarial support to Vice-President / Commercial Loan Operations including management of professional schedule; greeting and interacting with high-net-worth clients; maintaining up-to-date and accurate client files; supervising clerical assistant.

➢ Volunteered to participate on cross-functional team charged with the responsibility of evaluating new software applications; team's recommendation was implemented on bank-wide basis (transition to Microsoft Word from Corel WordPerfect).

➢ *Awarded President's Circle Distinction.*

Administrative Secretary – Branch Banking   (1.85 – 2.95)

Performed a wide variety of logistical, administrative, and customer satisfaction functions in support of branch banking team comprised of Vice-President / Consumer and Mortgage Loans and six loan officers at busy suburban bank branch in Webster, New York.

➢ *Received President's Award for Exceptional Customer Satisfaction/Branch Banking.*

Executive Secretary (1.72 – 1.85)

Accountable for providing secretarial and logistical support to dynamic executive team charged with developing and implementing the recently devised Individual Retirement Account initiative, bank-wide.

➢ *Received President's Award for Ingenuity & Innovation as member of IRA Team.*

Prior executive-level secretarial experience in academic, manufacturing and medical settings, including: the Alumni Relations office of Cornell University; Xerox Corporation; and The Genesee Hospital.

PROFESSIONAL DEVELOPMENT

Microsoft Office – Numerous courses, including Advanced Word

Bryant & Stratton; Rochester, New York - *Coursework in Bookkeeping & Accounting*

Total Quality Management for Banking (Three day-long workshops)

Steven Covey's Seven Habits of Highly Effective People (Two day-long seminars)

Excellent References Furnished Upon Request

Of course, an excellent cover letter accompanying this resume would be extremely helpful in explaining her goals and clarifying what she has to offer and hopes to achieve. However, notice here how the shift to a functional format makes it so much easier for the reader to quickly recognize how Mary's prior work experience directly relates to the responsibilities and expectations of the telephone receptionist role:

RELEVANT SKILLS & ABILITIES

Communications

- Highly articulate: Comfortable handling high volume of inbound calls with professionalism and warmth.
- Personable: Convey self-assurance and friendliness while quickly developing positive rapport with callers, putting them at ease while addressing a variety of inquiries and concerns.
- Accurate: Accustomed to taking detailed, complex messages for later research and follow-up.
- Discreet: Exercise the utmost tact and diplomacy at all times.

Computer Literacy

- Microsoft Outlook: Developed and sent e-mailings designed for existing and prospective clients;
- Microsoft Word: Highly skilled with advanced user training;
- Microsoft Access: Developed and maintained complex client databases;
- Microsoft PowerPoint: Created presentations from supervisor's notes; polished drafts to perfection;
- Internet: Skilled researcher with advanced training in proprietary databases and the "deep Web."

Again, this section would be followed by a reverse-chronological listing of her work history. (Mary's complete cover letter and resume appear in Chapter 8.)

Now, take a look at how the functional format powerfully shows that Aurelio Diaz, most recently a police lieutenant, has the demonstrated capacity to move into a new position that is dramatically different from his most recent experience. Can you guess what his new job target might be?

Aurelio Juan Diaz

6750 Marshall Highway ◆ Pittsburgh, Pennsylvania 15215
878. 223.7188 (Home) ◆ ADiaz@earthlink.net ◆ 878. 223.7188 (Cell)

CORE COMPETENCIES & ACHIEVEMENTS

Team Leadership and Management:
- Inspired and motivated diverse team members (including uniformed officers at all levels and civilians) to work together in developing common objectives to achieve organizational and community-wide goals.
- Trained, supervised, scheduled, and evaluated uniformed and civilian employees.
- Provided mentoring guidance to officers in a variety of areas including case development, evidence, search warrants and surveillances.
- Coordinate management of complex daily case load including: case consultation; initial reports; follow-up and investigative reports; witness / suspect statements; and state's attorneys' reports.
- *Led unit that consistently achieved significantly above average productivity ratings and was ranked #1 in the district for five consecutive years.*

Fiscal Management:
- Prepared and managed annual operating budgets in the $5.2 – $5.8 million range.
- *Reduced operating budget 14% by managing vacancy factors and identifying non-personnel cost savings, in response to mayoral directives for two consecutive years.*

Public Speaking, People Skills & Community Outreach
- Created and presented innovative narcotics education programs designed for multiple audiences including parent/teacher groups and a variety of civic organizations.
- Highly skilled with extensive training in the art of "reading" people via close observation of conversational style; body language; facial expression and eye movements.
- As founding President of the *Emilio Juan Diaz Foundation,* recruit and train volunteers; develop and coordinate annual special event; handle high-profile public relations initiatives; solicit donations in support of children's charities. Most recently, awarded $75,000 grant to the Childhood Cancer Survivors' Coalition.

PROFESSIONAL EXPERIENCE

APPLE VALLEY MUNICIPAL POLICE DEPARTMENT, Apple Valley, Wisconsin   1993 to Present
    Command Lieutenant (2004 – Present)
    Patrol Lieutenant (2000 to 2004)
    Administrative Lieutenant (1996 to 2000)
    Sergeant; Criminal Investigation Division (1993 to 1996)

OSHKOSH SHERIFF'S DEPARTMENT, Oshkosh, Wisconsin   1984 to 1993
    Patrol Sergeant (1990 to 1993)
    Police Detective; Criminal Investigation Division (1988 to 1990)
    Police Officer; Patrol Division (1984 to 1988)

If the functional format is the best choice for you, then the majority of your work experience will have already been presented in your summary section, so it's not necessary to repeat it in your work history section.

The excerpts of Mr. Diaz's resume should give you a sense of how a resume can significantly contribute to a successful major career transition. This talented police professional successfully identified capabilities, both natural and acquired, to demonstrate that he is equipped to take on the role of nonprofit agency director or development professional.

Following are several heading options for a reverse chronological work history section:

- Work History
- Professional Experience
- Employment Experience
- Employment History

If you use the functional format, following are several heading options for the functional section of your resume:

- Career Highlights
- Executive Experience
- Selected Projects and Highlights
- Relevant Accomplishments
- Relevant Skills and Abilities
- Core Competencies
- Significant Achievements

Educational Background

Prospective employers also tend to expect to see an education section on your resume. Again, depending upon your job target, this section may include detailed information about any college degrees, professional training, certifications, licenses, and other educational credentials.

This section may either precede or follow the work history section of your resume, depending upon several factors. For example, if you recently received or are currently pursuing a degree or other educational credential that is somehow directly relevant to your target job, then you'll want to locate your education section immediately following your summary and ahead of your work history. This applies especially to career changers and anyone else whose educational credentials are more important than their employment history in demonstrating their readiness to excel in the target job.

For example, let's imagine for a moment that you have expended what seemed at the time to be a superhuman effort to attend night and weekend classes in order to obtain your associate's degree in accounting. Perhaps you also have endured some degree of financial hardship to accomplish this. Let's further imagine that your new target job is in the public relations arena. How much detail do you think would be helpful to include about your degree on your resume? Most likely, not much! In this case, unless you also have course work related to public relations, your education section should follow your reverse-chronological employment history, which, in turn, should follow a functional statement of your skills and abilities most relevant to public relations activities.

Alternatively, let's imagine that, armed with your associate's degree, you're going after a position in a certified public accountant's practice. Not only should your accounting degree appear on your resume, but it may also be wise to consider including a few course titles that, based on your research, may be particularly relevant to the accountant's practice. Or, a candidate whose work toward the relevant degree is still in process might choose to handle the education section as shown here, following the summary:

SUMMARY

High-energy, seasoned accounting professional with successful track record in Payroll; Benefits Administration; Payables; Receivables; and General Ledger accounting.

EDUCATION

Bachelor of Science, Accounting   Anticipated, May, 2009
Montclair State University; Montclair, New Jersey
(Maintaining full-time employment while pursuing B.S. degree)

Selected Coursework:

➢ Introduction to Financial Management
➢ Developing Meaningful Management Information Reports
➢ General Ledger and Beyond: Income and P&L Statements
➢ Cost Containment Planning
➢ Foreign Currency & International Tax Filings

Training, Technical Proficiencies, and Other Qualifications

Hopefully, after working through the surveys in Chapter 1, you have a clear picture of your technical capabilities as well as a sense of the requirements of your target job. Whatever field you're in, most jobs now require employees to be comfortable using technology. Depending on the extent to which you're expected to be technologically savvy in your particular target field, remember to include a listing (brief or more in-depth and detailed) of your specific, hands-on technology skills and training. Following are additional education section formats designed for candidates with different areas of focus:

Education:

Bachelor of Arts, Arabic Languages, Magna Cum Laude, 2005
George Washington University; Washington, DC

Associate of Applied Science, Information Technology, 2003
Old Dominion University; Norfolk, Virginia
GPA: 3.9 / 4.0

***

Education:

Master of Business Administration (MBA)
Cleveland State University; Cleveland, Ohio

Bachelor of Science (BS), Marketing
Case Western Reserve; Cleveland, Ohio

Professional Training / Seminars:

Management Strategies for the New Millennium (2007)
The Xerox Corporation Leadership Training Institute

Dale Carnegie Institute:
The People Side of Process Improvement (2007)
Leadership Training for Managers (2006)
High Performance Teams (2005)

Stephen Covey:
Habits of Highly Effective Managers (2006)

Senior Leadership Training and NCO/Enlisted Technical Training
US Army Institute for Professional Development

***

Licenses, Certifications & Specialized Training:

OSHA Fork Lift License — Endorsements: Stacker; Walkie; Four-Wheel Sit Down; Tugger (2003)   Accident-free record

Advanced Cardiac Life Support Certification (ACLS) - Penfield Volunteer Ambulance (2002)

Specialized Training:

Hazardous Materials Handling	Back Safety & Proper Lifting
Emergency Evacuation Procedures	Blood-Borne Pathogens
Forklift Safety	Preventive Maintenance
ISO Quality Systems	Process Flow
ISO 14001	Expediting
Visual Quality Inspections	Hand Truck Operation

There are many other examples to guide you in the resumes included in Chapters 5 through 15.

Honors, Awards, and Special Recognition

One overarching consideration in deciding what to include on your resume is the degree of relevance to your target job. Determine whether you have received any recognition or accolades that relate to your job target, and evaluate the benefits of including them. It may be even more powerful to include one or two instances of special recognition in conjunction with the description of the position you held at the time. How about any volunteer activities or community involvement? How important do you believe it would be for prospective employers in your target field to know that you are actively involved in your community? What has your research turned up regarding their corporate or organizational culture in this area? Again, based on their direct relevance to your target job, determine if it is appropriate to include other extra categories, such as those shown here:

Honors and Awards:

Five-time Recipient of President's Gold Circle Award (2003-2007)

Regional Salesman of the Year (2006)

Voice of the Customer Award (Highest Customer Satisfaction Index) (2007)

Professional Memberships:

Florida Bankers' Association; 2002 – Present

Florida Association of Women in Banking (Recording Secretary, 2005); 2001 – 2006

National Association of Women Business Owners (NAWBO); 1999 – Present

American Association of University Women (AAUW); 2005 – Present

Century Club (Advisory Board member); 2004 – 2006

Community Involvement and Volunteer Activities:

Syracuse Chamber of Commerce – Membership Secretary, 2007 – Present

Liverpool Parent Teacher Association – Active Member, 2004 – Present

Greater Syracuse Youth Hockey – Volunteer Coach, 2003 – 2006

Syracuse Volunteer Ambulance Association – Volunteer Dispatcher, 1996 – 2006

Emergency Medical Technician (New York State-Certified)

Very few resumes contain all of these sections, as you will see by examining the samples later in this book. Likewise, the order may shift around, depending on what the prospective employer will consider important. The key is to select those sections that are appropriate and relevant to your particular scenario, with an eye toward your target job and expressing it forward.

Formatting and Design

First impressions are vitally important in your job search. With that in mind, the visual appearance of your resume is an important factor in capturing the attention of employers. You may ask, "Aren't design concerns strictly for artists and creative people?" Not necessarily! An attractive, visually appealing resume gives you an advantage over candidates with plain resumes. Imagine that a hiring manager has advertised a position on several major online job boards and in several regional newspapers. Within a week, there could be hundreds of resumes sent in response to the posting, all sitting on the HR (human resources) professional's desk. When that HR person starts scanning through the stack, if your resume catches his or her eye, your resume is more likely to end up in the pile that gets further consideration.

That doesn't mean you should use a bizarre typestyle, or print your resume on purple paper. You should, however, take the time necessary to prepare a resume that doesn't look just like everyone else's. The easiest way to achieve this is with typestyles (or fonts) other than Times Roman, which is the most widely used typestyle in business and on resumes. For every 100 resumes that I see, more than 80 of them are in Times Roman, which makes them all look very similar. Following are examples of some typestyles you might consider that will help distinguish your resume from the rest of the crowd. They're still clear and easy to read, and common to most word processing software, but subtly different from Times Roman:

Georgia	Tahoma	Arial
Garamond	**Verdana**	Century Schoolbook

Once you've finished following all the steps in this chapter and have a draft of your resume on the computer screen, experiment with different typestyles to see which one you like best. There are some cautions about using different typestyles if you are planning to send your resume electronically. These will be addressed in Chapter 4. Refer to the following chart displaying typestyles in various sizes to help you choose one that's best for you.

Comparison of Common Resume Typestyles and Sizes

Size	Roman	**Bold**	*Italic*
10-pt.	Arial Bookman Old Style Garamond Tahoma Times New Roman Verdana	**Arial** **Bookman Old Style** **Garamond** **Tahoma** **Times New Roman** **Verdana**	*Arial* *Bookman Old Style* *Garamond* *Tahoma* *Times New Roman* *Verdana*
10.5-pt.	Arial Bookman Old Style Garamond Tahoma Times New Roman Verdana	**Arial** **Bookman Old Style** **Garamond** **Tahoma** **Times New Roman** **Verdana**	*Arial* *Bookman Old Style* *Garamond* *Tahoma* *Times New Roman* *Verdana*
11-pt.	Arial Bookman Old Style Garamond Tahoma Times New Roman Verdana	**Arial** **Bookman Old Style** **Garamond** **Tahoma** **Times New Roman** **Verdana**	*Arial* *Bookman Old Style* *Garamond* *Tahoma* *Times New Roman* *Verdana*
11.5-pt.	Arial Bookman Old Style Garamond Tahoma Times New Roman Verdana	**Arial** **Bookman Old Style** **Garamond** **Tahoma** **Times New Roman** **Verdana**	*Arial* *Bookman Old Style* *Garamond* *Tahoma* *Times New Roman* *Verdana*
12-pt.	Arial Bookman Old Style Garamond Tahoma Times New Roman Verdana	**Arial** **Bookman Old Style** **Garamond** **Tahoma** **Times New Roman** **Verdana**	*Arial* *Bookman Old Style* *Garamond* *Tahoma* *Times New Roman* *Verdana*

Other commonly used design enhancements are **boldface**, *italics*, and <u>underlining</u>. When used appropriately, these elements can effectively draw attention to section headings, job titles, employer names, college degrees, notable achievements, and any other information you want to highlight. However, be forewarned: these enhancements only work to your advantage when they're not overused. For example, if you put half of your resume in bold print, you've defeated the purpose, as nothing will stand out. You may also consider using lines, boxes, columns, and other graphics to enhance the visual impact of your resume. Many of these enhancements are used in the sample resumes that appear in Chapters 5 through 15. One caution, however, if you decide to utilize graphics: "cute" does not work on a resume! Rather, your graphics must be appropriate to your profession and your industry, and enhance the overall presentation.

For example, in general, an engineer's resume should be conservative. The typestyle should be easy to read (for example, Tahoma or Arial), only simple lines or boxes should be used to offset any text, and it should be printed on white, ivory, or light gray paper. On the other hand, a graphic artist's resume should demonstrate that candidate's artistic capabilities. Typestyles can be less conservative (for example, Schoolbook, Garamond, or something more exotic, such as Brush Script or Freehand); designer lines, boxes, columns, and graphics can be used throughout; and paper selection should be unique (for example, blue, dusty rose, or pinstripe). The reader should be just as impressed with the visual presentation as with the content.

As you view the sample resumes throughout this book, take note of how design and formatting have been used to deliver an eye-catching and appealing presentation. Indeed, some of the samples are in this book as much because of their appearance as they are because of their content.

Chapter 4
Preparing Your Resume for Cyberspace

Congratulations! If you've made it this far, you should already have a well-written resume to use as a tool in your job search. By using the surveys described in Chapter 1, you defined who you are by identifying what you do well and what you enjoy doing. In Chapter 2, you learned about the five keys to building your successful resume. And Chapter 3 provided you with details on how to write and format your resume. These steps have led you through a process that should have resulted in a printed resume, which is what you most likely imagine when you think about resumes. You probably used a computer to create a word-processed document, and this is likely the version that you will mail or fax to prospective employers and recruiters, take on job interviews, and use as a networking tool. In effect, this is the "human-eye" version, because the overall design and even the paper choice are meant to appeal to readers as they hold that paper copy of the document in their hands.

Although your printed resume is a key component in your job search tool box, there are other versions of your resume that you'll find most useful as you embark on your job search. These days, employers and recruiters are relying more and more on e-mail and other online methods of transmitting and tracking information about job candidates. Therefore, it's vital to your job search success to have the proper electronic versions of your resume to complement your printed document, thus giving you the full set of tools.

E-resumes, the Wave of the Future

An e-resume, or electronic version of your resume, is important for two reasons. First, using current technology allows you to circumvent "snail mail" and get your job-search documents into the hands of the appropriate hiring authority quickly and efficiently. Second, the recipient can instantly share your resume with others who may have a stake in the hiring process. Imagine a human resources manager effortlessly forwarding your e-mailed resume to a hiring manager within minutes or even seconds of receiving it from you, the applicant.

In addition to the convenience of sending and receiving documents electronically, the electronic medium also allows employers to subtly test your capacity to use the technology. An executive recruiter once told me, "If a candidate can't e-mail me his resume [without any glitches], then he's probably not someone we really want to talk to." That doesn't mean you have to be a techno-geek, but it does mean that you need to have a basic understanding of e-resume design and distribution. That means you need to be able to create four versions of your resume and successfully integrate them into your job search. These four versions are:

1. E-mail attachments
2. ASCII text files
3. Scannable resumes
4. Web resumes

E-mail attachments

Chances are, whatever job target you plan to pursue, you'll find yourself e-mailing resumes to prospective employers and recruiters fairly regularly. It's likely that e-mailing will become your most frequently used method of resume distribution.

The e-mail attachment you send should be the word-processed version of your resume. I recommend that you prepare your resume in Microsoft Word because it is used by more than 80 percent of the business world, and you can be reasonably sure that your resume will arrive in the same format and presentation style as your carefully prepared original. If you do not use Word as your word-processing software, you run the risk of having your resume lose much of its presentation value—or worse yet, arrive in an unreadable state—because of format shifts. When that happens, the prospective employer will most likely delete the whole e-mail, and you will have missed your opportunity to interview for that job. If you're serious about your job search, it's worth it to purchase a copy of Microsoft Word; if not, use a friend's computer with an up-to-date version of Word loaded on it, or consider sending your resume in Rich Text Format (RTF), Portable Document Format (PDF), or as an ASCII text file. There are also "open source" versions of office applications available for free download from the Internet. If you're interested in exploring such possibilities, it may be an alternative to paying for the brand name in the box. Be aware, however, that there are no solid guarantees as to the reliability or compatibility of such "shareware."

When you prepare your resume for e-mail transmission, there are a few precautions to take that will ensure that your documents arrive in an attractive and readable format. With a variety of software and operating systems currently in use (including any number of versions of Word), your carefully formatted resume document may appear quite different when viewed and/or printed by prospective employers. This problem is only made worse by the countless different brands and models of printers on the market, each with its own printer driver. It's possible that your tightly formatted, two-page resume can wind up on four pages because of different default margins on the printer at the other end, or because of the use of an unusual font. It's tough to completely eliminate such issues, but following these guidelines can help minimize any problems:

- Use a minimum of 3/4-inch margins on all four sides of the page. Margins wider than 3/4-inch are okay, but anything less can lead to problems.

- Use common typestyles. Times New Roman and Arial are found in virtually all versions of Microsoft Word currently in use. That doesn't mean that you can't use other typestyles for your printed resume, but for the best chance of compatibility with those reading your e-mailed resume, use the recommended fonts.

- If you use any word-processing software other than Microsoft Word, consider saving the file in Rich Text Format (.rtf). In most word-processing applications, this is a choice from the **Save As** menu, and the .rtf suffix generally appears at the end of the file name when the document is saved. This file format is accepted by most software and overcomes many compatibility issues.

- Consider sending your resume attachment as a Portable Document Format (.pdf) if your resume has unique design elements (which are potentially corruptible by software compatibility issues) and if design skills are key to the position(s) you are pursuing. PDFs are viewed as graphics and are not editable, so they cannot generally be downloaded and stored in searchable databases. However, a PDF resume can be advantageous if your resume has unique design characteristics, as this format allows you to preserve your attractively designed document the way you intended it to appear.

- Send the e-mail attachment to yourself and to several friends who have different e-mail providers (AOL, Yahoo!, Hotmail, Gmail, and so on). This gives you the opportunity to see what your resume looks like when downloaded and opened, and gives you the opportunity to make any adjustments and correct any problems prior to sending it to an employer or recruiter.

Once your resume has been prepared for electronic transmission, you can send it just as you would any other attachment. Open your e-mail program, input the recipient's e-mail address, write a message, attach your resume, and send the e-mail message with the document attached. It's that easy and only takes a moment or two. However, you will want to carefully consider what you include in the subject line and the body of the e-mail message.

Your subject line should include the title of the position for which you are applying (and the job/vacancy announcement number, if applicable). You should also include the words "resume of," followed by your name. This format immediately alerts the recipient that you're responding to a posted job announcement and have forwarded your resume. Here's an example:

> **Director of Operations (#45893) – Resume of William Coles**

Perhaps you're not responding to a specific job announcement and are simply e-mailing your resume to a prospective employer or recruiter in anticipation of an appropriate opening. In such a case, use a headline similar to what you may have used in the summary section of your resume. This clearly identifies who you are and the type of position you are seeking. For example:

> **Vice President of Sales / Director of Business Development**

In the body of your e-mail, you can do one of the following:
1. Include a text version of your cover letter as your e-mail message, referencing that your resume is attached as a Word file.
2. Include a brief statement such as, "Please see the attached resume and cover letter in response to your recent job announcement for a _____."

Either of these choices is acceptable, but with the proliferation of text-heavy spam e-mails, a case can be made for using a message that is short and succinct, as option two suggests.

Following is an example of a Word resume ready for electronic submission:

Adam Loughran

1218 Steven's Creek Hill • Pultneyville, New York 14538 • (315) 216-1953 • AdamL@yahoo.com

CUSTOMER SERVICE / ORDER ENTRY – MACHINE TOOL INDUSTRY

Dynamic individual with strong technical skills and excellent customer relations capabilities. Successful track-record in order entry /customer service positions. Hands-on experience as machinist, aircraft mechanic, and chemical technologist. Strong ability to lead and motivate others to meet corporate objectives.

PROFESSIONAL EXPERIENCE:

2000 - Present   **Customer Service / Order Editor, Machine Tool Enterprises; Avon, NY**
Communicate with customers on issues relating to order entry, expediting shipments, and pricing /invoicing. Began as lathe operator and was promoted to Order Editor position.
- Confer with production planning and manufacturing to determine ship dates on ordered machines.
- Trace orders to identify delays and expedite delivery.
- Research and resolve billing discrepancies.
- Process returns of defective equipment.

Accomplishments:
Utilized Lotus 1-2-3 spreadsheet to develop software system for tracking production capacity and projected ship dates on ordered machines.
Received Attendance Awards annually 2000 - 2007.

1999 - 2000   **Grinder / Machinist, New Horizon Products; Syracuse, NY**
Ground precision metal parts to close tolerances (+/- .010").

1998   **Electronics Technician**
'Lectric Light Unlimited; Liverpool, NY *and* **Fletcher & Holmes; Solvay, NY**
(Temporary Assignments through The Employment Store)
Inspected and tested electronic systems. Identified source of malfunctions and effected repairs. Utilized oscilloscopes, multi-meters, and other test equipment.

1995 - 1998   **Aircraft Maintenance Technician, USAirways; Pittsburgh, PA**
Repaired and maintained hydraulic, pneumatic, mechanical, and electronic systems of jet and turbo-prop aircraft for regional airline.

EDUCATION:

2005   ***Rochester Institute of Technology; Rochester, NY***
Bachelor of Science in Management.

2001   **Associate of Applied Science, Business Administration**
Monroe Community College; Rochester, New York.
Graduated with Distinction / GPA: 3.73.

1999   **Tooling & Machinist Certificate**
Monroe Community College; Rochester, New York.

1995   **Certificate in Aircraft Maintenance**
Morrow School of Aeronautics; Springdale, Pennsylvania.

SPECIAL SKILLS / COMPUTER LITERACY:

Commercial Pilot / Flight Instructor - Instrument Rating.
Windows XP, Microsoft Office, Lotus Smart Suite, MAP, MRP, BAAN

ASCII text files

There may still be a few recruiters and employers who insist on receiving an ASCII text version of your resume. The advantages for the recipient include the fact that Internet viruses and worms can't hide in an ASCII text file. Even with sophisticated firewalls and virus protection in place, some businesses still do not accept e-mails with attachments. If this is the case, pasting your ASCII text resume into an e-mail message is the only way to send it electronically to those organizations.

ASCII text files are also useful when you need to paste your resume into an online job application. You can have the text version of your resume open on your computer at the same time you are viewing the online job application. By clicking back and forth between the two documents, you can copy and paste sections of your resume into the boxes provided on the application. Because this can save a great deal of time and prevent errors, an ASCII text version of your resume is a valuable tool for every job seeker. You can also be certain that an ASCII text file will be scannable, and can serve double duty in that regard. If someone asks for a scannable version of your resume and they do not open attachments, an ASCII text version of your resume is the document to submit.

Formatting an ASCII text resume is relatively simple if you follow these steps for Microsoft Word and similar word-processing programs:

- With your resume document open on the screen, choose **Save As** from the **File** menu.

- Select **Text Only**, **ASCII**, or **Plain Text** as your choice in the option box. You may want to give the file a slightly different name to differentiate it from your word-processed version. When you click **Save**, you will get a message warning you about losing content or formatting by saving the file in ASCII format. Ignore the message and click on **Yes** or **OK** (whichever your computer displays).

- Close the file and then reopen it. You will see that your resume has been stripped of all formatting and appears as left-justified text in the Courier font.

- Now set both the left and right side margins at 2 inches. This will center the text on the screen and optimize its readability when the file is reopened at some later time. This will also allow you to recognize any unusual line breaks that lead to awkward changes in format, which you can easily fix.

- Carefully proofread the resume for any glitches that may have occurred during the file conversion. You may wish to print the resume and proofread from a hard copy. Many people find it easier to spot errors on the printed page. You may see that many characters, such as quotation marks, dashes, or apostrophes, now appear as question marks or some other character. Simply replace these by typing in the appropriate character.

☐ Make any other adjustments that you feel will improve the readability of your text resume (for example, adding line returns, creating horizontal dividers to separate sections, and so on).

☐ Be sure to save the corrected version of your resume document.

☐ Proofread again, preferably after some time has passed, to ensure that you haven't missed anything.

Following is an example of an ASCII text resume:

— —

```
Adam Loughran
1218 Steven's Creek Hill
Pultneyville, New York 14538
(315) 216-1953
AdamL@yahoo.com

CUSTOMER SERVICE / ORDER ENTRY
MACHINE TOOL INDUSTRY

Dynamic individual with strong technical skills and excellent
customer relations capabilities. Successful track-record in
order entry/customer service positions. Hands-on experience as
machinist, aircraft mechanic, and chemical technologist. Strong
ability to lead and motivate others to meet corporate
objectives.


+++++++++++++++++++++++++++++++++++++++++++++++++++++++++++


PROFESSIONAL EXPERIENCE:

2000 - Present
Customer Service / Order Editor,
Machine Tool Enterprises; Avon, NY


Communicate with customers on issues relating to order entry,
expediting shipments, and pricing/invoicing. Began as lathe
operator and was promoted to Order Editor position.
- Confer with production planning and manufacturing to determine
ship dates on ordered machines.
- Trace orders to identify delays and expedite delivery.
- Research and resolve billing discrepancies.
- Process returns of defective equipment.
```

Accomplishments:

Utilized Lotus 1-2-3 spreadsheet to develop software system for
tracking production capacity and projected ship dates on ordered
machines.

Received Attendance Awards annually 2000 - 2007.

1999 - 2000
Grinder / Machinist,
New Horizon Products; Syracuse, New York.

Ground precision metal parts to close tolerances (+/- .010").

1998
Electronics Technician
'Lectric Light Unlimited;
Liverpool, NY and Fletcher & Holmes; Solvay, NY
(Temporary Assignments through The Employment Store)

Inspected and tested electronic systems. Identified source of
malfunctions and effected repairs. Utilized oscilloscopes, multi-
meters, and other test equipment.

1995 - 1998
Aircraft Maintenance Technician,
USAirways; Pittsburgh, Pennsylvania.

Repaired and maintained hydraulic, pneumatic, mechanical, and
electronic systems of jet and turbo-prop aircraft for regional
airline.

++
EDUCATION:

2005
Rochester Institute of Technology;
Rochester, New York
Bachelor of Science in Management.

```
2001
Associate of Applied Science, Business Administration
Monroe Community College; Rochester, New York.
Graduated with Distinction / GPA: 3.73.


1999
Tooling & Machinist Certificate
Monroe Community College; Rochester, New York.


1995
Certificate in Aircraft Maintenance
Morrow School of Aeronautics; Springdale, Pennsylvania.



SPECIAL SKILLS / COMPUTER LITERACY:


Commercial Pilot / Flight Instructor - Instrument Rating.


Windows XP, Microsoft Office, Lotus Smart Suite, MAP, MRP, BAAN
```

Scannable resumes

A scannable resume is a study in simplicity. Fancy typestyles, bold, and italics, and graphics such as borders, underlining, or unique symbols are stripped away to create a very plain version of your resume. The objective is to make your resume easily read and interpreted by scanning software used by employers and recruiters to file and track your resume in a database for later retrieval. To maximize the likelihood that this will happen smoothly, follow these guidelines to prepare a scannable version of your resume:

- Choose an easy-to-read font such as Times Roman or Arial.
- Avoid using bold, italic, or underlined type.
- Stick to type sizes of 11 point or larger (12 point is probably optimal).
- Make sure that only your name appears on the top line of the first page, followed by your contact information.
- At the top of each subsequent page, type your name on the first line, your telephone number on the second line, and your e-mail address on the third line.

- All of the text should be left-justified with a ragged-right margin.
- Be careful about using abbreviations. Widely used initialisms, such as BA for Bachelor of Arts, or acronyms such as OSHA (Occupational Safety and Health Administration) are fine to use, but if you have any doubts about the proper interpretation you should write it out.
- Eliminate borders or graphics, including horizontal or vertical lines, tables, and columns.
- Use common keyboard symbols such as the asterisk in places where you would use a bullet in your printed resume.
- Instead of using characters such as % or &, spell out the words ("percent" or "and").
- If slashes (/) are used, make sure you leave a space before and after each slash to ensure the scanner won't see it as a letter and misinterpret the word or phrase.
- Use a laser printer and print your document on smooth, white paper, rather than paper with any kind of texture, color, or pattern. White photocopy paper that you can purchase at any office supply store is fine for this purpose.
- Always use a paper clip; never staple the pages together.
- Mail the resume flat in a 9-by-12 envelope so it won't be folded. Unfortunately, the post office has dramatically raised postage rates on these so-called flats, but unless you're mailing out hundreds of resumes at one time, it's worth the few extra cents.

Scannable resumes are becoming somewhat passé with the wide use of e-mail, but they are still requested by some recruiters or employers, and thus should be an available tool in your job search toolbox. Again, an ASCII text resume can double as a scannable resume, but if you'd prefer to see your document in a typestyle other than Courier, you may wish to create a separate scannable document using Times, Arial, or one of the other more common typestyles available. Following is an example of a scannable resume:

Adam Loughran
1218 Steven's Creek Hill
Pultneyville, New York 14538
(315) 216-1953
AdamL@yahoo.com

CUSTOMER SERVICE / ORDER ENTRY – MACHINE TOOL INDUSTRY

Dynamic individual with strong technical skills and excellent customer relations capabilities. Successful track-record in order entry / customer service positions. Hands-on experience as machinist, aircraft mechanic, and chemical technologist. Strong ability to lead and motivate others to meet corporate objectives.

PROFESSIONAL EXPERIENCE:

2000 - Present
Customer Service / Order Editor, Machine Tool Enterprises; Avon, New York
Communicate with customers on issues relating to order entry, expediting shipments, and pricing / invoicing. Began as lathe operator and was promoted to Order Editor position.
- Confer with production planning and manufacturing to determine ship dates on ordered machines.
- Trace orders to identify delays and expedite delivery.
- Research and resolve billing discrepancies.
- Process returns of defective equipment.

Accomplishments:
Utilized Lotus 1-2-3 spreadsheet to develop software system for tracking production capacity and projected ship dates on ordered machines.

Received Attendance Awards annually 2000 - 2007.

1999 - 2000
Grinder / Machinist, New Horizon Products; Syracuse, New York.
Ground precision metal parts to close tolerances (+ / - .010").

1998
Electronics Technician
'Lectric Light Unlimited; Liverpool, New York and Fletcher & Holmes; Solvay, New York
(Temporary Assignments through The Employment Store)
Inspected and tested electronic systems. Identified source of malfunctions and effected repairs. Utilized oscilloscopes, multi-meters, and other test equipment.

1995 - 1998
Aircraft Maintenance Technician, USAirways; Pittsburgh, Pennsylvania.
Repaired and maintained hydraulic, pneumatic, mechanical, and electronic systems of jet and turbo-prop aircraft for regional airline.

EDUCATION:

2005
Rochester Institute of Technology; Rochester, New York
Bachelor of Science in Management.

2001
Associate of Applied Science, Business Administration
Monroe Community College; Rochester, New York.
Graduated with Distinction / GPA: 3.73.

1999
Tooling & Machinist Certificate
Monroe Community College; Rochester, New York.

1995
Certificate in Aircraft Maintenance
Morrow School of Aeronautics; Springdale, Pennsylvania.

SPECIAL SKILLS / COMPUTER LITERACY:

Commercial Pilot / Flight Instructor - Instrument Rating.

Windows XP, Microsoft Office, Lotus Smart Suite, MAP, MRP, BAAN

Web resumes

As technology continues to evolve, more and more job seekers are using Web resumes. Many job candidates are creating their own Websites where employers can view their resumes online. To create a Web resume, you will want to have your own URL (Website address), which you can set up on your own or with professional assistance.

Web resumes can vary greatly in their presentation. Some are merely an electronic, online representation of a candidate's printed resume that the employer can access to download and print. Others are highly designed Websites that function as online portfolios. You can include a link to your Web resume in any e-mails you send, making it possible for a prospective employer or recruiter to view your resume with just one click.

IT professionals and others who are techno-savvy can use their online portfolio to highlight a broad range of skills and achievements that are not practical to include on a conventional resume because of length restrictions. Consider including a complete listing of your technology skills and competencies, a complete listing of your technical training and certifications, and / or a complete listing of all of the projects on which you've worked. E-resumes and e-portfolios are also golden opportunities for technology professionals to demonstrate their technical prowess by designing the Website themselves.

The electronic portfolio concept can also be effectively used by other job seekers. A marketing executive might include successful marketing plans or advertising storyboards as pages on the Website. Or, a professional designer can include several pages of his or her designs as evidence of his or her creativity and innovation. Some candidates have included video clips introducing themselves and directing the viewer to other pages on the site. The opportunities you have to develop a powerful Web presentation are limited only by your imagination.

If you're adequately techno-savvy, creating an online portfolio can be advantageous to your job search as well as great fun. For most of the rest of us, whose core skills do not include Web development, hiring a professional to help may be the best course of action. You'll be surprised at how affordable this can be. To get a sense of what e-resumes and e-portfolios are all about, we suggest visiting these Websites:

www.blueskyportfolios.com

www.brandego.com

Transmitting an e-mail message that references your Web-based resume is easy to do. Instead of attaching a Microsoft Word document to an e-mail message, you simply include the link that will take the reader to the Website where your resume may be viewed, enlarged, printed, and evaluated by prospective employers and recruiters. What's more, it's easy to make changes to your Web-based resume if you need to update it, change certain information, add recent training, and soon.

Electronic Resumes—Design Considerations

	Word-Processed Resumes	**ASCII Text Resumes**	**Scannable Resumes**	**Web Resumes**
Typestyle/Font	Crisp, clean, distinctive (See recommendations in Chapter 2).	Courier.	Stick to the basics; Times Roman, Arial.	Choose fonts that look attractive on screen and reproduce well when printed.
Typestyle Effects	**Boldface**, *italics*, and <u>underlining</u> are all acceptable and recommended, as appropriate.	CAPITALIZATION is the only enhancement available.	CAPITALIZATION is the only enhancement thst will scan reliably.	A full range of design elements are available, including color.
Type Size	11-pt. or 12-pt. for body of the document. Use larger sizes (14,16,18) for name and headings.	12-point.	11-pt. or 12-pt. preferred.	11-pt. or 12-pt. for body of the document. Use larger sizes (14,16,18) for name and headings.
White Space	Use to optimize readability.	Separate sections to enhance readability.	Use liberally to maximize scannability.	Use to optimize readability.

Electronic Resumes—Production Considerations

	Word-Processed Resumes	ASCII Text Resumes	Scannable Resumes	Web Resumes
Text Format	Use centering, indents, etc., to create an appealing presentation.	Everything strictly flush left.	Everything strictly flush left.	Capitalize on the flexibility the Web offers to crate an appealing presentation.
Preferred Length	Generally, 1 or 2 pages; 3 pages is acceptable for senior-level canidates.	Length doesn't matter. Converting the resume will undoubtedly make it longer than the printed version	Length doesn't matter. Converting the resume will undoubtedly make it longer than the printed version.	Length is not critical, but be sure the site is well organized so that viewers can easily find what you most want them to see.
Preferred Paper Color	White, ivory, or light gray are most preferred	Not applicable.	Bright white or cream (natural). No patterns or shading that might interfere with scanning.	Paper is a non-issue; choose background colors that allow for readability and reproduce well if printed.

Chapter 5

Resumes for Parents Returning to Work

In this chapter, you will find resumes for moms and dads returning to the workforce after a hiatus. Job targets include:

Meeting Planner / Convention Services Representative
Event Planner / Fundraiser
Customer Service / Office Manager
Teacher's Aide / Para-Professional
Financial Planner
Customer Service / Account Manager
Athletic Director / High School Coach
Medical Billing

If you've been on the mommy track (or daddy track, as the case may be), you've devoted yourself to your family and probably worked harder than if you had held a "real job." But now that you're ready to get back into the conventional workforce, your challenge is to convince employers that you've got a wealth of skills to offer and are eager to demonstrate your capabilities. If this sounds like you, there are several key things to remember as you prepare your resume and cover letters. Here are just a few tips that you may find helpful:

1. Consider a functional format for your resume. This approach will allow you to highlight your past skills, regardless of when you acquired them or how long ago you may have last used them. This also has the

advantage of playing down the extended period of time that you have not held a paying job outside the home.

2. Show your volunteer experiences with full job descriptions as if they were paying jobs. If you held an officer or advisory board position with the PTA or your daughter's soccer league, you probably logged many hours and performed many organizational or managerial tasks. If you chaired a fundraising campaign at your child's nursery school or at your church, you most likely used a number of skills that can be relevant to your next employer. Be sure to include accomplishments from these volunteer experiences: How much money was raised? What initiative was advanced due to your efforts?

3. Lead with your strengths. Depending on your circumstances, your education or recent technical training may be your best asset for the job you are targeting. Even if you haven't completed your degree, it may be advantageous to show that you attended or are currently attending college, especially if your major relates to the targeted job.

4. If your technology skills are up to date, be sure to mention them prominently. Are you current on the newest version of MS Office? Have you used QuickBooks or some other accounting software? One concern employers have about hiring employees with any kind of employment gap is that their skills may be outdated or obsolete. If you've stayed current with computer skills or other technical proficiencies, make certain your resume reflects that fact.

On the following pages is an excellent example of a cover letter as well as several resumes for parents returning to the workforce.

Claire Majors

73 Reese Lane
Grand Falls, MN 56201

(505) 213-6918 or (505) 201-6918 (cell)
claire.majors@yahoo.com

January 12, 2008

Duane Larson, Director
Human Resources Department
University of Minnesota
PO Box 5555
Grand Falls, MN 56201

Dear Mr. Larson:

My qualifications and background are a great fit for the Conference Services Program Assistant position (#06-202) as listed on the University of Minnesota's Website. Here are some examples of how I have performed very similar duties:

- You need someone who can organize materials and manage an out-of-town conference. I've moved my family 13 times in 13 years.

- You need someone who can coordinate meeting arrangements. I've hosted a luncheon for a four-star general's wife and 20 others in my home. I've developed and coordinated volunteer teams to plan and host official social gatherings for as many as 500 culturally diverse guests.

- You need someone to produce and distribute packets, tickets, signs, nametags, brochures, registrations, mailing lists, rosters and database records. I have done these things, plus I am capable of writing the required database programs, if necessary.

- You need someone with exceptional interpersonal skills to welcome people to your office and to events. I have hosted NATO dignitaries known for strict protocol expectations, requiring finesse and the ability to think quickly "on one's feet."

- You need someone who presents a professional, friendly and helpful face across the desk and voice across the phone line. I have developed diplomatic skills through my work as Command Spouse, and am comfortable working with people of diverse rank, heritage, and culture.

With my Bachelor's degree in Business Administration, it may appear that I am overqualified for this position, but I assure you that I am genuinely interested in exceeding your expectations in the role of Conference Services Program Assistant. I look forward to participating in the off-base community that I have come to think of as my home, following my departure from the role of Command Spouse next month, when my husband will accept a new assignment.

I believe my skills and abilities would combine to make me a valuable member of the University Conference Services team, as summarized in the enclosed resume.

Thank you for your time and attention. I will call you soon to answer any questions.

Sincerely,

Claire Majors

Enclosure

Resume Writer: Jeri Dutcher

Claire Majors

73 Reese Lane
Grand Falls, MN 56201

(505) 213-6918 or (500) 201-6918 (cell)
claire.majors@yahoo.com

Planner/Coordinator/Manager

Career Command spouse skilled in international diplomacy and military protocol with experience in England, Okinawa, California, Florida, Kansas, Rhode Island, Illinois and Minnesota. Advisor, liaison, coordinator and planner for military, families and community. Equally comfortable interacting with people at all levels facing a variety of challenges (NATO four-star generals, PFC spouses with newborn infants, etc.). Routinely coordinate special events for up to 300 people.

Claire is a skillful manager who is an excellent team leader with great abilities to motivate people… She is highly versatile with a winning personality…"

- Former Supervisor

Accomplishments

Grand Falls Air Force Base

- Plan and coordinate with protocol office hundreds of annual military/community events to enhance relationship between military families and surrounding community, including events for families of deployed military members; military galas, fundraisers and open houses for as many as 300 people; luncheon events in my own and others' homes for 20 people including four-star general's wife. Because of military budget cutbacks, duties expanded from decorating and food ordering to include guest list coordination, invitation design, seating charts and cooking.

- Co-host official functions for 19 squadrons and 4 groups during 25 changes of command in past two years.

- Facilitate monthly meetings with key stakeholders to identify and meet needs of military families; serve as liaison and advisor among many groups on Air Force Base.

- Coordinate Key Spouse Program by recruiting and training individuals to fill support role at squadron level of Air Force Base.

- Publish squadron monthly newsletter, and various directories to keep community members informed and connected. Automated mailing lists.

- Advise Officers' Spouses Club on budgeting, fundraising, charitable contributions, social and educational programs and legal responsibilities. Implemented the first computerized budgeting program for the organization.

- Served on panel that interviewed and selected school board members for Air Force Base.

- Raised $11,000 in scholarship funds for children of military members through the Officers' Spouses Club charity auction (in October, 2005).

- Coordinated "Trip Around the World" dinner for Empire Arts fundraiser (April, 2005).

- Selected to judge Athena competition (February, 2005).

Resume Writer: Jeri Dutcher

Work History

Command Spouse (Volunteer)   1988 - Present
Grand Falls AFB, MN; NATO, High Wycombe, England; McDill AFB, Valentia, FL; Naval Air
Station, Newport, RI; Scott AFB, IL; Castle AFB, CA; Kadena AFB, Okinawa, Japan.

Neighborhood Watch Coordinator / Web Designer (Volunteer)   August 2002 - May 2003
Valentia, Florida
  + Recruited and organized block captains; created call chain.
  + Developed electronic database; distributed and gathered questionnaires; recorded
    results.

Volleyball Coach (Paid)
Taylor School, Grand Falls AFB, MN   October to December 2005
London West High School, High Wycombe, England   August 1998 - December 1999
  + Coached two seasons and coordinated week-long summer camp with international
    player and coach Debbie Sokol for Department of Defense England schools.

Computer Trainer and Database Developer (Volunteer)   September 1996 - May 1997
Armed Services YMCA, Newport, Rhode Island
  + Taught classes in Windows 95, Microsoft Word and Introduction to Computers.
  + Wrote Access database to track donations and newsletter recipients.

Previous paid and volunteer positions included the following:
    Contract Programmer Analyst / Help Desk Support (Betac, Belleville, IL)
    Programming Supervisor / Systems Programmer (Merced County, CA)
    Automated Data Processing Director (Kadena AFB, Okinawa, Japan)
    Sales Manager (American Computers)
    English Teacher (Okinawan International School)
    Substitute Teacher (Department of Defense Schools K-12, Okinawa, Japan)
    Systems Analyst (Boeing Computing Services, Wichita, KS)

Education

Lincoln State University, Kansas, **Bachelor of Science, Business Administration**

Private Pilot License, 1995

BEVERLY J. ELLIS

777 Wingate Drive ◆ Wilmington, NC 28412 ◆ Phone: (219) 543-2109 ◆ bellis3@hotmail.com

CUSTOMER SERVICE/OFFICE ADMINISTRATION

INSIDE SALES • ORDER PROCESSING • INVENTORY CONTROL

Accomplished professional with extensive experience in customer service and supervision. Seasoned expert in problem resolution and client relations. Able to direct staff in a fast-paced environment and deliver sound decisions under pressure. Strong ability to communicate with internal and external customers, face-to-face and over the telephone. Ability to operate autonomously or as part of team. Proven track record of meeting and exceeding customer and company expectations.

QUALIFICATIONS

CUSTOMER SERVICE: *Sales Support, Problem Resolution, Product Selection*

Hired as facility receptionist, answering a four-line switchboard, and quickly advanced to positions with expanded responsibilities and increased customer interaction. Supported outside sales staff; apprised customers of order status; resolved problems.

- Helped customers with product selection and special order placement. Expedited order fulfillment. Handled walk-in counter sales traffic.
- Traveled with outside sales reps in NC / SC territory and met with key account representatives. Responded to customer questions and resolved shipping issues through in-house and vendor follow-up and coordination.
- Selected to operate on-site customer tool crib for Manufacturing International.

SUPERVISION: *Material Handling, Inventory Control, Tool Crib*

Oversaw operation of material handling equipment repair and spare parts inventory department. Monitored on-hand stock movement and reported on intra-company transfers. Updated inventory control and customer databases.

- Supervised and scheduled seven forklift repair mechanics. Determined client sense of urgency and re-routed / re-directed repair personnel to meet need.
- Received 35+ calls per day regarding order status, part availability and product maintenance. Notified clients upon receipt of special orders and shipped material per customer requirements.
- Managed beginning-to-end operation of on-site tool crib. Sold tools and supplies, issued purchase orders and invoices. Compiled daily business activity reports. Operated with minimal outside intervention.

ADMINISTRATION: *Order Processing, Billing, Shipping*

Took, clarified and edited customer orders and entered them into company database. Completed medical insurance claim forms. Posted payment to customer accounts. Covered switchboard and processed incoming mail.

- Filed and followed-up on in / out patient insurance claims for 124-bed hospital facility.
- Generated stock delivery and transfer tickets. Billed customer accounts and sent out monthly statements.
- Supported office operation with filing, owner administrative support and other essential duties.

WORK HISTORY

Parker Memorial Hospital
Laurinburg, NC (1999 – 2005)
Insurance Clerk/Customer Service

Wilmington Wholesale Supply Company
Laurinburg, NC (1994 – 1999)
Materials Handling Parts Manager; Manufacturing Tool Crib Coordinator; Inside Sales; Counter Sales;
Receptionist / Data Entry

◆ ◆ ◆

Resume Writer: Dawn Bugni

Annmarie Guevarra Aleman

2368 Elm Run Drive ● Bethesda, MD 20850 ● 301.641.9238 ● aga@verizon.net

OBJECTIVE/ PROFESSIONAL PROFILE

Bilingual communicator (fluent in English and Spanish) with excellent organizational skills seeking a permanent position in education. Currently pursuing a Bachelor's degree in education. Creative problem-solver; dedicated and driven to succeed. Able to put others at ease and build strong, positive relationships with children and adults.

EDUCATION

University of Maryland; College Park, MD
> Bachelor of Science, Education, Anticipated Graduation, 2009

Towson University, Towson, MD
> Bachelor of Arts, Graphic Design, Cum Laude, 1997
> Golden Key National Honor Society, 1996 - 1997

Montgomery College, Rockville, MD
> Associate of Arts, Business Administration, 1988

VOLUNTEER EXPERIENCE

Carderock Springs Elementary School, Bethesda, MD   2004 - Present
Parent Volunteer
Assist teachers in the classroom (Room Mother, 2005-Present; Classroom Aide, 2004-2005).
Plan, organize and participate in fundraising events (Co-chaired Silent Auction which raised $4,000; and Viva Italia! Dinner which raised $2,500).

American Cancer Society, Relay for Life, Baltimore, MD   1998 - 2002
Organizer/Participant
Assisted with all aspects of annual events held to raise funds for cancer research, and celebrate cancer survivors.

PROFESSIONAL EXPERIENCE

Montgomery County Public Schools, Rockville, MD   2005 - Present
Substitute Teacher
Teach pre-school to 7th grade and special education, as needed. Creatively engage students in learning; able to build positive rapport with students and with parents.

Mary Kay, Inc., Bethesda, MD   2002 - Present
Sales Representative
Self-motivated, customer-focused sales representative, determined to succeed. Consistently exceed goals. Recruit, and train new representatives. Provide strong leadership and support. *Achieved President's Club and Honor Society status 2003, 2004, and 2005.*

Maryland Communications, Inc., Columbia, MD   1998 - 1999
Graphic Designer
Created advertisements, brochures, posters, exhibits, and logos. Managed in-house marketing needs. Used effective communication skills and design expertise to meet clients' visual media goals. Consistently brought projects to successful completion within extremely tight deadlines. *Proficient in Illustrator, Photoshop, PageMaker, and QuarkXPress.*

> **Resume Writer: Sheri Hawes**

Melanie Daws

1930 Peters Mill Road, Suwanee, GA 30066 ▪ 877-470-3260 ▪ medaws@yahoo.com

SUMMARY OF QUALIFICATIONS

A successful financial services professional with more than 10 years of experience building service-related partnerships and expanding the customer base for reputable financial institutions.

- Establish customer trust and account loyalty
- Interact well with team members at all levels to ensure organizational goals are achieved
- Excel within highly competitive environments where leadership skills are the key to success
- Proven success in training, coaching, counseling and managing staff to its fullest potential
- Highly skilled in conducting needs analysis, educating clients on investment options and providing solutions

Client-Focused ▪ Analytical ▪ Flexible ▪ Results-oriented ▪ Team Player ▪ Self-Motivated ▪ Sales-Driven

KEY ACCOMPLISHMENTS

- **Promoted to Teller Supervisor** in little over a year by demonstrating excellence in the areas of coaching, team development, and management
- Developed **strong rapport** and offered excellent customer service, resulting in **20% of local credit union members** requesting me to consult exclusively with them regarding their financial needs
- **Initiated coaching and mentoring program** for new hires that was modeled & implemented at all branches.
- **Led teller sales team in referral campaign** which enhanced front-line service operations
- **Established dual control measures, audit logs, and key controls** for two new branches, resulting in "outstanding" audits
- **Managed financial services department** during Senior Financial Service Representative's absences
- **Mediated highly sensitive situations** in connection with settling deceased clients' accounts
- Participated in **community-wide events to enhance the institution's visibility**
- Received **excellent audits** for four consecutive years
- **Promoted to Head Teller** of a new branch after only six months of employment
- Ranked #1 among tellers branch-wide in cash reconciliation accuracy
- **Set up and organized teller department** for a new branch

PROFESSIONAL EXPERIENCE

MANAGEMENT & EMPLOYEE DEVELOPMENT
- Managed teller staff of nine for branch and drive-through banking operations
- Directed work flow to comply with institution's policies and procedures
- Hired, coached and counseled staff
- Conducted performance appraisals and disciplinary actions for six direct-reports
- Served as Acting Branch Manager during Branch Manager's absence
- Developed creative solutions for customer-related inquiries and escalated issues

SALES
- Consistently exceeded sales goals
- Prevented loss of accounts by highlighting the features and benefits pertinent to client's needs
- Cross sold banking products and services (mortgages, loans, credit cards, financial solutions)
- Facilitated monthly sales meetings
- Processed loan applications
- Opened new accounts (savings, checking, business accounts, money market and CDs)

Resume Writer: Nicole Darby

Melanie Daws   - 2 -

ACCOUNT MANAGEMENT & CLIENT RELATIONS
- Consulted with customers to understand their financial objectives and provide creative options
- Obtained and evaluated credit reports to determine membership eligibility
- Consistently handled financial transactions with accuracy (deposits, withdrawals, foreign currency)
- Acted as the primary contact for client requests that required special research or detailed explanations
- Processed a wide variety of requests via telephone, fax, mail and e-mail

OPERATIONS
- Performed branch opening and closing procedures
- Managed and secured cash and negotiable items necessary for daily bank operations
- Completed monthly audits for cash drawers, ATMs and key control
- Balanced ATMs and negotiable items (cashiers' checks, money orders and travelers' checks)
- Prepared and submitted various reports based on weekly staff meetings and internal communications
- Reviewed and approved all vendor activity, including office supply purchasing
- Opened and maintained safe deposit boxes

RETIREMENT PLANNING
- Opened and closed traditional, Roth and Coverdale Investment Retirement Accounts
- Processed IRA contributions, rollovers, minimum distribution requests and direct transfers
- Supported 25 branches with IRA-processing procedures, CD and new account requests
- Conducted daily support activities and compliance audits for 25 satellite branches

WORK HISTORY

Associated Markup Credit Union Financial Services Representative	04/01-05/05 Norcross, GA
Ironplan Bank Teller Supervisor	03/00-03/01 Alpharetta, GA
Top Flight Credit Union Teller Supervisor	09/96-12/99 Miami, FL
Head Teller	06/95-09/96
Teller	09/94-06/95

EDUCATION & TRAINING

American Intercontinental University **BS in Business Administration**	06/03-06/04 Atlanta, GA
Miami Dade Community College **AA in Business Administration**	10/98-06/00 Miami, FL

IRA Essentials & Advanced Training (2003)   Basic Credit Union Financials (2002)
Financial Services (2002)   Platform Training (2000)
Fraud Prevention (2000)   Teller Coaching / Counseling (1998)
Leadership Development (1997)   Managing for Success (1997)
Teller Training (1996)   Sales / Service (1996)

DEBBIE FOLEY

23 Garden Court
Princeton, NJ 08540
(609) 464-4019 • dfoley@msn.com

CUSTOMER SERVICE / CLIENT RELATIONS

High-energy, Results-Oriented Professional • Superb Telephone Communication Skills
Resourceful Multi-Tasker • Flexible & Adaptable • Dependable Under Pressure • Lifelong Learner
Record of Top-Notch Customer Care across Multiple Environments

CORE STRENGTHS

Communication Skills	Conflict Resolution	Self-Starter
Time Management	Relationship Building	Effective Listener
Training / Mentoring	Attention to Detail	Computer Literate

SUMMARY OF QUALIFICATIONS

Sales Representative, Coldwell Banker, Morris Plains, NJ   2001–Present
- Prospect and network to generate leads. Work primarily with first-time home buyers purchasing single or two-family homes, walking clients through the mortgage process with value-add service.
- Mentor new realtors within the office on policies, procedures, computer software, and best practices.

Notary Signing Agent, Princeton, NJ   2001–Present
- As a Notary Public, work with mortgage lenders and signing companies to ensure loan documents are properly signed and notarized.

Substitute Teacher K-12, Princeton Public School System, Princeton, NJ   2001–Present
- Implement daily lesson plans and classroom activities. Manage class sizes up to 30 students.
- Establish rapport with students to maintain order and an efficient learning environment. Classroom philosophy includes communicating with students with respect and patience.

CAREER HISTORY

Independent Sales Consultant, Tupperware (8 years)
Pastor's Assistant, Christian Reformed Church, Largo, FL (2 years)
Cafeteria Staff, Mildred Helms Elementary School, Largo, FL (2 years)
Private In-Home Daycare Provider, Largo, FL (2 years)
Assistant Branch Manager, California Savings & Loan, Lafayette, CA (2 years)
Sales Assistant, Prudential Securities, Los Angeles, CA (2 years)
Sales Assistant, Oppenheimer & Co., Los Angeles, CA (2 years)

EDUCATION & TRAINING

Bachelor of Arts in Communications with a minor in Business University of Delaware, Wilmington, DE
Substitute Teaching Seminar (September 2003)   William Paterson University, Wayne, NJ

Resume Writer: Laurie Berenson

JEREMEY BREYER

2704 Hacienda Plains Drive ✳ Tampa, FL 24739 ✳ j.breyer@att.net ✳ 446.901.2771

OBJECTIVE: ***Athletic Director*** *position that will utilize leadership skills as coach of top-ranked Tampa Academy basketball team as well as professional background in business development and sales.*

- Highly effective in establishing and managing relationships with administrators, faculty, parents, and students to boost program awareness. Excellent scheduling and prioritization skills, effectively managing concurrent multi-faceted activities.
- Maintain active alliances with local and regional athletic directors, coaches, and support staff across several leagues and sports, plus contacts within local media and reputable online athletics consulting resources.

COACHING & ATHLETIC INSTRUCTION

HEAD COACH, GIRLS' VARSITY BASKETBALL, TAMPA ACADEMY, TAMPA, FL　　　**6/00 – PRESENT**
Plan and coordinate all activities for a cohesive and competitive high school girls' basketball team. Helped establish Tampa Academy's relationship with the Positive Coaching Alliance to build communication and support among players. Within one year, brought team to its first ever FCA playoff (with six subsequent FCA showings).

Commitment to the team and to TA Athletics has led to the following achievements over the past seven seasons:
- Placed 4th in both the Tampa Academy Invitational and the Thespa Valley H.S. Spartan Classic　　2006
- Reached 2nd round of FCA Playoffs, only to lose in overtime　　2005-2006
- Won the Tampa Academy Invitational Basketball Tournament　　2004-2005
- Finished 3rd in ALC South two years in a row behind Florida's top-ranked teams　　2003-2005
- Reached 2nd round of FCA two years in a row behind Florida's top-ranked team　　2003-2005

PHYSICAL EDUCATION TEACHER, ALCOTT ELEMENTARY SCHOOL, TAMPA, FL　　　**09/01 – 6/02**
Developed comprehensive Physical Education program, including organizing Alcott Elementary Field Day. Left this position after nine months to become a full-time father while coaching girls' varsity basketball on part-time basis.

SALES, BUSINESS DEVELOPMENT & OUTREACH

ACCOUNT EXECUTIVE, LMS GLOBAL SERVICES, TAMPA, FL　　　**06/99 – 08/01**
- Developed new accounts by identifying and consulting with prospects on infrastructure solutions options
- Leveraged project management skills to bring several concurrent campaigns to successful conclusion

OFFICE ADMINISTRATOR, COHEN & ASSOCIATES REALTORS, TAMPA, FL　　　**03/98 – 06/99**
- Assisted in the daily operation of $120 million sales office

REGIONAL SALES COORDINATOR, FOUNDERS MAGAZINE, MIAMI, FL　　　**11/96 – 05/97**
- Developed and managed southern Florida territory, achieving 44% increase in client base
- Created and presented successful multi-media sales presentations to upper-level management

SALES REPRESENTATIVE, SPRINT, TAMPA, FL　　　**04/96 – 10/96**
- Secured new accounts in voice, data, and video solutions through networking and direct mail campaigns

ASSOCIATE VICE PRESIDENT, TAMPA YOUTH FOUNDATION, MIAMI, CA　　　**06/95 – 01/96**
- Directed acquisition of $3.6 million in contributions out of $21 million total.
- Increased card value 15% year-over-year by designing strategic account development plans
- Managed the nation's first ever $1 million campaign effort at The University of Miami

EDUCATION

Bachelor of Science in Political Science, Minor in Creative Writing
Florida State University, Tallahassee, FL

Resume Writer: Cliff Flamer

TATIANA KOMENICI

TatianaK@aol.com
24449 Civilian Road ■ Tinker AFB, OK 88223
405.555.5432 (H) ■ 405.555.6678 (C)

MEDICAL BILLING AND CODING PROFESSIONAL

Dedicated medical billing and coding professional with training and experience in office management, accounting and billing procedures. Excellent success rate recovering unpaid debts.

Qualification Highlights

✓ Thorough understanding of medical billing and claims coding for physician payments and patient reimbursements. Experience working with wide range of insurance companies; in-depth knowledge and familiarity with specific procedures required by private insurance companies, Medicare and Medicaid.

✓ Outstanding communication skills demonstrated while working with physicians, coworkers, representatives of insurance companies and governmental agencies. Provide exceptional customer service in assisting patients with seamless and complete transactions.

✓ Over six years of office management experience coordinating daily operations including accounting, payroll, taxes, and claims functions.

✓ Expert in Microsoft Office applications, company database, and accounting software.

✓ Recently completed AHIMA certification.

EDUCATIONAL BACKGROUND

OKLAHOMA CITY COMMUNITY COLLEGE, Oklahoma City, OK
Certified, AHIMA Certification in Medical Reception/Coding and Billing, 2007

OKLAHOMA CITY COMMUNITY COLLEGE, Oklahoma City, OK
Associates of Applied Science Degree in Office Management, 1996

PROFESSIONAL EXPERIENCE

SIMS FINANCIAL, Oklahoma City, OK   2000 to 2005
Debt Collector

Contacted debtors of clients represented by SIMS to attain debt reduction and recovery. Initiated contact with parties past due 60 days and tracked claims to understand reason for delinquency. Worked with debtors to resolve insurance problems, and developed payment plans manageable for all parties. Researched cold case files in an effort to collect payment on older unpaid claims.

■ Brought in over $17,000 in recovered revenues in nine months, a record for the office.

SMITH & STONE MEDICAL, Del City, OK   1994 to 2000
Medical Office Manager

Supported two physicians in daily operations and office management for a busy family medical practice. Accepted payments, coordinated billing, accurately input data into main database to gather relevant information along with financial and billing data for later use in receivables, payables, and payroll reports. Utilized medical codes and submitted claims filing both HCFA and UB-92 forms. Re-engineered communication and workflow processes, significantly improving efficiency to increase time available for patient - physician interaction.

COMMUNITY INVOLVEMENT

American Red Cross – Oklahoma City Chapter; Semi-Annual Blood Drive Volunteer   2000 to Present
United Way – Volunteer Campaign Coordinator   1998 - 2004

Resume Writer: Kris Plantrich

Chapter 6
Resumes for People With Gaps in Their Work History

In this chapter, find resumes for people who, for whatever reason, have recent gaps in their employment. Job targets include:

Events Manager
Administrative Support Professional
Office Support Specialist
Financial Analyst / Auditor
Quality Assurance Professional
Sales and Marketing Professional
Firefighter / Emergency Response Professional

If you've been out of the workforce for a while due to an illness or injury, family obligations, or the inability to find continuous gainful employment in your chosen field, you probably have some gaps on your resume. Whatever it was that kept you from working is behind you now, and you're ready to get back to work. Your challenge is to show employers that your skills and expertise overshadow any prolonged absences from the job market. As you anticipate your return to work, there are several key things to remember in preparing your resume and cover letters. Here are just a few tips that you may find helpful:

1. Consider whether a functional resume will serve you best. This approach will allow you to highlight your past skills, regardless of when you acquired them, as well as play down the extended periods of unemployment.

2. Be creative in accounting for your time away from the workforce. Never make false statements—dishonesty will ultimately come back to haunt you. However, if you cared for an elderly relative for a few years, it's legitimate to list this on the resume as "private caregiver for elderly family member" and include duties such as coordinating medical appointments and administering household budgets. If you volunteered for a human service agency or were active in any organized networking groups, these activities can also be included as recent experience.

3. Put your best foot forward by organizing your resume to show the training, qualifications, or experience that will most impress the prospective employer. This may mean that education would appear near the top of the resume, or, using the functional format, skills from several years ago would be featured at the beginning of the resume. Your guiding light in deciding what comes first is the relevance to your target job.

4. If your technology skills are up-to-date, be sure to mention them prominently. Are you current on the newest version of MS Office? Have you used QuickBooks or some other accounting software? One concern employers have about hiring employees with any kind of employment gap is that their skills may be outdated or obsolete. If you've stayed current with your computer skills or other technical proficiencies, make certain your resume effectively reflects this.

On the following pages is an excellent example of a cover letter as well as several resumes for candidates with gaps in their work history. (Note: Some of the resumes contained in this chapter were written by Canadian or Australian resume professionals for candidates seeking work in those countries. With this in mind, we have left in place the accepted spelling, grammar, and wording used in those countries. Even if you're not looking for work in Canada or Australia, the overall format and structure of these documents may prove helpful to you in preparing your job-search documents.)

Jennifer Miller

432 Wells Street ■ Eagle, WI 53119
(262) 594-3377 ■ jennifer.miller@gmail.com

January 15, 2008

Ms. Amy Randolph
Adventures for Life
2077 Burke Street
Milwaukee, WI 53233

Dear Ms. Randolph:

Bringing focus, professionalism, and enthusiasm to an organization and its clients has been a constant throughout my career. My demonstrated strengths in building relationships and ensuring the proper execution of project plans will enable me to excel in the *Hospitality Events Manager* position with Adventures for Life.

My responsibilities in both professional and volunteer capacities provide me with the knowledge, experience, and skills required to succeed in this position. Day-to-day tasks at which I have excelled include conducting facility tours and orientation sessions, handling detailed administrative functions, and communicating with customers. In leadership roles, I have planned and managed special events of all sizes, including developing creative themes, hiring outside service providers, guiding volunteers, and supervising on-site activities.

As a marketing manager for RDI Industries, I managed numerous projects to ensure the accurate, consistent, and timely communication of marketing messages to different target audiences. Duties also involved quickly assessing and defining goals, leading cross-functional teams, and adhering to strict deadlines. Prior to earning my Bachelor's degree, I worked for Browning Grocers and gained extensive experience interacting directly with a broad array of customers. My progression with this grocery retailer provided me with insight into how to develop viable strategic plans that are achievable in the field environment.

After caring for a family member and more recently, completing a contract assignment as the manager of a whitewater-rafting resort, I have been working in an interim position in the hospitality industry. I am eager to contribute my professional capabilities to a dynamic organization with a strong mission, such as Adventures for Life.

The enclosed resume captures only the highlights of my background and capabilities, and a personal interview would provide the opportunity for me to answer any questions you may have about what I enthusiastically offer to Adventures for Life in the Hospitality Events Coordinator role.

I look forward to learning more about your expectations for the position and how I can contribute to your organization's success. I hope to speak with you soon.

Thank you.

Sincerely,

Jennifer Miller

Enclosure

Resume Writer: Julie Rains

Jennifer Miller

432 Wells Street ▪ Eagle, WI 53119
(262) 594-3377 ▪ jennifer.miller@gmail.com

Profile

Accomplished, action-oriented professional with excellent communication, organizational, time-management, and relationship-building skills. Background includes:

- Event Planning for Business, Development, and Social Events attended by 10 to 500+ people
- Project Management including Cross-Functional Team Leadership and Vendor Management
- Concept Development & Tactical Execution
- Marketing Communications including Creative Services Management

Professional Experience

SALMON RIVER LODGE, McCall, ID   January 2006-December 2007
Program Manager *(contract position)*

- Managed the rafting program and assisted in the general management of a private resort.
- Planned activities associated with guest arrivals. Determined schedules and directed staff responsible for readying lodging areas as well as preparing welcoming events and dinners.
- Led orientations to include general briefings and individual discussions regarding skill levels.
- Created and executed whitewater rafting plans, supervising guides, interacting extensively with guests, and ensuring adherence to safety guidelines.

December 2003-December 2005

Provided care for a terminally ill parent and settled estate, Milwaukee, WI, Dec. 2003-Oct. 2005
Earned certification as a **Whitewater Rafting Guide Leader** and **Swiftwater Rescue Professional** through the **California Whitewater School**, **Arcadia, CA,** November 2005-December 2005.

RDI INDUSTRIES, Houston, TX   October 1996-December 2003
Internet Marketing Manager

- Planned and managed the execution of numerous concurrent projects to support the needs of the marketing offers and programs group as well as the public relations staff.
- Directed the updating of various Internet and intranet sites for multiple market segments (e.g., youth market and business-to-business market).
- Oversaw the development, approval, and deployment of updated site content, visuals, and navigation; ensured a highly positive end-user experience by providing accurate, easy-to-find information aligned with content disseminated through advertising campaigns.
- Managed cross-functional teams that included outside creative-services agencies and web-design firms as well as internal IT developers and marketing-communication managers.

Accomplishments:

- Conceptualized and implemented a marketing intranet that equipped field staff with easily accessible, up-to-date information on offers.
- Successfully established and developed resources that enabled the company to generate competitive responses, meeting aggressive lead times of three weeks or less.
- Integrated sponsorship of the 2002 Winter Olympics into the company's web presence.

Business Marketing Communications Manager

- Established a distinct marketing-communications area for business-to-business initiatives.
- Managed communication aspects of new product launches by receiving direction from offer managers and product managers, overseeing the development of up to 60 market-specific versions of collateral per channel, and securing approval of content from legal staff.

Accomplishments:

- Created an online program that provided direct sales representatives with nationally consistent, legally approved sales flyers customizable with contact information.
- Achieved consistency of product references in marketing collateral and POS materials by developing processes for reporting all references and tracking material inventories.

Resume Writer: Julie Rains

Jennifer Miller   (262) 594-3377 ▪ jennifer.miller@gmail.com ▪ page 2

Prior Positions with RDI Industries: started as executive administrative assistant to the President of the Southwestern Region; gained working knowledge of marketing communications and advertising functions as marketing specialist and advertising specialist.

Attended University of Wisconsin from 1992-1995 and held the following positions while earning my degree:

- **Business Manager, Financial Directions, Milwaukee, WI, March 1993-December 1993:** supervised office operations of a financial consulting firm.
- **Marketing Coordinator, Hege & Shepherd, L.L.P., Milwaukee, WI, March 1994-April 1996:** supported marketing and client-relations activities for 90-attorney firm by overseeing the execution of special events; started in an entry-level position, worked as an assistant supervisor, and progressed to the business development role.

BROWNING GROCERS, INC., Milwaukee, WI   **July 1983-August 1992**
Bakery Buyer
- Devised and oversaw execution of merchandising plans for 112 in-store bakeries in four states.
- Defined product mix for a 400-item product line, evaluating new products, analyzing feedback from store managers, and conducting yearly product reviews to select best-in-class items.
- Managed in-store presentation and sales of products by creating merchandising guidelines, visiting stores to review displays, arranging vendor training of store staff, producing weekly newsletters with contests, and organizing weekly sales promotions and holiday events.
- Gathered, analyzed, and presented information on the weekly sales and promotions of two districts (24 stores) for executive-level meetings with the President, CEO, and senior managers.

Accomplishments:
- Designed management tools that tracked the impact of product promotions on sales and profits.
- Developed a wedding cake program in collaboration with a product vendor.
- Planned and managed the annual product show to showcase items available for the holiday season: conceptualized theme; coordinated the presentation of items at 190 booths; hosted 450+ attendees; and created an ordering book for use by store managers in placing holiday orders.
- Started in entry-level position and progressed to the buyer position.

Education

Bachelor of Arts, *magna cum laude,* UNIVERSITY OF WISCONSIN, Milwaukee, WI   **1995**
- **Major in Computer Information Systems; Minor in Marketing.**
- Developed marketing plans for a non-profit agency and financial consulting firm, and generated product ideas for a sports-marketing company, working as a team member on class projects.

Professional Development: Optimizing Performance through Effective Interactions, Partnerships: Creating Synergy, Trust and Valuing Differences, Interpersonal Managing Skills.

Activities

HABITATS FOR YOU   **2004-Present**
- **Volunteer** and past **Vice President, Board of Directors** of non-profit, environmental education organization. Assist with operations to include delivering educational programs to school and community groups. Managed fund-raiser that generated over $20,000 by soliciting donations from area businesses, arranging ticket sales, and emceeing the event.

EVENT PLANNING   **2002-Present**
- Plan weddings for up to 200 guests. Collaborate with bridal couples to define event themes, preferences, and budgets. Evaluate, select, engage, and direct service providers such as caterers, musicians, and florists. Ensure adherence to facility requirements and supervise on-site activities.

CASSANDRA RABINOWITZ

201 W. Village St. • Phoenix, AZ 85098 • (Home) 602.238.2183 • (Mobile) 602.252.6032 • cass201@gmail.com

OFFICE ADMINISTRATION PROFESSIONAL

SKILLS AND COMPETENCIES

- Self-motivated, accomplished administrative professional who readily accepts new challenges.
- Fast learner with demonstrated initiative and dedication to achieving organizational goals.
- Highly conscientious in the planning, follow-through, and organization of projects.
- Dependable team player with successful track record as team leader.
- Friendly personality; relate well and work cooperatively with diverse personalities.
- Computer proficiencies include Microsoft Office, Corel WordPerfect, and bankruptcy-specific software.

EMPLOYMENT HISTORY

DEBT RELIEF LEGAL SERVICES ✧ PHOENIX, AZ   MAR 2002 TO PRESENT
Office Manager
Bankruptcy law office handling an average of 25 cases per month, at times reaching a high of 40 in one month.
Promoted from Secretary to Office Manager two months from hire date based on excellent performance.
Perform variety of Office Management roles highlighted below:

Financial Manager
Manage all aspects of office Payroll, Accounts Receivable and Accounts Payable.
- Research and negotiate with suppliers in order to secure the most economical options available.
- Collect and process payments; follow up on delinquent accounts.
- **Successfully work within $30,000 office supplies budget.**

Case Manager
Sole employee responsible for debtor case files throughout entirety of process. Notify creditors when issues arise; resolve concerns with creditor's attorneys; counsel clients on proper budgeting; prepare documents for clients' signatures; deliver final copies to court.
- **Selected by attorney** to appear during bankruptcy hearings in court.
- **Research relevant case law** for use by attorney in existing cases.

Human Resources Manager
Recruit, interview, hire, supervise and evaluate performance of secretarial staff of two.
- **Manage office payroll**
- **Mediate conflicts** with challenging clients

CATHOLIC CHARITIES OF SOUTHWEST ✧ PHOENIX, AZ   FEB 2000 TO MAR 2002
Head Secretary (of three Secretaries)
Served in leadership secretarial role managing appointments for therapy team. Managed intake process for three different programs: Family Service, Family Reunification and Child Welfare Departments. Explained to incoming clients the entire intake process for each department. Processed client and insurance billing, accounts receivable / payable and scheduled management meetings.
- **Initiated a fundraiser that netted over $10,000** to benefit abused children in two foster families for the holiday season.

PRIOR TO 2000, held several challenging part-time positions in various industries, primarily in hospitality.

EDUCATION / TRAINING / MEMBERSHIP

Maricopa Area Legal Support Professionals – Active member since 2003 (Served on Board 2004 – 2005)
Monthly Bankruptcy Seminar, Scottsdale, AZ – Attended monthly since 2002
Paradise Valley Community College, Paradise Valley, AZ – Certified Nursing Assistant (CNA), 1997

Resume Writer: Nancy Walkup

Cheryl St. Angel

20 Forest St. #6
Burton, NH 03846

Phone: (603) 555-2932
Email: Cstangel197@hotmail.com

OFFICE SUPPORT PROFESSIONAL

SKILLS SUMMARY

Communication Skills

- Friendly demeanor with pleasant speaking voice and manner
- Greeted customers politely & professionally both on telephone and in person
- Took messages precisely; made certain each message was directly & accurately delivered

Office Support Skills

- Handled multiple telephone line systems
- Proficient in use of dispatch radio
- Managed office supply inventory
- Organized filing systems
- Accurately filed documents for efficient retrieval

Customer Service

- Assisted customers with key consumer information and directional guidance
- Assisted customers with special purchases, such as gift certificates
- Maintained positive attitude and resolved concerns expressed by upset or angry customers

Strong Work Ethic

- Reliably and consistently punctual
- Willing and eager to go the extra mile to get the job done right the first time
- Developed strong understanding of industry protocols and what information to share with customers
- Exercised discretion and tact

WORK EXPERIENCE

Product Assembler: TempPlace (Hi-Def Systems), Burton, NH	2006
Packing Associate: TempPlace (Locks Packing), Burton, NH	2006
Customer Service Associate: Mall One Plaza, Standish, NH	2005
Sales Associate: Cumberland Farms, Worthington, NH	2004
Sales Associate: Worth's Oil Service, Worthington, NH	2002–2004
Receptionist: H & R Block, South Lempster, VT	2002

EDUCATION

Program Support Internship: Future Works, Stowe, VT	2006–2007
GED with specialization in Retail Sales: WorkCorps Center, Lempster, VT	2002

REFERENCES AVAILABLE ON REQUEST

Resume Writer: David Phreaner

ALAN B. WENDT

362 Nightengale Drive   (502) 555-3751
Louisville, Kentucky 40001   alan.wendt@egmail.com

FINANCIAL ANALYST • AUDITOR

Analytical problem-solver with Master of Accountancy and MBA degrees, and seven years of experience auditing automotive, transportation, warehousing, defense, and consumer products companies. Experience highlights include:

Auditing:	• Eliminated $30,000 in annual expenses by identifying process weakness. Client recovered an additional $80,000 in unclaimed freight-allowance credits.
	• Eight years of experience in uncovering savings for numerous organizations.
Research:	• Co-authored paper on impact of Sarbanes-Oxley on corporate financial reporting that was published in *Accounting Matters* for 2005 Conference on Business Issues.
	• Provided research services for accounting faculty at the University of Louisville.
Process Improvement:	• Developed five-year workflow and staffing projections for Grants Department that included recommendations for using technology to improve productivity.
Project Management:	• Directed eight-member team in faculty needs-assessment project that culminated in implementation of faculty-mentoring and classroom-technology programs.

EDUCATION AND HONORS

Master of Accountancy – University of Louisville, Louisville, Kentucky, 2006
Master of Business Administration – University of Louisville, 2006
Dean's List • Beta Alpha Psi • GPA: 3.8 / 4.0

Bachelor of Arts – Purdue University, West Lafayette, Indiana
Major: Communications; Minor: Mathematics
Distinguished Student Award • Dean's List • Teaching Assistant • Paid Internship

EXPERIENCE

Research, Teaching, Administration: Three years of experience
Graduate Research Assistant, University of Louisville (2004-Present)
Intern, Purdue University, Center for Instructional Services (1986)

Transportation / Manufacturing: Seven years of experience
Vehicle Assembly Technician, Toyota Motor Company (1999-2002)
Contract Service Provider, Southern Warehouse and Cartage (1995-1999)

Auditing: Eleven years of experience
Accounts Payable Auditor/Consultant, Rogers Associates (1987-1995)
Grants Specialist/Accountant, Mississippi State University, Grants (1990-1992)

COMPUTER SKILLS

Microsoft Excel, Access, Word, and PowerPoint, Great Plains
LogicNet, CCH, RIA Checkpoint, FARS, QuickBooks, Research Insight, and CompuStat

Resume Writer: Eileen Davis

LYNN AUDREY POWELL

9518 La Vista View Lane • Dallas, TX 75240 • (214) 380-9750 • E-mail: lpowell@hotmail.com

QUALITY SPECIALIST

Award-winning Quality Specialist with over five years of experience, and a history of success ensuring compliance with both domestic and international laws and standards. Able to write and implement policies and procedures that consistently meet or exceed regulations. Exceptional communication and organizational skills, with superior attention to detail. Excellent training and presentation skills. Software proficiencies: Visio, Word, Excel, Outlook, and PowerPoint. System proficiencies: SAP, AS400.

KEY QUALITY COMPETENCIES

- Audit Management
- Verification Activities
- Device Law / Regulations
- CAPA System

- ISO Management
- Document Maintenance
- Regulatory Compliance
- Process Implementation

- Quality Inspections
- ISO Training
- Quality Reporting
- Supplier Management

CAREER CHRONOLOGY

CARUTHERS MEDICAL DEVICES, Plano, TX (5 years)
This division of Fortune 500 parent company manufactures x-ray system components.

Quality and Logistics Manager
Ensure compliance with ISO 13485:2003, 21 CFR 820 (FDA) 93/42/EEC (European Medical Device Directive), Canadian Medical Devices Regulation, and the organization's quality objectives; perform all document control activities; manage the calibration program; perform final quality inspection of medical devices manufactured at facility.

Achievements:
- **Won the coveted "Caruthers Management Award of Excellence"** for achieving ISO 13485:2003 certification.
- **Hand-selected to perform ISO Management Representative functions.**
- **Reduced defect rate from 2.2% to 0.7%** by implementing assembly process improvements.
- **Secured CE-mark for a family of nine models;** created and maintained product technical files for each model.
- **Lowered shipping costs by $18K in 2006** by implementing cost-control measures.
- **Supervise, train, and coach a staff of two,** including a material planner and material handler.

Resume Writer: Robyn Feldberg

MOCKINGBIRD ELECTRONICS, LLC, Lewisville, TX (7 years)
Senior Import/Export Specialist
Ensured the electronic transmission of export data to U.S. government via the Automated Export System (AES); coordinated clearance and delivery of import shipments with customs brokers and carriers; coordinated export shipments with overseas officers, sales, freight forwarders, and carriers.

Achievements:
- **Performed internal quality audits** to meet company goal of complying with ISO 9002 quality objectives.
- **Successfully prepared documents for export shipments to comply with domestic and international laws;** documentation included commercial invoices, bills of lading, certificates of origin, export declarations, export license applications, letter of credit banking documents, and FDA Certificates for Foreign Governments.

EDUCATION

UNIVERSITY OF TEXAS, Austin, TX
Bachelor of Science in Organizational Management
- **Graduated with honors.**
- **Self-financed 100% of tuition and books** by working full-time throughout college.

CONTINUING COURSEWORK

- Internal Auditor Training for FDA Regulated Industries (ISO 13485:2003), 2005
- Application of Risk Management Devices: Compliance with ISO 14971, 2005
- Radiation Safety, 2005
- Best Practices for Managing Inventories and Cycle Counts, 2004
- Problem Solving and Decision Making, 2004
- Internal Auditor Training for FDA Regulated Industries (ISO 13485:2003 and ISO 9001:2000), 2004
- Product Safety for Medical Devices, 2003
- The European Medical Device Directive, 2003
- Understanding and Implementing the New ISO 13485 Standard, 2002
- Quality System Regulation for the Medical Device Industry, 2002
- Internal Auditing to ISO 9002 with the A_2Q Method™, 1999

PROFESSIONAL INVOLVEMENT

AMERICAN SOCIETY FOR QUALITY (ASQ)
Member in Good Standing

CELIA WALTERS-MONROE

70 Bombay Lane • Dix Hills, NY 11787
CMonroe@hotmail.com • **(631) 545-9182**

SALES PROFESSIONAL

Strategic Marketing • *Business Development* • *Retail Merchandising*

Highly experienced professional with expertise in sales, operations and business management. Offer solid track record of increasing profits through customer base expansion. Diverse sales experience, along with strong relationship-building skills and the capacity to thrive in high-pressure environments, contributes to the ability to deliver impressive sales results in a wide variety of settings. Broad skill set includes advertising design and promotions, team development and training. Proficient in all standard business software and office practices. ***Core competencies include:***

- Operations Oversight
- Customer Relations
- Budget Planning & Control

- Brand Development
- Sales Closing Techniques
- Advertising & Sales Promotions

- Customer Base Expansion
- Teambuilding & Leadership
- Product Demonstrations

PROFESSIONAL EXPERIENCE

BOSTON PIANO COMPANY – East Hills, NY   2004-Present

Sales & Marketing Consultant

Principal sales and marketing consultant for this established retail piano company.

Develop new business through vigorous telephone contact. Assess customers' needs and target appropriate products and service solutions; respond to inquiries and resolve concerns. Conduct product demonstrations and special sales promotions with focus on profitability.

Key Contributions:
- Generate substantial revenue increase through use of proven sales techniques including up-selling and cross-selling.
- Recommend and implement operational efficiency improvements to advance company objectives.

INDEPENDENT MOBILE CATERING UNIT – Smithtown, NY   1998-2004

Operations Manager

Established and operated Mobile Catering Sales unit serving locations throughout Suffolk County, NY.

Developed new sales accounts, adjusting routes accordingly. Created strategic marketing plans and creative merchandising approaches. Managed budget, financial statements and all related administrative tasks.

Key Contributions:
- Prospected and maintained productive working relationships with third-party vendors to increase profitability.
- Leveraged strong interpersonal skills and extraordinary multitasking capability to successfully manage thriving business.

COMMUNITY LIFE– Kings Park, NY   2002-2003

Promotions Director

Coordinated advertising and sales promotions for this established weekly community newspaper with 30 editions and circulation of over 435,000.

Coordinated all aspects of newspaper advertisement design and production. Directed outside sales promotions and events to secure new customers.

...continued...

Resume Writer: Karen Bartell

CELIA WALTERS-MONROE   •   Page 2

Key Contributions:
- Increased sales revenue by 18% and significantly enhanced profitability during first year.
- Orchestrated highly productive outside sales and promotional events.

CUSTOMER CONNECTIONS, INC. – Medford, NY   1996-1998

Sales Associate / Office Manager

Coordinated sales and service for this established distributor of outdoor sheds.

Directed all aspects of outdoor shed sales and service from setup to revenue collection. Scheduled construction jobs, prepared invoices and conducted related administrative procedures. Managed equipment and supply purchasing.

Key Contribution:
- Coordinated all aspects of major corporate base relocation to significantly enhance operations with minimal disruption of service.

JUD THOMAS LIMOUSINE SERVICE – Fort Lauderdale, FL   1994-1996

Director of Operations

Developed creative sales and marketing promotions for this start-up Limousine Company.
- Built and expanded customer base through effective prospecting and strategic marketing techniques. Managed operations including driver dispatch, routing, scheduling and vehicle-tracking.

TED SMILEY FURNITURE – Port Charlotte, FL   1990-1994

Sales Associate

Sold products and provided customer service for this established retail dealer of fine home furnishings.

Assessed customers' needs and recommended appropriate merchandise solutions. Coordinated sales closings, and resolved customer concerns.

EDUCATION AND CREDENTIALS

University of Phoenix, Scottsdale, AZ
Coursework underway leading to Bachelor of Science in Business Administration, Sales Concentration

---

PROFESSIONAL DEVELOPMENT

Effective Sales Techniques & Approaches - Dale Carnegie Institute, 1994

Jonathan Colby
1003 Blackberry Street
Jeter, New Hampshire 03398
(603) 515-3396

Fire Prevention & Protection Services Professional

Relevant Firefighter Experience

- Performed detailed equipment checks on fire trucks and related apparatus.
- Conducted maintenance inspections on firehouse facilities and grounds.
- Actively participated in trainings in the following:
  - Incident stabilization
  - Life safety
  - Property conservation techniques.
- *Certifications:*
  - *FireFighter 1 (FF1)*
  - *Cardio-Pulmonary Resuscitation (CPR)*
  - *Basic Life Support (BLS)*
  - *Automatic Electronic Defibrillator (AED)*
- *Coursework in Certified Emergency Vehicle Operation and Two-way Radio Communication.*

Animal Caretaker Experience

Catered to a variety of animal needs to maintain good health (feeding, exercising, washing, and replacing bedding). Assisted Veterinarian in making farm calls to address the needs of large farm animals. Performed administrative tasks including filing, answering phones, and scheduling appointments.

General Labor Experience

- Filled a variety of roles in the areas of heavy and light-manufacturing.
- Carried out various duties in connection with residential house construction and remodeling.
- Performed maintenance and repairs to residential swimming pools.
- Completed a variety of landscaping projects of all sizes.

Work History

Corestaff Temporary Services, Tremont, NH	6/06-8/06
Lakes Carter Veterinary Hospital, Tremont, NH	9/05-1/06
Smith's Vehicular Systems, Tremont, NH	10/04-9/05
Copperfield Animal Hospital, Copperfield, NH	5/04-8/04
Copperfield Emergency Services, Copperfield, NH	4/03-8/04
T-Tec.LLC, Copperfield, NH	5/03-12/03
Woodburn House, Copperfield, NH	12/02-5/03
HighBoy Farm, Geery, MA	5/02-11/02

Excellent References Available Upon Request

Chapter 7

Resumes for Skilled Trades People, Technicians, and Factory Workers

In this chapter, find resumes for hands-on working people, including:

Security Systems Installer
Industrial Maintenance Electrician
Truck Driver / Equipment Operator
Boiler Operator / Stationary Engineer
HVAC Technician
Heavy Equipment Mechanic
Auto Body Shop Manager

If you make your living working with your hands and don't work in an office all day, sitting in front of a computer to write your resume may not be something that comes easily to you. If you've been around for a few years, you probably remember when you didn't need a resume for these types of jobs. Times have changed, and even technicians, skilled trades people, and construction workers need to present themselves to employers with a well-written resume. If you work in one of these fields, there are several key things to remember as you prepare your resume and cover letters. Here are just a few tips that you may find helpful:

1. Document your training and knowledge. If you're a technical person, you've probably attended a number of training schools for installing and/or repairing various models and brands of equipment. Identify

those that will really matter to a prospective employer and make sure they're included on your resume under "technical training" or some other appropriate heading.

2. Recognize what your accomplishments are and be sure to include them on your resume and in cover letters. Many workers in these types of positions don't believe that they have any accomplishments—they just show up for work and do a great job, working hard every day. But if you make a suggestion that saves time or improves quality, that's an accomplishment. If you are singled out as someone who's great at teaching the new kid the ropes, or training coworkers more formally in new job skills, these are accomplishments. Did you complete your apprenticeship in three years instead of four? Any of these things can be included on your resume as an accomplishment, or highlighted in a cover letter if they are particularly relevant to the targeted job.

3. Show your range of experience. If you're an electrician, do you install network and telephone cables as well as 110-volt and 220-volt service? Do you operate a bulldozer and also drive over-the-road trucks? Are you a plumber who works with pneumatics and hydraulics as well as water and sewer lines? In each case, you want to include this information on your resume, most likely in your summary or technical skills section.

4. Highlight any technical skills that set you apart from the crowd. Do you use wireless technology to track inventory in a warehouse? Are you competent with state-of-the-art test equipment? Have you been trained to install or repair equipment that's new to the market? Do you use CAD/CAM software to create drawings? Any of these things can distinguish you from the dozens of other job applicants you might be competing against, and including them on your resume may give you an edge.

On the following pages is an excellent example of a cover letter as well as several resumes for skilled trades people, technicians, and production workers. (Note: Some of the resumes contained in this chapter were written by Canadian or Australian resume professionals for candidates seeking work in those countries. With this in mind, we have left in place the accepted spelling, grammar, and wording used in those countries. Even if you're not looking for work in Canada or Australia, the overall format and structure of these documents may prove helpful to you in preparing your job-search documents.)

MIKE E. JOHNSON

105 Rosemary Lane
Dallas, Georgia 30156

Residence: (678) 568-0783

June 26, 2008

Brent Gillette, Vice President
Human Resources
Global Security Systems, Inc.
1221 Peachtree Boulevard
Atlanta, Georgia 30119

Re: Security System Installer position

Dear Mr. Gillette:

This letter of introduction is in response to your recent announcement advertised in the *Atlanta Journal & Constitution* for a Security System Installer. The enclosed résumé highlights my experience, qualifications and accomplishments.

As my resume reflects, I bring solid experience in a wide variety of areas related to this position. My work history includes installing home alarm and fire prevention systems along with their control panels; installing electrical power supplies; and I am knowledgeable in reading wiring diagrams. I have a wealth of customer service experience and am committed to achieving organizational objectives without sacrificing customer satisfaction. My strong work ethic and dedication to the highest moral standards are second to none. Additionally, I possess organizational, multi-tasking, and time management skills necessary for success in the Security System Installer position.

Please contact me at your convenience to discuss in detail your expectations for the position and how my background and skills can contribute to the continuing success of Global Security Systems, Inc. I look forward to hearing from you soon.

 Thank you for your consideration.

Sincerely,

Mike E. Johnson

Enclosure

Resume Writer: Shannon Branson

MIKE E. JOHNSON

105 Rosemary Lane   Residence: (678) 568-0783
Dallas, Georgia 30156

SECURITY SYSTEM INSTALLER

Conscientious, efficient, and detail-oriented professional with two years of experience providing superior technical support and customer service in fast-paced, profit-driven environments. Experienced in installing industry-standard security and fire prevention systems. Adept at meeting tight deadlines without sacrificing quality of service. Highly skilled in evaluating and solving complex problems. Excellent communication skills; able to quickly establish rapport with customers, colleagues and management. Reliable and trustworthy.

Core Competencies and Characteristics:

- Home Security System Installation
- Wiring Diagram Interpretation
- Control Panel Installation
- Fire Prevention System Installation
- Safety Procedure Compliance
- Troubleshooting / Problem-Solving
- Judicious and Discreet
- Detail-Oriented
- Customer-Focused

Computer-literate with proficiencies in Microsoft Office

PROFESSIONAL EXPERIENCE

Installation Assistant   **2006**
Fire Prevention, Inc.   **Dallas, Georgia**

- Installed, programmed, maintained, and repaired security and fire alarm systems and related equipment ensuring compliance with local code regulations and taking appropriate safety precautions.
- In accordance with design specifications, installed electronic power, communications, and control panel equipment.
- Analyzed operation of malfunctioning electrical system equipment and conducted sequential tests to locate sources of malfunction. Followed blueprints and wiring diagrams to repair and/or replace electrical wiring, conduits, tubing, circuits, fixtures, or equipment as appropriate.

Server   **2004 – 2005**
Riley's Bar & Grill   **Dallas, Georgia**

- Provided extensive customer service to diverse customer base for this well-known, national restaurant chain; handled customer concerns and disputes in a friendly, courteous manner.
- Maintained excellent rapport with customers, staff, and management to facilitate teamwork, professionalism, and increase sales.
- Accountable for large sums of cash on a daily basis.
- Implemented suggestive selling techniques on store promotions to increase consumer purchasing and promote items of interest.

EDUCATION

High School Diploma, Paulding High School, Dallas, Georgia, 2004.

Excellent References Furnished on Request

Resume Writer: Shannon Branson

Montana J. Moore, Jr.

110 Nine Mile Rd., Kinston, NC 26666 ▪ (919) 287-3611 ▪ (919) 319-3611 Cell ▪ montanamoore@yahoo.com

Industrial Maintenance/Electrician

Extensive experience in industrial machine maintenance and electrical work. Superb technical aptitude and highly skilled in use of measuring tools and equipment. Knowledge of Lean Manufacturing principles. Energetic, gets along well with associates, good safety record and great work ethic.

Comments from Employers' Letters of Recommendation:

"He believes in giving an honest days work and taking responsibility for his actions."
"Mr. Moore's attendance record is quite impeccable. And his attitude is always positive."
"He responds decisively in crisis situations and gets the job done right the first time."

Achievements

- *Received **Values in Action Award** for voluntarily traveling to South Africa to establish the Affinity FDR (Foldable Disposable Respirator) line. Trained African associates to build foldable respirators and maintain equipment*
- *Earned **Perfect Attendance Award** for 2003 and 2004*
- *Recognized for two **Safety Suggestions** which were implemented during 2001 – 2004*

Work Experience

Jones Pulpwood Manufacturing, New Bern, NC   02/2006 – Present
Maintenance Mechanic
- Perform machinery maintenance, troubleshooting, repairing, upgrading and installations in high-volume, dynamic environment
- Perform predictive and preventive maintenance on wide range of equipment
- Read and interpret mechanical prints, electrical wiring diagrams, AC / DC, pneumatic diagrams, and hydraulic diagrams
- Repair ac/dc electrical controls, pneumatic equipment, and hydraulic equipment
- Fabricate equipment using arc and gas welding techniques
- Dismantle devices to gain access to and remove defective parts
- Adjust functional parts of devices and control instruments to ensure optimal functioning
- Set up and operate drill presses, grinders, and other metalworking tools to fabricate and repair parts

Actus Lend Lease, LLC, Jacksonville, NC   *09/2005 – 02/2006*
Maintenance Repairman
Performed maintenance on military housing—electrical, sheet rocking, plumbing, and roofing.

Resume Writer: Billie Jordan

Montana J. Moore, Jr.   **Page Two**

Major Safety Appliances Company, Kinston, NC   **06/2001 – 05/2005**
Industrial Maintenance Electrician
- Installed, maintained and repaired machinery, equipment, physical structures, and pipe and electrical systems in commercial and industrial establishments
- Reviewed specifications, blueprints, manuals and schematic drawings
- Inspected and tested machinery and equipment with electrical and electronic test equipment
- Located damaged air and hydraulic pipes on machines and measured, cut, threaded and installed new pipe
- Repaired broken parts, using brazing, soldering and welding equipment and hand tools
- Cleaned and lubricated shafts, bearings, gears and other machinery parts
- Installed and repaired electrical apparatus including transformers, wiring and electrical and electronic components of machinery and equipment

Global Services Corporation, Jacksonville, NC and San Francisco, CA 08/2000 – 04/2001
Electrician
Installed highly sensitive computer cable; installed and repaired electrical panels; installed conduit; installed and punched down Cat 5 Cable in conduit.

Dynamite Industries, Inc., Apollo, NY   **05/1996 – 07/2000**
Sr. Maintenance Mechanic/Maintenance Coordinator
Repaired and maintained stamping presses, surface grinder mills and other equipment. Performed general maintenance including electrical, plumbing and painting. Prioritized and scheduled repair work. Coordinated with contractors and vendors for roofing issues, HVAC, water authority, waste water management, and state regulatory agency. Helped build Safety Team and worked with team to correct non-conforming equipment to expectations.

Hospital Central Services Cooperative, Inc., Apollo, NY   **02/1985 – 05/1996**
Maintenance Mechanic First Class
Repaired industrial laundry equipment including washers, dryers, extractors, and folders. Installed gas lines, water lines, and electrical wiring. Welded mild steel, cast iron, and stainless steel. Performed hydraulic and general plant repair work.

United States Army and Army Reserves   **06/1970 – 07/1990**
Maintenance Mechanic
Performed wheel and track maintenance (tanks and fighting vehicles) and fuel and electrical systems repair. Commended for initiative, conscientiousness, and competence.

Education/Training

Introduction to Lean Manufacturing - Coastal Carolina Community College, Jacksonville, NC (2004)
Lean Manufacturing - Coastal Carolina Community College, Jacksonville, NC (2004)
The Quality Advantage - Dynamite Industries, Inc. (1999)
Forklift Operator Training Class - Allegheny High Lift, Inc. (1999)
Forklift Safety - HCSC Laundry (1995)
Hydraulics/Pneumatics; Welding; Industrial Wiring –
Central Westmoreland Career & Technology Center, Apollo, NY (1993)
Diploma - Hempfield Area Senior High School, Apollo, NY

Recognition

Outstanding Commendation (US Army)
National Defense Service Medal and Letter of Appreciation
Battalion Commander's Coin

DONALD SHEA

424 74th Avenue South, Grand Falls, MN 56201(218) 924-1633   **donald.shea@online.net**

EQUIPMENT MAINTENANCE MECHANIC / TRUCK DRIVER

QUALIFICATIONS & CERTIFICATIONS

- High energy individual with solid track record of reliable performance as truck driver and equipment maintenance professional.
- Hands-on supervisor who teaches by modeling expected behavior and receives high ratings for employee supervision skills, plant knowledge, and dependability.
- CDL (Class A) with HazMat endorsement; over two million accident-free miles.
- OSHA-certified forklift operator; experienced operating pay loaders, backhoes and skid-steer loaders.
- Minnesota State Board of Health certification: visual emission ratings.
- Minnesota 2nd Class Engineer license (Grade B).
- National Institute for Uniform Licensing of Power Plant Engineers (3rd Class)

EXPERIENCE

UNIVERSITY OF MINNESOTA, Grand Falls, MN   November 1997 to Present
Heating Plant Shift Supervisor (Operator II), September 2000 to Present

- Maintain uniform heat source through 12 running miles of lines by fueling high-pressure boiler, operating, monitoring, maintaining, and repairing related equipment.
- Supervise eight operators, two on each shift; fill in for absent employees as needed.
- Communicate clearly orally and in writing with subordinates and superiors.

Heating Plant Operator (I), November 1997 to September 2000

- Fire boilers, run coal-handling and ash-moving equipment; monitor gauges.
- Clean, repair and maintain boilers, pumps and other equipment.

CENEX, Grand Falls, MN   1981 to 2003
Fuel Transport Driver, part-time occasional.
- Picked up and delivered petroleum products in Minnesota, North Dakota, and Manitoba.

MIDTOWN OIL INC., West River, ND   April 1985 to October 1997
Fuel Transport Driver
- Picked up and delivered petroleum products in Minnesota, North Dakota, and Canada.
- Hired and supervised three part-time drivers; maintained truck.

Prior positions (all in Grand Falls, MN):
Managed Grand Falls Repair, Ltd., an auto body repair franchise. Delivered dry freight to 48 states and Canada as truck driver for Residual Materials and as driver / trainer for Northland Transport. Sold new and used vehicles, managed four sales people and oversaw entire operation as co-owner and -operator of Westar Sales/Lease. Served as Missile System Analyst Specialist in USAF, receiving certification and Outstanding Maintenance Standard Evaluation team reviews from SAC Headquarters. Selected from all analysts in SRAM missile field nationwide to develop in-field training program for modifications to missile system at SAC Headquarters in Omaha, NE. One of two selected from 50-member squadron to train B-52 bombing navigators/officers in flight on missile guidance system.

EDUCATION

Truck Driver Training Certificate, received Outstanding Student in Trade and Industrial Section Award.
North Country Community Technical College, Grand Falls, MN

Electronics Technician (11 months training in certificate program)
IOWA ELECTRONICS INSTITUTE, Des Moines, IA

SMITHTON (IL) HIGH SCHOOL, diploma.

Resume Writer: Jeri Dutcher

JOSEPH PORTERFIELD

joeport@yahoo.com

342 Blackbird Road • Petrolia, Pennsylvania 16050   613-288-1773

BOILER OPERATOR
Steam Plant • Environmental Monitoring • Water Treatment

In the Boiler Room, Joe has always taken his role as Production Operator with the seriousness that is necessary to produce a quality product, efficiently and with high regard to the safety and environment of his fellow employees and the community around the plant. Because of his knowledge in the fundamentals of plant equipment and operations, Joe is confident when making suggestions for plant improvements. He works well coordinating the maintenance of his equipment with minimal downtime and process interruptions.
—Gordon H. Cogley
Production Superintendent

As an operator, Joe was very helpful to me on [the installation of a gas-fired boiler] and other projects. He offered numerous suggestions that greatly improved the projects. Joe is eager to learn, conscientious, and I fully expect him to excel in whatever employment endeavor he pursues.
—Eric Bright P.E.
Senior Electrical Engineer

[Joe] is able to work unsupervised and make critical decisions involving the operation of millions of dollars worth of equipment. He follows safety procedures and has made a continuous effort for improvement. Over the years, Joe's recommendations and suggestions have led to a more streamlined operation and cost savings.
—Gary B. Smith,
Safety Specialist

► 15⁺ years of experience operating, servicing, maintaining, and repairing steam and hot water boilers. Assess boiler conditions, evaluate results, and recommend solutions, e.g., system modifications, to improve performance and operations. Perform pipe fitting as needed.

► Broad-based experience in all critical aspects of coal-fired and gas-fired boiler technology and design, including process engineering, mechanical design, fluid mechanics, hydraulics, fuel systems, fuel performance and pressure parts. Analyze boiler water for acidity, causticity, and alkalinity.

► Strong project management expertise. Adept at recognizing/launching steps needed to attain objectives. Thrive on challenges to overcome obstacles with solutions that are technically sound and financially feasible.

► Self-motivated to work independently; equally competent working as member of a team. Exceptional interpersonal and communication skills.

► Verify operating conditions by reading meters and gauges or automatic recording devices at specified intervals. Maintain equipment in prescribed operating ranges. Record operation and maintenance actions.

PROFESSIONAL EXPERIENCE

Specter Chemical Corporation – Parker, Pennsylvania   *1974 – Present*
FIREMAN A
Operate and maintain steam plant, water filtration systems, and mechanical equipment, e.g., pumps and air compressors, to provide utilities through steam, compressed air, and water, for 300-employee facility, manufacturing resin to bond steel belts to rubber in tires.

- Provide steam to plant from three gas-fired boilers at two pressures: 150 lbs. and 250 lbs. Commended for exemplary attendance and safety record.
  - In 1998, switched coal boiler to gas boiler, producing 100,000 lbs. per hour of 150-lb. steam. Put Pillard-Burner inside boiler. Part of team to start and operate boiler.
  - In 1996, installed Indeck boiler 150 lbs. – 250 lbs., producing 150,000 lbs. of steam per hour to meet growing needs of expanding company.
  - Played key role in replacing two coal-fired boilers and starting up two gas-fired boilers that were installed in 1990.
  - Started up Nebraska boiler 150 lbs. – 250 lbs., producing up to 150,000 lbs. of steam per hour.

Resume Writer: Jane Roqueplot

Joe is an asset to our production team as well as an individual that exhibits an excellent work ethic. He rarely needs guidance or supervision, but willingly adds his extensive knowledge base of boiler house operation to make problem-solving much easier for me. He is consistently successful in improving his skills associated with continued operational efficiency and easily adapts to our integrated computer control system updates.

Joe has a knack for spotting equipment problems before they cause significant delay and presses for preventive maintenance to avoid the possibility of long power outages. Steam production is the heart of our plant, and Joe plays a significant role in communicating with over a dozen sub-operations in the chemical process to keep their specific units online.

Joe meets and exceeds the stringent safety guidelines established for our plant. In addition, he readily applies his thorough knowledge of environmental emission standards so timely adjustments are made to the boiler systems. His proficiency in this area has saved our plant fines and paperwork.

—Terrence L. McGuirk
Shift Supervisor / Dept.
Supervisor

Joe is knowledgeable in water treatment, both filtration and resin softening. He has operated both gas and coal-fired boilers, maintaining a steady load for the plant. He also has experience operating both electric- and diesel-powered air compressors.

—Fred Rupp,
Boilerhouse Superintendent

Specter Chemical Corporation, *continued*

- Observe and interpret readings on gauges, meters, and charts indicating boiler operation status. Adjust controls to ensure safe and efficient boiler operation and to meet demands for steam or high temperature water.

- Manage water treatment program by using products that conform to Indspec's water treatment and zero discharge standards. Complete Boiler House Title V Permit Compliance daily.

  - Apply, monitor, and adjust chemical applications, e.g., EDTA, to maintain the internal integrity of heat transfer surfaces, sodium sulfite to removal oxygen and prevent internal damage associated with oxygen attack.

  - Ensure maximum capacity and effluent quality for protection of downstream equipment critical to steam generation and production by maintaining function and accuracy of critical pretreatment equipment, e.g., multimedia filters and sodium zeolite water softeners.

  - Maximize operational efficiency of unit by cycling the internal water chemistry to maximum limits to efficiently conserve water, chemicals, and fuel consumption.

  - Ensure CEMS units are operational at all times. Ensure pounds per million BTU of NOx do not exceed standards of .110 and .05 for boiler # 9 and #10 respectively.

- Participated in implementing ISO 9001 – 2000 and SAP.

- During annual plant shut-down for maintenance, perform pipefitting of 1" – 16" pipes and install new valves. Operate 3-ton and 10-ton forklifts.

- Manage operation of boilers for peak performance:

  - #4 boiler: 50,000 lbs. per hour; coal travel grate
  - #8 coal boiler converted to gas; 100,000 lbs. per hour; Pillard burner
  - #9 Nebraska boiler, 150,000 lbs. per hour; Coen burner
  - #10 Indeck boiler, 150,000 lbs. per hour, Pillard burner
  - Moore controllers for boilers: 351, 352, 353

M & N Excavation – Petrolia, Pennsylvania   *1991 – 1994*
OWNER/OPERATOR

- Managed excavation company that dug basements, water and gas lines. Secured contracts with several area cemeteries.

- Developed reputation for performing quality work with excellent customer satisfaction.

- Successfully sold flourishing business.

MICHAEL A. FITZGERALD

4787 Panera Lane · Lapeer, MI 48446 · (247) 445-8701 · mfitzgerald@sbcglobal.net

INSTALLATION TECHNICIAN (HVACR)

Heating • Ventilation • Air Conditioning • Refrigeration

Trained and dedicated HVACR professional with broad-based knowledge and hands-on, industry-related experience encompassing over 20 years as a Mechanic with additional training in heating and cooling repair, and installation. Consistently meet production goals and quality standards. Strong trouble shooting and diagnostic expertise. *Coursework includes*: Heating Systems I & II, Sealed System Installation, Basic Mechanical Refrigeration, Architectural Blueprint Reading, Air Conditioning Fundamentals and Duct System Fabrication.

RELEVANT EXPERIENCE

FLINT CENTRAL HEATING AND COOLING, Flint, MI   2005
HVACR Assistant
Gained hands-on experience installing heating and cooling systems in new construction commercial and residential buildings. Performed ductwork manufacturing and installation.

MECHANICAL EXPERIENCE

JC's TIRE, Lapeer, MI	2005 to Present
ATLAS FORD, Atlas MI	2001 to 2004
JOHN SHAW FORD, St. Clair Shores, MI	2000 to 2001
MIKE FITZGERALD AUTO REPAIR, Lapeer, MI	1992 to 1999
JONESTOWN AUTOMOTIVE, San Diego, CA	1991 to 1992
ROBERTS CHEVROLET, San Diego, CA	1984 to 1990
SUNNYVALE UNOCAL, San Diego, CA	1983 to 1990

Mechanic
Hired to examine and repair various mechanical problems on all vehicles including front-end alignment, front-end and steering components, brakes, and light repairs. Follow checklists to ensure all vital parts are examined: belts, hoses, steering systems, spark plugs, brake and fuel systems, wheel bearings, and other potentially troublesome areas.

- Cultivate loyal customer relationships resulting from honest discussions of vehicle problems with decisions on repair and future maintenance requirements.
- Test drive vehicles; test components and systems, using equipment such as infrared engine analyzers, compression gauges, and computerized diagnostic devices.
- Investigate and adjust repaired systems to meet manufacturers' performance specifications.

FORMTECH JOINT SYSTEMS, Santa Fe, CA   1999 to 2000
Press Operator
Operated a power press, power brake, and hydraulic press according to specifications. Set stops on machine bed, changed dies, and adjusted components, including ram or power press, when making multiple or successive passes.

- Installed, aligned, and secured gears to machine bed, using gauges, templates, feelers, shims, and hand tools.

TRAINING & CERTIFICATIONS

Certificate of Achievement in HVACR, MOTT COMMUNITY COLLEGE, Flint, MI—2006
Universal Certification EPA Technician License, MOTT COMMUNITY COLLEGE, Flint, MI—2005
Auto Brakes and Braking Systems, MI DEPARTMENT OF STATE—2002
Auto Front End and Steering, MI DEPARTMENT OF STATE—2002

Resume Writer: Erin Kennedy

CHARLES L. DENNISON

541-123-4567 (hm) • 541-234-5678 (mb) • charles_dennison@gmail.com

MASTER HEAVY EQUIPMENT MECHANIC

Offering 15 years of Heavy Equipment Specialization

Well-qualified master heavy equipment mechanic with six years of experience in fast-paced, high-volume shop and more than 18 years of relevant machinery experience. Motivated, hard working, reliable, and productive with proven ability to deliver high quality work and excellent customer satisfaction. **Competencies include:**

- ► Specialized LeTourneau training
- ► Heavy equipment maintenance
- ► Engine, transmission, rear end rebuilding
- ► Home construction

- ► Safety training
- ► Metal fabrication
- ► Welding / Mig Welding
- ► Cutting torch

Maintain fully functioning private shop with ability to supply own tools and painting equipment.

QUALIFICATION HIGHLIGHTS

- • Increased the water pump life of a T-model CAT from two weeks to six months by leveraging auto racing industry standards to increase the belt tension and layer in an antifreeze additive.

- • Improved safety of a John Deere 330 shovel by widening the step to prevent operator injury.

- • Replaced an outdated 8V92 motor with a series 60 Detroit motor of a LeTourneau. Additionally, modified motor mounts, exhaust, and wiring to ensure machine recognition by the Series 60 Detroit motor.

- • Designed and built new seatbelt brackets for fleet of 14 forklifts to increase operator safety.

WORK HISTORY

HEAVY EQUIPMENT MECHANIC   1989 – Present
Turnstile Plywood Company – Albany, Oregon
Formerly Johnson Industries Plywood

Promoted through successively responsible positions as one of two mechanics charged with repairing and maintaining 52 pieces of machinery. Order parts, plan projects, manage vendor relations, maintain machinery logs, and ensure compliance with environmental laws.

Machinery Expertise:
Golf carts • Three-wheeled scooters • Man lifts • Carry deck cranes • Miller gas powered welders
8000-11000 pound Hyster forklifts • CAT T-MOD 8000 forklifts • Tenant sweepers • John Deere 644 Block wheel loaders 966 CAT Bucket loaders • Bobcat skid steer • Pond boats • LeTourneau.

SAW OPERATOR / FORKLIFT DRIVER   1989
Sensyne Moulding Plant – Albany, Oregon

TRUCK DRIVER / MECHANIC   1987 – 1989
Farside Wood Products – Albany, Oregon

ADDITIONAL QUALIFICATIONS

Designed and built 2,500 square foot, two-level home in partnership with wife, serving as General Contractor for entire project. Project scope included felling and clearing six truckloads of timber; backhoe and ground preparation for septic and services; groundwork, plumbing, windows, doors, plywood sheeting, siding, painting, heating, molding, concrete driveway, and sidewalk completion; and hiring of construction staff to assist with foundation, roof, and framing. House completed in three years while working 70+ hours at Turnstile Plywood.

Crane Operator Certification • Forklift Driving Certification
Four years' metal shop • Two years' auto shop • One year wood shop and small engine studies

123 Main Street • Albany, OR 97321

Resume Writer: Jared Redick

ROBERT COOKE

222 Main Avenue • College Point, NY 11356 • Cell (718) 622-5999 • Home (718) 993-2525
Rcooke@aol.com

AUTO BODY SHOP MANAGER

Versatile auto body technician and shop manager with more than 16 years of experience that includes bodywork, chassis-straightening, electrical systems, mechanical repairs, painting, welding, and assembly. Demonstrated excellence in managing high-volume workload while maintaining highest quality standards.

TECHNICAL SKILLS

General Equipment: Full range of *Hand Tools, Air Tools, and Hydraulic Tools*
Frame Straightening Equipment: *Flat Rack, Chief Equipment, Continental Pulling, Carolina Pulling Systems*
Painting Systems: *PPG, Sherwin-Williams, Sikkens, DuPont, House of Color, Behr, all types of enamels*
Welding Techniques: *Plasma Cutting, MIG Welding*

EXPERIENCE

AUTO BODY COMBO TECHNICIAN   01/1998 to Present

Performed all-around collision repair services for the following auto body shops:

B & J Collision, Brooklyn, NY (10/2004 – Present)
Mitchell Collision, Flushing, NY (03/2001 – 10/2004)
Ace Collision, Long Island City, NY (12/1998 – 03/2001)
Palmer Automotive, Queens Village, NY (01/1998 – 11/1998)

Innovative problem-solver. Perform collision repairs in all service areas including: bodywork, chassis repair, painting, welding, mechanical, and final assembly. Filled in wherever needed in order to maintain seamless workflow, meet time-sensitive deadlines and ensure the highest level of customer satisfaction at all times.

- Maintain workload of 20 – 25 auto repairs per week.
- Supervise activities of various shop technicians and drivers.
- Provide accurate cost estimates to insurance adjusters.

AUTO BODY SHOP OWNER / OPERATOR   06/1990 to 12/1997

Owned and managed two successful Auto Body repair shops

Ace Auto Works, Yonkers, NY (03/1995 – 12/1997)
Built successful auto body repair business from the ground floor into a thriving enterprise with more than $1.5MM in annual revenues. Managed day-to-day business operations, supervised staff of repair specialists, and provided hands-on repair service in all areas of shop.

- Developed active fleet servicing business with local companies that accounted for 30% of total revenues.
- Established additional profit center by purchasing, repairing and re-selling cars acquired at auctions.
- ***Cultivated relationships with local tow truck company and parking garage representatives that generated steady referrals for repair business.***

Magic Touch, College Point, NY (06/1990 – 03/1995)
Purchased existing repair shop and expanded operations to include additional profit centers.

- Expanded core business to include active towing service with three tow trucks.
- Established relationship with the NYPD as an approved towing service.
- Built specialty niche business rebuilding classic automobiles.

EDUCATION / LICENSURE

Auto Body Repair Program Diploma – Davis Technical School, New York, NY

New York Fire Department Certificates:
Certificate of Fitness Permit for Use of Oxygen and Acetylene
Certificate of Fitness Permit for Operation of Air Compressor
Certificate of Fitness Permit for Supervision of Spray Paint

Resume Writer: Tom Albano

Chapter 8
Resumes for Retirees

In this chapter, find resumes for folks retiring from full-time careers and transitioning to new challenges.

Retiring As:	Target Position:
Executive Assistant	Part-Time Receptionist
Postmaster	Retail Customer Service Representative
Manufacturing Process Technician	Church Custodian
Police Officer	Consultant to Law Practice
Sales & Marketing Executive	Financial Services / Sales
Chief Executive Officer	Management Consultant

If you have recently retired or are about to retire, but aren't ready to completely quit working, you may decide to pursue a life-long dream job or choose to take a position that's less demanding, thus affording you the opportunity to smell the roses. When you find yourself in one of these scenarios, there are several key things to remember as you prepare your resume and cover letters. Here are just a few tips that you may find helpful:

1. Be aware that you don't have to include every job you've ever held. Your first job as a junior sales representative in 1972 is usually going to be of less interest to an employer than what you've done in the past 10 to 15 years. If you've been in your current or most recent position for

five years or more, it's probably sufficient to focus on that position and summarize the rest of your career.

2. Think about which of your skills and experiences are most relevant to the type of position you are now seeking. Those are the skills you want to emphasize on your resume. This may mean that you will want to use the functional format for your resume in order to highlight skills that may not have been called upon in your most recent job.

3. Consider whether your volunteer experiences are relevant to your new career goal. For example, if you've been a youth soccer coach for many years as a volunteer and now would like to pursue coaching at the high school or college level as a profession, your volunteer experiences in that area may be the most relevant information on your resume.

4. Avoid giving away your age by including dates of graduation. This relates back to the first tip, as well. If you started your first job in 1968, the prospective employer doesn't need a PhD in math to figure out that you're either 58 or 62, depending on whether you went to college or not. It's okay to leave graduation dates off your resume and lop off the first 10 or 20 years of your work history. If that early experience is relevant, however, use the functional format to highlight it without tying it to a specific time frame.

On the following pages is an excellent example of a cover letter as well as several resumes for retirees pursuing new career challenges.

Mary Frances Rowley

1018 Crystal Valley Overlook • Honeoye Falls, New York 14472
(585) 624-7579 • MaryR@yahoo.com

January 13, 2008

Mr. George Arnold
Managing Partner
ResumeSOS.com
625 Panorama Trail
Rochester, New York 14625

Dear Mr. Arnold:

Please accept this letter and enclosed resume as my expression of strong interest and enthusiasm for the position of **Telephone Receptionist and Appointment Manager** as listed in a recent edition of the Rochester *Democrat and Chronicle.*

My expertise has been enhanced by a career spanning a wide variety of settings that include banking; academia; manufacturing; and human services. If you are looking for someone who is accustomed to working in dynamic situations under demanding time constraints, and who is comfortable interacting with culturally diverse customers, then please consider me for your opening.

Planning to retire within the next month from my position at Bank of America, I believe my key competencies mesh well with your expressed needs. A recent performance appraisal included the following remarks from my supervisor, Vice-President of Trust & Estate Planning:

> *"Mary is extraordinarily gifted in making clients with diverse backgrounds, and often under trying circumstances, feel at ease... She has a terrific 'telephone personality,' and is somehow able to convey her natural warmth and charm over the phone... She runs a tight ship... I rely on her to exercise the utmost discretion, and she is completely capable of interacting with clients on my behalf... I am saddened that she plans to retire, as she will be virtually impossible to replace."*

As the enclosed resume barely scratches the surface of my areas of expertise, I would welcome the opportunity to speak with you in person to discuss how my background can address your needs. Please feel free to contact me to arrange a mutually convenient date and time.

Thank you.

Sincerely,

Mary Frances Rowley

Enclosure

Resume Writer: Gail Smith Boldt

Mary Frances Rowley

1018 Crystal Valley Overlook • Honeoye Falls, New York 14472 • (585) 624-7579 • MaryR@yahoo.com

PROFILE:

Accomplished executive assistant with extraordinary communication skills and keen attention to detail. Excellent capacity to work independently without direct supervision or as productive and supportive team member. Demonstrated track record of exceeding expectations; willing to enthusiastically volunteer for challenging assignments and consistently recognize total customer satisfaction as the highest priority. Personable; gifted in developing quick, warm, productive rapport with individuals at all levels. Superb telephone personality; accustomed to working with highly confidential information, exercising strictest levels of discretion, tact and diplomacy. Skilled in Microsoft Office Suite applications.

RELEVANT PROFESSIONAL EXPERIENCE

BANK OF AMERICA; Rochester, New York
Executive Assistant (3.02 – 6.08)
Accountable for a range of support functions, including managing the schedules of the Vice-President / Trust and Estate Planning; handling confidential client information; providing secretarial support on ad hoc basis for team of five Certified Financial Planners; greeting high-net-worth clients; and maintaining office equipment.
- ➢ Selected to serve as mentor to recently recruited administrative support personnel.
- ➢ Chosen to participate as member of team developing new employee orientation programs.
- ➢ ***Received President's Award for Exceptional Customer Satisfaction based on results of client survey conducted over 18-month period.***

Administrative Secretary (2.95 – 3.02)
Provided confidential secretarial support to Vice-President / Commercial Loan Operations including management of professional schedule; greeting and interacting with high-net-worth clients; maintaining up-to-date and accurate client files; and supervising a clerical assistant.
- ➢ Volunteered to participate on cross-functional team charged with the responsibility of evaluating new software applications; team's recommendation was implemented on bank-wide basis (transition to Microsoft Word from Corel WordPerfect).
- ➢ ***Awarded President's Circle Distinction.***

Administrative Secretary – Branch Banking (1.85 – 2.95)
Performed a wide variety of logistical, administrative, and customer satisfaction functions in support of branch banking team comprised of Vice-President / Consumer and Mortgage Loans and six loan officers at busy suburban bank branch in Webster, New York.
- ➢ ***Received President's Award for Exceptional Customer Satisfaction / Branch Banking.***

Executive Secretary (1.78 – 1.85)
Accountable for providing secretarial and logistical support to dynamic executive team charged with developing and implementing then newly devised Individual Retirement Account initiative, bank-wide.
- ➢ ***Received President's Award for Ingenuity & Innovation as member of IRA Team.***

Prior executive-level secretarial experience in academic, manufacturing, and medical settings, including:
The Alumni Relations office of Cornell University; Xerox Corporation; and The Genesee Hospital.

PROFESSIONAL DEVELOPMENT

Microsoft Office – Numerous courses, including Advanced Word

Total Quality Management for Banking (Three day-long workshops)

Steven Covey's Seven Habits of Highly Effective People (Two day-long seminars)

Andrew Carnegie's How to Win Friends & Influence People (Two day-long workshops)

Resume Writer: Gail Smith Boldt

TERRY FRANKLIN
827 Murray Road • Summerville, PA 15864 • 635-852-1388

LOGISTICS • DISTRIBUTION • SALES • CUSTOMER SERVICE

▶ Dedicated team player with solid work ethic, superb attendance record, and respect for following rules. Place value on quality and doing the job right the first time. Accurately complete detailed reports. Versatile and adaptable to changing priorities and situations.

▶ Readily visualize target / identify problems and implement steps required to attain goals / resolve issues. Skilled observer; collect facts and data to make informed decisions. Respond to challenges in a forthright and cooperative manner. Succeed through persistence and resolve.

▶ Respected team leader with record of inspiring high morale and productivity in an atmosphere of respect and courtesy. Savvy time management skills.

EMPLOYMENT HISTORY

Rowan Company, Harmony, PA   *2005 – Present*
PARTS DRIVER
• Deliver parts to area parts stores, gas stations and repair shops as needed.

Harmony High School, Harmony, PA   *2005*
MAINTENANCE WORKER
• Worked as member of team, cleaning school building and grounds. Repaired road and parking area surfaces for optimal, safe driving conditions.

United States Postal Service   *1970 – 2005*
POSTMASTER, Jefferson, PA *(1989 – 2005)*
SUPERINTENDENT POSTAL OPERATIONS, Summerville, PA *(1983 – 1989)*
SUPERVISOR OF MAILS, Newell, PA *(1979 – 1983)*
DISTRIBUTION CLERK / FLEXIBLE CLERK - CARRIER, Newell, PA *(1970 – 1979)*
Directed operations of postal facility, supervising 6 - 40 employees. Developed operating budgets, maintained files and records; submitted timely reports; evaluated procedures and initiated efficiency and productivity improvements; purchased supplies and services. Worked retail window, serving needs of customers. Performed distribution tasks.
• Select achievements include:
  - Generated up-selling results by educating customers on availability of various products and services.
  - Scheduled training / development sessions for employees to improve safety awareness, enhance employee morale and improve retention.
  - Held operating costs and expenditures in proper relationship to authorized budgets. Performed labor relations negotiations with unions to avert dissatisfaction and maintain good working environment.
  - Chosen in 1997 as member of assessment team charged with evaluating and identifying defects of POS ONE System at offices in Dallas, Texas and Rockville, Maryland prior to nationwide roll-out of software to postal facilities. Identified 500$^+$ defects that were corrected by NCR prior to roll-out.
  - Selected to assess productivity, efficiency, and performance of other offices. Made recommendations that enhanced workflow and cut operating costs.

MILITARY

U.S. Marine Corps, Disbursing Clerk, Honorable Discharge

EDUCATION / TRAINING / CLEARANCE

PA Child Abuse History Clearance, 2005

Selective Sampling of Postal Service Training:
- Postmaster Development Seminar
- Train the Trainer
- Convince Me About Safety
- Management Safety
- Labor Relations - Field Managers

- Mail Processing Supervisor
- EAS Selection Methods
- Operation Training
- Defensive Driving
- Injury Compensation

- Associate Office Management
- OMAS Training Program
- Absence Control
- Mail Classification
- Basic Math and Electricity

Business Administration Coursework, Newell Business College

Resume Writer: Jane Roqueplot

Howard M. Campbell

1224 Beeson Street SW
East Sparta, OH 44556
330-444-5555

CUSTODIAL / MAINTENANCE / REPAIR

Dedicated to the belief that a well-presented facility is the cornerstone of its image in the public eye. Reputation for a meticulous attitude toward work projects. Step forward to meet short-term deadlines. Interpret and follow written or verbal instructions equally well. Work successfully independently or when partnering with others to meet a common goal. Strong mechanical inclination. Excellent communication skills with people on all levels. Possess initiative, resourcefulness, punctuality, and a solid work ethic.

SUMMARY OF SKILLS

- Carpentry
- Painting
- Plumbing
- Safety & Security

- Building Maintenance
- Emergency Evacuation Procedures
- Equipment Installation & Moves
- General Custodial Services

- Electrical Wiring
- Roofing Repairs
- Special Event Set-up
- Groundskeeping

RELEVANT EXPERIENCE

Good Shepherd Church, Minerva, OH (9/95–11/03)
CUSTODIAN
Performed general cleaning of three-floor facility. Efficiently provided set-up and teardown for special events like weddings, banquets, and funeral dinners. Completed commonplace tasks such as changing light bulbs, stripping|waxing of floors, parking lot|walkway snow removal.

Customer Service: Assumed all responsibility for maintaining a clean, well-kept environment for all users of church facility with a conscientious, thorough approach.

Initiative: Promptly responded, providing timely assistance on short notice when set-up was needed for funeral dinners. Conscientiously conserved heat by maintaining thermostat at low levels when facility was vacant. Willingly accepted responsibilities outside of job description with enthusiasm.

Security and Safety: Voluntarily contributed expertise in handling upkeep and maintenance of fire extinguishers and smoke detectors. Always replaced burned out light bulbs promptly. Skillfully painted wheelchair ramp for disabled church members to improve visibility. Entrusted to close and lock church facility 365 days a year. Effectively implemented practice drills for existing fire evacuation plan.

Strategic Problem Solving: Competently organized a team of church members on short-term notice to expedite clean-up of flooded basement due to ruptured hot water tank.

OTHER EXPERIENCE

Tasty-Flavor Foods, Akron, OH (6/76–2/08)
LABORER
Expertly loaded flavor injection machine. Operated electric forklift to unload incoming trucks and move skids. Ran packaging machines. Performed minor machine adjustments.

MILITARY

United States Navy – 4 years – Honorable discharge

Resume Writer: Barbara Kanney

JIM HUGO

Veteran law-enforcement professional with excellent investigative skills, the ability to communicate effectively with others, and demonstrated expertise in managing investigative assignments

SUMMARY OF QUALIFICATIONS

- Accomplished detective and patrol officer with more than 25 years of law enforcement experience.
- Top-notch investigative and interviewing skills. Incisive, perceptive, and thorough.
- Recognized authority known for making accurate assessments and sound judgments. Highly successful in substantiating allegations and developing compelling arguments.
- Organized and effective. A seasoned professional who is able to remain focused on big picture goals.
- Open, upfront communicator with no-nonsense style. Effective in building rapport and developing productive relationships with people at all levels.
- Successful in consistently building strong cases and effectively preparing for court proceedings.

KEY ACCOMPLISHMENTS

Leadership & Service Excellence

- Established solid record of accomplishment in law enforcement as both a detective and a patrol officer, earning recognition for exemplary leadership and service. Among achievements, selected by prosecutor's office to participate on Collision Analysis Reconstruction Team and Emergency Response Team.
- Won three Officer of the Year awards (1986, 1991, and 1999) for outstanding service as patrol officer and detective in Bedford Township.
- Recognized for leadership ability, named patrol officer-in-charge of five-member squad after only six months with Bedford department.

Law Enforcement Expertise

- Built reputation for strong investigative and interrogation skills, consistently building strong cases that frequently resulted in indictments and convictions.
- Led burglary investigation, forming task force with law enforcement agents from other communities that led to successful prosecution in spree of 70 to 80 burglaries across six-county area.
- Earned recognition for showing good judgment and restraint in highly-charged situations. For example, intervened in possibly deadly domestic abuse case, safely disarming and restraining man with known psychiatric issues, without physical harm to involved parties.
- Established record of success in investigating broad range of fraud (insurance fraud, check kiting, credit card fraud, etc.) and embezzlement cases. Elicited confession that netted suspect in 10-state check cashing scam. Solved inside job at bank involving $175,000 in stolen funds.

PROFESSIONAL EXPERIENCE

BEDFORD TOWNSHIP POLICE DEPARTMENT, Bedford, NY   1981 to 2006
Detective/Patrol Officer-in-Charge/Patrol Officer

As detective, conducted criminal investigations, interviewing and interrogating witnesses and suspects. Processed crime scenes and collected and preserved evidence. Prepared criminal cases for court presentation. Also investigated unattended and sudden deaths, fatal/serious motor vehicle accidents, and firearm applications. As patrol officer-in-charge, supervised five-member patrol shift.

---

6 MANNERS ROAD ◆ WHITE PLAINS, NY 10610 ◆ (914) 287-0001 ◆ hugo3@yahoo.com

Resume Writer: Carol Altomare

David Tanzer

21 Woodgrove   Cell: 714/264-6523
Anaheim, CA 92801   davidtanzer@sbcglobal.net

SALES / BUSINESS DEVELOPMENT

Productive, motivated, and goal-driven sales professional who has substantially increased market share and profits by successfully selling products and services to business owners and executive decision makers in a wide range of industries. Developed relationships with clients by providing personalized service, evaluating needs and recommending solutions. Gained customer trust, loyalty and satisfaction as well as repeat business and referrals with product knowledge, creative presentations, responsiveness, and integrity. Frequently exceeded sales quotas.

AREAS OF EXPERTISE

Account Management	Large Ticket Sales	Regional Sales
Account Retention	Lead Development	Relationship Building
Business Development	Market Expansion	Resolving Client Concerns
Cold Call / Outside Sales	National Sales & Accounts	Revenue Growth
Convert Desires Into Needs	Negotiations / Strong Closer	Solution Selling
Creative Sales / Cross-selling	Presentations / Follow-up	Strategizing Customer Needs
Customer Service / Support	Pricing & Sales Analysis	Territory Development
Exceed Sales Quotas	Prospecting / Telemarketing	Territory Management

PROFESSIONAL EXPERIENCE

SBC, INC., Headquarters: Albany, NY   1979 – 12/07
The second largest regional / national print and interactive Yellow Pages agency in the U.S. providing consulting and placement services for Print and Internet Yellow Pages, Local Search, SEM and SEO Advertising.

New Business Director - Western U.S. Region (1989 – 2007)
Responsible for marketing and inside / outside sales of print and Internet Yellow Pages advertising to large regional and national advertisers that buy Yellow Pages advertising in a minimum of 20 directories across three states with an annual spend of at least $100K. Average annual billing per account: $400K.

Account Executive, (1979 – 1989)
Responsible for premise sales, marketing and creative design of print Yellow Pages advertising to small and medium size businesses within the state of Wisconsin.

Achievements:
- Consistently met or exceeded annual sales quotas, which ranged from $1.2M to $1.8M in annual billable revenue since 1990.
- Won the President's Club Award in 1981, 1982, 1987, 1991 and 1995. Won the Executive Club Award in 1985, 1993, 1998, 1999, 2001 and 2002. Won the Sales Achievement Club Award in 1980 and 1988 for recognition of long-standing sales performance on a company-wide basis.
- Enhanced the prestige of our company by building a relationship with Kawasaki Motor Corp. over a two-year period and negotiating a $1.5M contract.
- Sold a $1.2M contract to Aramack Uniform Supply, a Fortune 500 company, by demonstrating our company's proprietary directory selection model and strategic approach to more effectively communicate our marketing initiatives to their field managers.
- Increased market share through extensive phone cold calling, relationship building, and on-site meetings to thoroughly analyze a prospect's needs and goals. Designed customized solutions including value added services.

Resume Writer: Pearl White

David Tanzer	714/264-6523	Resume – Page 2

PROFESSIONAL EXPERIENCE

Achievements (continued):

- Achieved higher sales by selling additional advertising to existing clients and selling new prospects on the advantages of utilizing our advertising services.
- Expanded the account base with persistent prospecting and follow-up, developing honest, trusting relationships and always exceeding client expectations by helping them grow their businesses.
- Overcame objections and closed contracts by cultivating rapport and conveying a sincere desire to assist clients and prospects solve their needs and problems.
- Developed new business by using Hoover's online and Lexis / Nexis as prospecting tools and to research potential new clients.
- Increased sales by recommending the development of new sales collateral materials to senior management to showcase new products, capabilities, features, and benefits in fresh and unique ways.
- Generated sales and good will by attending clients' annual conventions and meeting with their dealer / franchise networks. Created Yellow Pages advertising sales leads by attending several annual industry trade shows.

EDUCATION and TRAINING

- B.S. Degree: Psychology, University of Michigan

- Sales Training and Motivational Seminars by Dale Carnegie, Anthony Robbins, and Zig Ziglar

PROFESSIONAL AFFILIATIONS

- Association of Directory Marketing (ADM)

- National Yellow Pages Publishers Association (NYPA)

TECHNICAL SKILLS

- Proficient with current Microsoft Office Suite and ACT! (customer relationship database)

- Internet research with an emphasis on Hoover's online and Lexis/Nexis

Edward T. Cohen

234 Industrial View
Princeton, NJ 08540

609.987.6543
edwardtcohen@superlink.net

BUSINESS CONSULTANT / ANALYST
with proven track record in:
Executive Management, Program Management, and Engineering

Offering industry experience in:
Manufacturing, Telecommunications, Pharmaceuticals, & Financial Services

SUMMARY OF QUALIFICATIONS

- Monitor, analyze, and report on budget performance and spending status
- Communicate effectively with clients and staff
- Champion changes to streamline processes and improve efficiencies
- Analyze data and recommend strategies to ensure delivery of objectives
- Manage project planning process; including timelines, forms, and internal communication
- Develop and manage vendor programs and negotiate changes with vendors and clients
- Initiate standards and quality controls
- Assign project resources, including manpower, schedules, costs, to maximize returns

PROFESSIONAL EXPERIENCE

Business Analysis
- Used Internet and graphic arts to design business strategies
- Optimized work-flow, layouts of all facilities
- Negotiated all parameters into a final workable solution
- Used robotics and automated production facilities
- Utilized Operations Research techniques for project management
- Developed computerized models to manage 1.5 MM square feet of manufacturing space

Project Management
- Designed goal-directed organizational structure and operational procedures that met an array of project objectives
- Supervised over 100 employees at high quality printing company
- Administered and upgraded new facilities and technology, including servers, networks, software, pre-press, web, sheet fed, and digital printing presses
- Spearheaded planning of plant expansion, including design of manufacturing processes
- Coordinated work with architect, other engineering groups and department managers
- Managed projects to retool and engineer automated manufacturing operations

Marketing and Sales
- Managed sales group and a client-oriented production staff
- Increased sales by 50% year-over-year for 15 straight years
- Served Fortune 1000 clients, including IBM, Merck, Merrill Lynch, Dow Jones, and KPMG
- Increased market share; improve customer relations
- Optimized pricing and production
- Sped flow of information; improved databases

Resume Writer: Beth Woodworth

Edward T. Cohen

Resume	**609.987.6543**
Page – Two	**edwardtcohen@superlink.net**

PROFESSIONAL HISTORY

Business Analyst	*Smith and Barney*, Princeton, NJ
Program Manager and Business Analyst	*Alliance Graphic Design,* Princeton, NJ
Chief Executive Officer	*Crest Lithographers, Inc.,* New Brunswick, NJ
Engineer	*Johnson & Johnson*, New Brunswick, NJ
Engineer	*Western Electric Company,* Trenton, NJ

PROFESSIONAL LEADERSHIP

- **President:** Industrial Industries of Metropolitan New York 1990-1995
- **Board Member:** Metropolitan Industrial Engineering Association
- **Guest Instructor:** American Institute Industrial Engineering
- **Guest Instructor:** City University of New York
- **Presenter:** New Jersey Department of Labor

EDUCATION

Master of Business Administration – New York University
Bachelor of Science, Industrial Engineering – New York University

COMPUTER SKILLS

Microsoft Certified Software Engineer (MCSE)

Microsoft: Windows NT Systems Administration, HTML, Visual Basic, Front Page, Windows 98, Microsoft Project, Word, Excel, Access, PowerPoint, Outlook

IBM: Lotus Notes, System 36, AS/400, RPG; **Adobe:** Acrobat, Photoshop, Illustrator

Other: Quark, Oracle, JavaScript, HTML, COBOL, FORTRAN

Chapter 9
Resumes for Ex-offenders

In this chapter, find resumes for people recently freed from jail or prison and seeking to rejoin the workforce. Job targets include:

Health Educator
Shipping & Receiving Coordinator
Facilities Maintenance Manager
Custodian / Maintenance Technician
Restaurant Manager
Youth Services Director

Everyone's life includes some bad choices, but some bad choices carry much graver consequences than others. If you're an ex-offender, you fully understand that, and hopefully, at this point, are on your way to recovering from those consequences. Landing and holding a job will be a key component to your success on the outside, and you will want to demonstrate on your resume that you have skills prospective employers need and the desire to contribute positively to their organization. As you anticipate your return to work, there are several key things to remember in preparing your resume and cover letters. Here are just a few tips that you may find helpful:

1. Show your work experience and accomplishments while in prison as a job. Your work experience on the inside may be where you gained some of your best qualifications, especially if you have little or no work experience on the outside. It's legitimate to show "The State of New

York" or "The State of Illinois" as your employer for the time you were inside; or, if you are more comfortable, list the facility (for example, "Clinton Correctional Facility" or "Los Angeles County Jail") as your employer. Include any volunteer work, as well. Even if you weren't paid, you gained experience and learned skills while doing it. When you get to the job interview, you'll need to be forthcoming about your incarceration, but on your resume there's no need to state it explicitly.

2. Be sure to document any skills training or more formal education you may have completed. This may include workshops on anger management or team building, for example, or training in Microsoft Office or skilled trades. You may have had the opportunity to further your education by completing a GED or pursuing a college degree. Show that on your resume by stating that you attended the sponsoring institution. Again, when you get to the interview you may have to disclose your incarceration, but on the resume it's not necessary or even recommended.

3. Look to your work history prior to your incarceration for transferable skills. If you received training for a new career in prison, examine your job duties at previous positions and identify skills that will be relevant in your new job target. Skills such as strong record-keeping or customer service capabilities or an aptitude for math are transferable to many diverse career opportunities.

4. If you aren't already, get connected with the information superhighway. Being reachable by e-mail is becoming more and more essential to a successful job search. You may not be able to afford your own computer right away. However, if you participate in a program to help you find a job, there may be resources available to help with providing computer access. If not, public libraries in many cities and towns offer free Internet access to anyone with a library card. Once you have access, you can easily set up a free e-mail account through Yahoo!, Google, Hotmail, or some other service. Computer access also affords you the opportunity to research potential employers and track down job openings.

On the following pages is an excellent example of a cover letter as well as several resumes for candidates returning to the workforce following an incarceration. (Note: Some of the resumes contained in this chapter were written by Canadian or Australian resume professionals for candidates seeking work in those countries. With this in mind, we have left in place the accepted spelling, grammar, and wording used in those countries. Even if you're not looking for work in Canada or Australia, the overall format and structure of these documents may prove helpful to you in preparing your job search documents.)

HANK CHRISTO

Telephone: 25 College Street
(03) 9808 4100   West Melbourne, Victoria, Australia 3003

16th April 2008

Mr. John Abernathy
Prisoner Release Agency
Department for Correctional Services
GPO Box 900A
MELBOURNE, Victoria, Australia 3003

Dear Mr Abernathy:

John Jenkins, the prisoner liaison officer at the Parkville pre-release facility, suggested that I write to you concerning a non-advertised opening which he believes you may have for a **Health Issues Educator**.

Over the last seven years, I have been a Seminar Presenter and HIV Peer Educator to young and adult offenders, ex-offenders, and those at risk of offending or re-offending. This role has extended since 2004 to working as a volunteer with the AIDS Council of Victoria.

I have been trained to counsel and advise on safe sex, substance abuse, and HIV, and over the seven years have planned and presented seminars to school students, community groups and prison communities. and delivered individual counselling to youth and adults at risk. Personal life experience has reinforced my ability to achieve particular empathy with the target group.

Through working in the Health Issues Section of a prison library, I have developed a strong network of service and resource providers throughout Australia and overseas.

I look forward to discussing with you the strengths I could bring to this position.

Yours sincerely,

Hank Christo

Resume Writer: Brian Leeson

HANK CHRISTO

Telephone: 25 College Street
(03) 9808 4100   West Melbourne, Victoria, Australia 3003

HEALTH ISSUES EDUCATOR

Career Summary

Peer educator trained to counsel and advise on safe sex, substance abuse, and HIV, with experience over a four-year period of presenting seminars to school students and delivering individual counselling to youth and adults at risk. Personal life experience has reinforced my ability to achieve particular empathy with young and adult offenders, ex-offenders, and those at risk of offending or re-offending. Experienced in planning and presenting educational seminars to schools, community groups and prison communities.

KEY COMPETENCIES

- Communicating • Liaising • Planning and Organising • Networking
- Behavioural Management • Presenting • Facilitating • Counselling

RELATED SKILLS

- Counselling before and after HIV testing   • Advising on Universal Infection Control
- Planning and organising seminars on personal health topics – HIV risk, safe sex, substance and alcohol abuse, behaviour management
- Presenting challenging health topics to student groups
- Establishing and maintaining in-house libraries on health issues
- Behaviour management, assessment of risk behaviour and risk situations
- Networking and liaising with similar organisations to achieve resource sharing

RELATED ACHIEVEMENTS

- During a period of community detention, organised and presented seminars on health risk issues to high school students and community groups under the encouragement and supervision of a prison liaison officer, with excellent feedback including requests for annual repeats.
- Upgraded and maintained the Health Issues Section of a prison library through networking information agencies and locating and downloading internet material.
- Initiated networking between individual prison Health Committees statewide, achieving resource sharing and structured educational programs for inmates.

RELATED EXPERIENCE

Volunteer
AIDS Council of Victoria   2004 – Present

Seminar Presenter and HIV Peer Educator
Department of Correctional Service, Victoria   2000–2007

RELEVANT EDUCATION & TRAINING

Volunteer Training
AIDS Council of Victoria   2004

Counselling Strategies
Centre for Personal Relationships, Victoria   2004

Certificate in HIV Counselling
Peer Education Training, Melbourne, Victoria   2000

Resume Writer: Brian Leeson

James A. Peters
2 Main Street, Hartford, CT 06120   860-789-9876   peterjames@yahoo.com

Material Handler

- High-energy, dependable Material Handler with successful track record of over 10 years
- Experienced delivery driver and forklift / pallet jack operator with excellent safety history
- Demonstrated attention to detail
- Additional training and experience in processing invoices and shipping / receiving functions
- Skilled in inventory-related activities including stocking, order selecting, hand packing, wrapping, palletizing, loading and unloading trucks
- Trained and comfortable using all power tools and hand tools
- Proficient in Microsoft Word, Excel, PowerPoint, Outlook, and various Internet applications
- Valid CT driver's license – excellent safety record

WORK EXPERIENCE

Building and Grounds Maintenance / Material Handler / Kitchen Worker   2006 - Present
Cheyney House, Hartford, CT

- Effect minor plumbing repairs as well as electrical installations
- Employ carpentry skills in the areas of flooring (linoleum, tile, hardwood, sub-flooring); framing; deck construction; drywall work, siding, window replacements, additions, renovations, demolitions and roofing
- Install poured concrete (floors and foundations)
- Paint a variety of surfaces with accuracy and care
- Drive delivery truck and forklift; process invoices; coordinate inventory, shipping and receiving
- Operate floor buffing machines; sweep, mop and vacuum floors
- Maintain sanitary, pristine restroom facilities
- Keep up facility's grounds: operate snow blowers, mowers, trimmers, and rake leaves
- Prepare food; cook; serve; and clean kitchen

Building and Grounds Maintenance / Laundry Laborer / Material Handler /   1992 - 2006
Production Worker / Kitchen Worker / Tutor / Clerk
Dept. of Correction, State of CT, Niantic, CT
Participated in activities similar to those listed above, plus:

- Maintained automobiles; painted snowplows; and cleaned roadside areas
- Operated industrial sewing machines: produced uniforms and mattresses
- Ran metal stamping machines to produce license plates
- Constructed and assembled:
    - Metal beds, desks, bookshelves and cabinets
    - Victorian wooden railings for Habitat for Humanity housing
- Tutored GED students in math and reading
- Provided clerical support to educational staff

Independent Contractor   1991 - 1992

- Installed and repaired electrical equipment
- Employed carpentry skills in the areas of flooring (linoleum, tile, hardwood, sub-flooring); framing; deck construction; drywall work, siding, window replacements, additions, renovations, demolitions and roofing
- Operated construction tools and equipment including bobcats, chainsaws, hand and power tools

Resume Writer: Joanne Shugrue

James A. Peters (Résumé – Page Two)

Material Handler   1990 - 1991
B&D Industries, Hartford, CT
- Operated pallet jack; processed invoices; coordinated inventory, including shipping & receiving, stocking, order-selecting, hand packing, wrapping, palletizing, loading and unloading trucks

EDUCATION & CERTIFICATIONS

College Courses – General Studies (10)	1993 - 2006
Certificates in Interpersonal Skills & Health Issues (15)	1992 - 2006
Certificate in Auto Mechanic Repair Technician	1999
Certificate in Horticulture	1999
Certificate in Culinary Arts	1998
Certificate in Metal Machining	1997
Certificate in Carpentry	1996
Certificate in Building Maintenance	1995
Certificate in Forklift Operating	1994
Certificate in Computer Skills and Word Processing	1993
High School Diploma	1992

VOLUNTEER WORK

Material Handler   1985 - 1991
Food Share, Niantic, CT

RALPH MARTINEZ
21 Butler Drive
Amityville, New York 11701
631 732 8492 (Home); 631 231 5775 (Cell)
E-Mail: Martinezray@optonline.net

Facilities Maintenance / Management

Highly skilled in Facilities Maintenance Manager role. Demonstrated capabilities in handling projects from inception to completion, training, and supervising staff. Solid track record of adhering to preventive maintenance programs. Strong facilities management background includes coordinating effective custodial operations. Excellent proficiencies in Electrical, Carpentry, Plumbing, and HVAC. A resourceful, quality-focused self-starter with reputation for excellent troubleshooting and communication abilities.

SELECTED HIGHLIGHTS

Electrical
- Managed and coordinated all aspects of multiple residential wiring projects. Met all deadlines. Successfully conformed to all electrical utility, municipal and / or town code requirements.

- Developed and implemented a preventive maintenance program for emergency lighting system covering eight buildings.

- Installed a complete base board heating unit within three days resulting in complete customer satisfaction.

- Provided orientation, trained, and supervised new electrical assistants resulting in measurable performance improvements.

Refrigeration
- Troubleshot and resolved refrigeration problems, and implemented a preventive maintenance program, effectively preventing future system failures.

- Investigated and repaired faulty refrigeration units, achieving minimal downtime and no food spoilage.

- Conducted on-the-job training for refrigeration students which contributed to excellent job performance.

- Supervised and coordinated the cleaning of a commissary which received recognition from management for cleanliness.

PROFESSIONAL EXPERIENCE

SOUTHAMPTON COLLEGE, Southampton, NY, 2003 – Present
Facilities Maintenance Mechanic

A & M CONSTRUCTION, INC., Deer Park, NY, 2000 - 2003
Construction Supervisor

SHOP COMMISSARY, Woodbourne Correctional Facility; Woodbourne, NY, 1996 - 2000
Clerk Typist

FACILITY MAINTENANCE, Woodbourne Correctional Facility; Woodbourne, NY, 1993 – 1996
Instructional Aide in Air Conditioning and Refrigeration

Previous Experience:
Worked as an Electrician for a Facilities Maintenance Department of State University.

Resume Writer: Bob Simmons

Ralph Martinez Resume (Page Two)

EDUCATION & CERTIFICATIONS

ADELPHI UNIVERSITY, Garden City, NY
Currently pursuing a Master of Science degree in Technical Systems Management

DOWLING COLLEGE, Farmingdale, NY
Bachelor of Science degree in Industrial Technology/Facility Management, 2005

National Association of Plumbing-Heating-Cooling Contractors (NAPHCC)
Type I CFC Technical Certification

Mobile Air Conditioning Society (MACS)
MACS Technician Certification

COMMUNITY ACTIVITIES

President of the Collegiate Science and Technology Entry Program (CSTEP) Club
Board Member of the Distinguished Speakers Program
Board Member of Multicultural Committee
Team Leader of the American Cancer Society Relay for Life fundraising event

SCHOLARSHIPS

Charles O. Schmidt Memorial Scholarship
Dr. Horst Saalbach Scholarship
Ferdinand Laurentian Engelhardt Memorial Scholarship

OTHER AWARDS

Award of Merit, The School of Engineering Technologies
Farmingdale Spirit Award, CSTEP
First Prize – Community Essay Contest, Southampton College

Quan A. Olarinde

1239 First Street, Apartment B2
Plattsburgh, New York 12901
518-327-9212 ✦ QuanO9212@aol.com

Building Maintenance / Custodian

Over two years of building maintenance and cleaning experience

o Maintained a wide variety of floor surfaces including wood, cement, tile and carpet
o Performed preventive and routine maintenance on equipment and machinery
o Kept up outdoor grounds in all types of weather using a variety of equipment
o Set priorities to meet goals and exceed expectations in fast-paced environment
o Worked cooperatively with individuals of widely different backgrounds; skilled in conflict resolution

Related Abilities and Experience

- **Floor and Production Area Maintenance**

- Swept, mopped, scrubbed, and vacuumed floors using appropriate cleaning products
- Collected scrap materials for recycling from production work areas; cleaned shop floors
- Cleaned walls, ceilings, windows, equipment and building fixtures
- Applied paint, waxes and sealers to wood and concrete floors

- **Equipment Maintenance**

- Performed preventive and routine maintenance on a variety of equipment
- Notified management promptly of concerns for needed repairs
- Troubleshot and replaced defective parts on machines and equipment

- **Building & Grounds Maintenance**

- Removed snow and ice from parking areas, driveways and sidewalks
- Used front-end loader, snowplow, snowblower, and shovel to move snow
- Performed preventive and routine painting, plumbing and electrical repairs
- Mowed lawns and grounds using power mowers, tractors and appropriate attachments
- Seeded, watered, and applied protective coverings to new grass growth areas
- Applied herbicides, fertilizers and pesticides using spreaders and spray equipment

Work History

Building Maintenance - Clinton County Correctional Facility, Dannemora, New York
March 2005 to April 2007
Teller - Albank Savings Bank, Albany, New York
March 1999 to January 2005

Education and Training

Building Maintenance Training, Clinton County Correctional Facility, Dannemora, New York
May 2005 to April 2007

High School Diploma / GED - 1998

Resume Writer: Andrea Howard

Michael A. James   333 South Main St. # 2D · Sacramento, CA 95824
916-200-5123

RESTAURANT MANAGER

- Versatile manager with restaurant and retail management and supervisory experience.
- Friendly, outgoing personality comfortable working cooperatively with other team members as well as independently to achieve agreed-upon goals.

Successfully maintain high level of attention to detail even in dynamic, fast-paced environments.

- Well-developed skills in crisis management, intervention, and conflict resolution.
- Comfortable developing positive rapport with individuals of diverse backgrounds.

PROFESSIONAL HIGHLIGHTS

Management / Supervision
- Over 12 years of management and supervisory experience in retail, industrial and medical environments
- Supervised up to seven employees in a department
- Coordinated staff work schedules
- Conducted periodic employee performance appraisals for direct-reports
- Controlled inventory: monitored merchandise inventories; ordered supplies
- Managed cash flow

Customer Service
- Over 15 years of experience in direct customer contact, providing excellent service
- Responded to customer inquiries; provided requested information
- Resolved customer concerns across wide spectrum of customer bases (including restaurant guests; shoppers; wholesale vendors; retailers; doctors; research associates; and patients)

Medical and Counseling
- Informed and counseled individuals regarding medical test results (including AIDS)
- Coordinated group activities for mentally ill residents
- Performed, processed, and logged medical lab procedures on patients including:
  - Blood and arterial draws
  - Urinalysis
  - Vitals - blood pressure, temperature, respiratory rate, heart rate

WORK EXPERIENCE (*1995 to Present*)

House Supervisor	Main Street Homeless Shelter	Sacramento, CA
Cook	Tony's Gourmet Pizza	Sacramento, CA
Phlebotomist	El Centro Pathology	Los Angeles, CA
Lab Assistant	Los Angeles Hospital	Los Angeles, CA
Lab Assistant Manager	L.V. Plasma	Las Vegas, NV
Shipping & Receiving	RTM Corporation	Las Vegas, NV

EDUCATION

Medical Technician Certificate	Los Angeles Community College	Los Angeles, CA

Resume Writer: Beth WoodWorth

Jaime Luis Brownhouse

1234 New Town Lane, Issaquah, WA 98029
(425) 904-8304

Target: Assistant Director, Center for Troubled Youth

PROFILE

Dynamic individual with keen business understanding and an enthusiastic attitude. Genuine, passionate desire to reach out to troubled young people, open lines of communication to help them understand the consequences of their choices, and facilitate providing the resources and tools they need to improve their lives. Hard worker who is willing to learn; currently enrolled in business management classes.

QUALIFICATIONS

- Excellent financial management skills.
- Strong communication skills; proven track record of developing and maintaining loyal clients.
- Extraordinary memory for names and faces.
- Demonstrated strength in marketing without advertising, within extremely limited budgets.
- Skilled in creating, recognizing and optimizing business opportunities.
- Creative and innovative: ability to achieve outstanding results with limited resources.
- Bilingual— Spanish / English.

EXPERIENCE

Men's Correctional Facility, Spokane, Washington, 2001-2008
Assigned position of **Kitchen Supervisor**

- Directed activities and performance of 23 men in the preparation, service, and cleanup of meals for inmates.
- Applied strong leadership, conflict resolution, and mediation skills. Monitored and kept records of kitchen inventory. Commended for consistently excellent management and job performance.

Self-Employed throughout Washington and Oregon, 1995–2001
Manufacturers' Representative

- Built, expanded and maintained loyal customer base.
- Created and nurtured extensive network of contacts.
- Effectively managed cash flow; maintained accurate bookkeeping records.
- Polished communications and mediation skills.

Construction Laborer, part-time positions, various employers, throughout Oregon, 1987–1995

- Developed finish-carpentry skills and learned to operate various pieces of heavy equipment. Worked cooperatively with crews with diverse backgrounds and personalities.

TRAINING / EDUCATION

Business Management, Piedmont Community College; Issaquah, WA (Currently enrolled)
Diploma, New Town High School, New Town, WA

VOLUNTEERISM

Tutor / Advisor, Navigators (Youth Group), Piedmont Community Church (2005 – Present)

Resume Writer: Janice Shepherd

Chapter 10
Resumes for Recent Immigrants

In this chapter, find resumes for:

Account Manager / Marketing Representative
Administrative Assistant
Laboratory Technician
Designer
Auditor
Travel Agency Manager
Pharmaceutical Sales Executive

If you're a new arrival to the United States or Canada, you face many challenges in adjusting to the culture, the language, and the lifestyle. Along the way, you'll find that the culture of the workplace may be much different, and, most importantly for our discussion here, your job search will likely be a bit different than what you may have been accustomed to in your country of origin. The advice offered here is valid for the United States and Canada, and reasonably applies to Australia, as well. (Take note that we have included at least one resume for a candidate relocating from South Africa to Australia. The countries are different and there are some cultural differences, to be sure, but the fundamental principles involved in launching a new career in a new country are similar.) Here are a few tips to help you prepare a resume and cover letters that will advance your job search and win you interviews:

1. Be your own advocate. Whether on your resume or your cover letter, or in person at a job interview, don't be afraid to tell employers about your accomplishments. In some parts of the world, modesty and a certain level of reserve are highly valued. However, what might seem like bragging in other cultures is almost a requirement for job seekers in the United States and Canada. Take to heart the advice in Chapters 2 and 3, and include many accomplishments on your resume and in your cover letters.

2. Clarify everything on your resume. You may hold a certification or university degree whose name is unfamiliar to employers in your new country. There may be other technical terms that lose something in the translation. Add an extra parenthetical line explaining that the credential in question is the equivalent of an American (or Canadian or Australian) college or university. An American employer may have never heard of the prestigious university in your homeland that is comparable to Harvard or Princeton in the United States. An extra line explaining the admissions standards or the institution's reputation may help an employer understand the value of your education at that school.

3. If English is not your first language, have someone who is adept in English (preferably a native speaker who also writes well) review your documents and help you get the language right. Especially in resumes, there are many nuances to word choices and usage. American English is a decidedly different dialect from that of our British or Australian cousins. Spelling, grammar, and the vernacular usage of certain words vary between these countries, and these variations are most noticeable in the written language. Even though Canada is right next door to the United States, in most cases Canadians follow the British model for spelling and grammar rather than the U.S. model. That said, neither is right or wrong; it's just a matter of knowing which to use depending on where you are sending your resume.

4. In the United States, including your immigration status near the bottom of the resume is a good idea. Certain types of visas require employer sponsorship, which may or may not be an issue for some employers. If you're a permanent resident alien or otherwise possess immigration status that allows you to live and work in the country without restriction, including that on your resume assures employers that they won't have to deal with any extra red tape in order to employ you. Some government jobs require U.S. citizenship, and if you are a naturalized U.S. citizen, you may want to state that on your resume. In countries other than the United States, it's recommended that you check with that nation's immigration authorities to determine your eligibility for work in that country.

On the following pages is an excellent example of a cover letter as well as several resumes for candidates seeking employment in their new country. (Note: Some of the resumes contained in this chapter were written by Canadian or Australian resume professionals for candidates seeking work in those countries. With this in mind, we have left in place the accepted spelling, grammar, and wording used in those countries. Even if you're not looking for work in Canada or Australia, the overall format and structure of these documents may prove helpful to you in preparing your job search documents.)

Inger V. Holstrom

84 Crystal Springs Crescent • Syracuse, New York 13212 • 315.903.2184
Inger.Holstrom@frontiernet.net

January 12, 2008

Mr. Trevor J. Denslow
President and Chief Executive Officer
Xtraordinary Advertising and Marketing, Unlimited
2128 Main Street
Syracuse, New York 13212

Dear Mr. Denslow:

You know how competitive your business is. In order to succeed, a sales professional needs to be innovative, creative, personable, and disciplined. I offer these qualities, plus enthusiasm and a strong desire to succeed. Having recently immigrated to the U.S. from Scandinavia (fully eligible to work in the U.S.), I am eager to apply the knowledge and experience that made me a successful Sales Representative / Account Manager in Europe to a new opportunity with a Syracuse-based firm. With this goal in mind, I have enclosed a resume for your review and consideration.

Among my key capabilities relevant to a sales position with your firm are the following:

➢ **Adaptability:** During my 12-year career, I have worked in the hospitality, entertainment, telecommunications, and marketing industries, achieving success in each business setting.

➢ **Professionalism:** I am equally comfortable consulting with senior managers of major corporations on multi-million dollar campaigns and addressing the needs of small business owners seeking cost-effective solutions that meet their modest needs.

➢ **Confidence:** Since the age of 10, I have been an on-air personality, entertainer, and consummate sales professional. I have the stage presence and poise to be effective in high-pressure sales situations, plus the ability to build rapport and promote trust with decision-makers at all levels.

➢ **Organizational Skills:** In addition to sales successes, I have served in Project Manager / Event Coordinator roles, with accountability for high-profile marketing campaigns with multi-million dollar budgets.

➢ **Results:** In virtually all of my professional experiences, I have met or exceeded expectations and played an integral role in several major business successes.

No piece of paper can adequately portray the range of skills and abilities that I can bring to a Sales / Account Management / Customer Relationship Management role. I encourage you to contact me so that we can arrange a mutually convenient time for an initial meeting to discuss your needs and how I can fulfill them. Please feel free to call or e-mail me at the number / address shown above.

Thank you for your time and attention. I look forward to speaking with you soon.

Sincerely,

Inger V. Holstrom

Enclosure

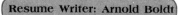

Inger V. Holstrom

84 Crystal Springs Crescent
Syracuse, New York 13212
315.903.2184
Inger.Holstrom@frontiernet.net

SALES / ACCOUNT MANAGEMENT / CUSTOMER RELATIONSHIP MANAGEMENT
Telecommunications • Advertising • Event Planning / Marketing • Hospitality Industry

Personable and engaging sales professional with established track record of representing an array of products and services to corporate accounts in European markets. Exceptional customer relations, negotiation, and project management skills.

CAREER HIGHLIGHTS

Recruited by ScandiaNet, Sweden's largest telecommunications provider, to participate in the launch of web-based directory service best described as an online yellow pages. Joined company in telemarketing role, cold calling small business customers, and was quickly promoted to Key Account Manager position. In this high-profile role, developed and presented proposals to senior decision-makers at large global firms, including Pepsico, Emerson Electric, Playstation, and Saatchi & Saatchi. Negotiated agreements and closed deals with these major advertisers for new website focusing on a young adult audience.

Selected to serve in Marketing Coordinator role for firm specializing in "last-link" marketing campaigns, which included product sampling, product demonstrations, and event marketing. Responsibilities included lead generation, high-level sales presentations (CEO and CFO level), planning and coordinating event logistics, and negotiating with celebrities to participate in high-profile events. Consulted with Ogilvy & Mather (one of Europe's leading ad agencies) to develop and present proposal to their client, Seagram and Sons. Managed large-scale public events that occurred in four different cities simultaneously to kick off the highly successful launch of their latest Seagram's' Gin product.

Marketed trade show booths to major corporations throughout Europe and globally for convention facility with over 4,200,000 square feet of indoor exhibition space and ten acres of outdoor display areas. Successfully sold out convention space in less than three months; developed new "Computer Commons" concept for convention and sold out all available slots.

Recruited to manage bar and wine collection for gourmet restaurant featuring the cuisine of Provence. Property was listed in Michelin Guide (two stars). Managed inventory, including wine cellar; handled purchasing and vendor relations; and supervised security staff. Hired and supervised "singing waiters," a renowned feature of the restaurant.

Launched start-up business at age 17. Developed unique entertainment concept and marketed this concept to night clubs and bars. Booked an average of 70 shows during a two-month season at venues throughout Sweden. Cold-called club managers, presented concept, negotiated arrangements, and closed sales. Recruited and auditioned performers, and coordinated travel and logistics related to operating this touring show. Managed business for four years before profitably selling to a leading competitor.

Successfully auditioned at age 12 for host role on prime-time children's television show that aired nationally throughout Sweden. Served in this role for two years, interviewing guests, voicing features, and hosting live on-air contests as part of the show format.

Inger V. Holstrom

Resume – Page Two
315.903.2184/ Inger.Holstrom@frontiernet.net

PROFESSIONAL EXPERIENCE

SCANDIANET; Stockholm, Sweden
Key Account Manager   May 2006 – Jan. 2008
Called on high-level corporate decision-makers to present proposals for online directory advertising. **Exceeded all targeted goals calling on major corporations and large advertising agencies.**

Sales Coordinator   Apr. 2005 – May 2006
Played a key role in the launch of online directory service. Frequently exceeded monthly goals; selected to deliver motivational presentations to fellow team members. **Promoted to Key Account Manager role.**

ZENITH TEMP AGENCY; Stockholm, Sweden
Sales Coordinator / Project Manager – "Kommunal Teknik Sweden"   Dec. 2004 – Mar. 2005
Sold out display booths at major convention center for promoters of business-to-business trade show. Called on prospects in Norway, Denmark, and Sweden, adding numerous new contacts to customer database.

FRESCH APPROACH; Hammarstrand, Norway
Marketing Coordinator   Jan. 2003 – Dec. 2004
Scheduled and executed high-level sales presentations with senior managers at major corporations and large ad agencies. Developed proposals and managed execution of event marketing and product sampling campaigns that led to successful introduction of new products to the marketplace.

CAFÉ DE PROVENCE; Stockholm, Sweden
Bar Manager   Jan. 2002 – Jan. 2003
Managed purchasing of wines and spirits for this fine dining restaurant. Supervised bar staff and auditioned / hired singing waiters.

AGENCY NOUVEAU; Stockholm, Sweden
Sales Executive / Show Promoter (Partner)   1996 – 1999
Founded this business, with a partner, at the age of 17. Solicited managers of night clubs and entertainment venues to book entertainment at locations throughout Sweden. Managed all aspects of business operations. **Profitably sold this business to competing company.**

PROFESSIONAL DEVELOPMENT

Sales Team Training – Six Weeks – ScandiaNet (Sweden)
Hotel & Restaurant Management Training – Completed first 12 months of 18-month course.

Computer Literate: Windows; MS Office

PERSONAL

Permanent Resident Alien / Married to U.S. Citizen
Fluent in English, Norwegian, and Danish; Native Speaker of Swedish

Excellent Letters of Recommendation Available at Time of Interview

ESTELLA MARTINEZ

P.O. Box 875
Sunland Park, New Mexico 78953   estellamartinez@jci.com

Residence: (505) 566-0258
Office: (915) 307-6542

ADMINISTRATIVE ASSISTANT

Highly efficient, judicious administrative professional with nine years of dedicated experience in office administration, multi-faceted clerical projects, international employee relations, customer service, special event planning, and translation. Confident in all aspects of office operations, including calendar management, record keeping, scheduling, order processing, and preparing professional correspondence. Exceptional time management and organizational skills with keen attention to detail. Noted ability to work and communicate well across cultures.
• Computer proficiencies include Microsoft Word, Excel, & PowerPoint
• Bilingual with fluency in English and Spanish.

PROFESSIONAL EXPERIENCE

SMITH CONTROLS, PLANTS I, II, AND C.O.E.   Cd. JUAREZ, CHIHUAHUA, MEXICO
Administrative Assistant   **1998 TO April, 2008**
Recognized for and rapidly promoted to a variety of administrative positions with increased responsibility for worldwide leader in the manufacture and supply of automotive interiors with annual sales exceeding $32M. Position highlights:

- Interfaced with representatives of multiple internal departments and outside agencies on a daily basis to provide comprehensive administrative assistance to Plant Managers.
- Composed and distributed correspondence: Quality Assurance meeting minutes; executive messages; monthly operations reports.
- Made travel arrangements and scheduled meetings.
- Translated simultaneous and consecutive sessions from English to Spanish and vice versa to ensure accurate communication among management, employees, and visitors from the United States.
- Procured purchase orders for office supplies ensuring appropriate signature approval.
- Prepared and tracked expense reports, credit card statements, and other accounting information.

Human Services Representative
- Specially selected to serve in this highly-sensitive position during the 18-month absence of incumbent.
- Implemented employee disciplinary actions as appropriate, such as verbal and written warnings and / or suspensions.
- Tracked employee schedules to ensure compliance with policies and procedures.
- Processed and routed all new employee documentation to verify eligibility for employment, ensure appropriate testing and medical reports were complete.
- Implemented measures necessary to ensure compliance with occupational health and safety laws.

Receptionist
- Served as the primary point of contact for customers, management, and employees, greeting visitors in a professional, courteous manner.
- Operated multi-line telephone system; maintained appropriate etiquette and demeanor.
- Distributed incoming mail, faxes, and other highly sensitive correspondence.

Special Event Planner
- Managed all aspects of special events including holiday gatherings, picnics, and other occasions.
- Selected and scheduled venues; prepared announcements and invitations; selected and managed caterers and other service providers.

EDUCATION & TRAINING

New Horizons High School, Anthony, New Mexico, Diploma, 1996.
Specialized in computer training.

References Available Upon Request

Resume Writer: Shannon Branson

Xiao Yin Zhang

96 Mountain Road, Unit 10-D Rapid City, South Dakota 57701
(605) 829-6368 • xyz1028@yahoo.com

CAREER GOAL

Position as an **Associate Laboratory Technician** with a biotechnology research and development facility studying genetics and cellular / molecular biology.

PROFILE

- Strong theoretical background in life / physical sciences combined with work experience involving micro-biological testing, as well as, zoological interaction / behavioral observation of a variety of animals.
- Demonstrated hands-on skill in the preparation of lab samples and analytical techniques requiring precision, resourcefulness, dedication, and a well-organized approach.
- Experience in coordinating, monitoring, ordering, and inventorying lab supplies.
- Adept in technical writing with well-developed research, analytical, and documentation abilities; comprehensive vocabulary of scientific terminology.
- Personable and collaborative team participant, compliant with department standards, and articulate in verbal communications.
- High level of productivity, with proven initiative, time management, and multitasking capabilities; adaptable to frequent change and erratic work schedules.
- Computer literate: MS Word, Excel, and PowerPoint as well as data entry on Laboratory Information Management System (LIMS); sophisticated Internet research skills.
- Language fluency in English and Mandarin.

TECHNICAL SKILLS

- Practical knowledge and expertise in various laboratory equipment / procedures including microscopes … slit-to-agar … machine … lab burner … incubator … centrifuge … fluorometer … pH meter … gas chromatograph … polymerase chain reaction (PCR) studies … gram staining … enzyme restriction … electrophoresis process
- Genetic testing: biochemical … cytogenic … DNA … prenatal.

EDUCATION AND RESEARCH

Washington University, Rapid City, SD

Coursework underway leading to Master of Science degree, Zoology
- Research zoologist at Bear Country USA, Black Hills State Park.
  Engaged in 18-month supervised field study involving ova and embryo transfers to increase the grizzly bear population, using black bears for gestation.

Anticipated 2009

Bachelor of Science in Biology with concentrations in Zoology / Cellular Biology

May 2007

Veterinary Medical Research Institute, Beijing, China
Zoology student and veterinary lab assistant
- Observed and documented giant panda behavior and biology in a controlled laboratory setting.
- Awarded scholarship by the government of China to continue education and participate in veterinary research in the United States.

2003–2005

EMPLOYMENT

Black Hills State Park Zoo, Rapid City, SD
Animal Keeper
Earning living expenses while attending and conducting research at Washington University
- Tend over 200 different types of wild and exotic animals, including mammals, amphibians, reptiles, birds, and insects within a 15-acre zoo.
- Maintain safe and sanitary animal enclosures.
- Train and supervise volunteer zookeeping assistants.
- Assist in-house veterinarian in the planning and execution of varied medical procedures.
- Administer medication and obtain / document vital signs and developmental data.
- Monitor animals' day-to-day behavior and social interactions among their species as well as zoo patrons.
- Report notable behavioral deviations to appropriate medical and operational authorities.
- Use diverse animal capture methods for transference, medical assessment, and treatment.

2005–Present

CITIZENSHIP STATUS

Entered the United States under F-1 student visa in 2005.
Currently a permanent resident, eligible for U.S. citizenship in 2009.

Resume Writer: Melanie Noonan

THERESA ABRITZO, DESIGNER

900 East 11ᵗʰ Street, #4J ▪ New York, NY 10009 ▪ 212.555.1212 ▪ theresa.abritzo@email.com

RETAIL ▪ PRIVATE LABEL ▪ WHOLESALE

Talented, profit-generating home furnishings designer; nine years of experience with dinnerware, gift items, textiles, and lighting.

KEY AREAS OF EXPERTISE

- Research & Forecasting
- Luxury & Mid-Tier Products
- Spec & Technical Drawings
- Ceramics, Glass, Naturals, Synthetics
- Brand Identity & Support
- Photoshop CS2, Illustrator CS2
- 3D Prototypes
- Factory Communications
- Team Management

PROFESSIONAL EXPERIENCE

Senior Designer, DESIGN SOLUTIONS, LTD – MELBOURNE, AUSTRALIA   2003 – Present

Lead strategic planning and design for this Australian company, creating home furnishing lines and directing breadth and depth of each category. Developed company from a limited interior and graphic design practice to a highly respected housewares design source, supplying several stores including Casper Harris, Wells & Robert, and Home. Work closely with buyers to create designs that support color palettes, price points, and functional crossover requirements. Forecast season designs and trends; direct overseas factories in India, China, and Thailand, using detailed technical and hand drawings to communicate designs. Develop 50 products under five different housewares categories annually – taking product from idea to store shelves within eight months. Portfolio: *www.abritzo.com.*

- Designed contemporary table lamp with sales spanning multiple seasons and requiring two production drops for single store.
- Created dinner set chosen to replace longstanding stock set at high-end department store; new design available year-round.
- Devised company's restructure; developed tiered approach with differentiated brands, materials and price points for each market.

Owner, SANCTUARY; MELBOURNE, AUSTRALIA   1998 – 2003

Founded and ran small volume, high-end home furnishings business; products included vases, serving trays, floor rugs, bookends, lighting and tables using luxury fabrics, woods, ceramics, and leathers. Grew product line from eight designs in first year to over 26 by 2001. Clients included retail stores, specialty boutiques, interior designers, contractors, and architects. Recruited and managed team of freelancers and worked closely with accountants to calculate markups and oversee A/R, A/P, and payroll. Portfolio: www.abritzo.com.

- Realized $180,000 AUD turnover (about $135,000 US) with initial product line in first year of business.
- Consistently quadrupled markup over cost. For example: produced bedside lamp at $65 AU cost and retail price of $250 AU; created leather embossed side table at cost $317 AU / price $1500 AU retail.
- Featured in numerous magazine articles and books: Wallpaper, Living Australia, Square Rooms Singapore, Marie Claire, Metropolitan Home and Fine Furniture International.
- Exhibits include Space Uptown (Heights Hotel, New York City) and 180 Turns (Stilwerk, Berlin).

Designer, NABLE GREY DEPARTMENT STORES; SYDNEY, AUSTRALIA (4 MONTH CONTRACT)   1998

Brought into this national retailer to design tabletop and gift items in line with new market position / company re-branding. Worked closely with development team and overseas factories to communicate specifications.

EDUCATION

Bachelor of Design, INDUSTRIAL DESIGN; MELBOURNE UNIVERSITY   1997

Resume Writer: Kimberly Schneiderman

ANIL MEHTA, CPA

227 Scarberia Avenue
Ajax, Ontario L1T 4V6
Cellular Telephone: (289) 157-2169
E-mail: amehta@thewrightcareer.com

PROFESSIONAL PROFILE

An accomplished Senior Auditor with global expertise and a solid track record of performing auditing functions for major banks, investment companies, brand-name hotel chains and retailers, Internet service providers, and international automotive dealerships. Highly motivated and experienced, with a proven ability to work beyond the parameters of the role and to prioritise effectively to meet deadlines. Resourceful and intuitive; excel at leading and coordinating field work teams, presenting practical business solutions to accounting issues, and providing timely information to management. Acquired a sound understanding of, and ability to apply existing accounting and auditing standards, including International Financial Reporting Standards (IFRS) and US Generally Accepted Accounting Principles (GAAP). Achieved CPA designation. **Core strengths** include:

- Financial Analysis
- Risk Assessment
- Internal Control Assessment
- Business Process Review
- Global Experience

- Financial Statements & Disclosures
- Audit Compliance
- Team Leadership

- Full-cycle Audit Management (planning, fieldwork & wrap-up)
- Documentation
- Client Relationship Management
- Project Management

SPECIAL SKILLS

- Auditor Work Station (AWS)
- CaseWare
- Audit Command Language

PROFESSIONAL EXPERIENCE

FREEDOM TAX SERVICE, Scarborough, Ontario   Jan 2006 – May 2008
Senior Tax Accountant

Recruited to provide diverse accounting, payroll and tax-preparation functions for an independent tax firm. Interfaced with Company's corporate office on technical and operational issues at the local level.

- Streamlined accounting processes which immediately improved efficiency in this franchise.
- Collaborated with staff to resolve tax issues; ensured proper discounting of returns and kept tax refund shortages to a minimum.
- Acted as primary contact between the organization and Canada Revenue Agency (CRA) on issues relating to individual and corporate tax returns.
- Prepared payroll and source deduction remittances to CRA and filed GST returns on a periodic basis.
- Produced daily and weekly management reports to monitor the profitability of individual profit centres.

ERNST & YOUNG, Mumbai, India   1998 – 2004
Assurance & Advisory Business Services
Senior Accountant

Initially hired to perform analytical reviews; devise audit programs; plan and test internal controls. Through a series of promotions, attained the rank of **Senior Accountant**. **Nominated as CaseWare and ACL Champion** within the Mumbai office.

- Used AWS on all major jobs and formulated strategies for testing and documentation of UBPs (Understanding Business Processes) and PCAFs (Program for Controls and Analysis Forms).
- Worked in partnership with engagement team to share all client knowledge; kept senior management apprised of all audit and accounting issues.
- Provided on-the-job training for junior audit staff and supervised teams of up to seven members.
- Thoroughly and constructively reviewed team members' work for accuracy and completeness and to ensure sufficient evidence was gathered and correctly documented to support the audit opinions.
- Executed appropriate use of electronic working papers, audit tools and sources of knowledge to streamline audit processes.
- Determined that all engagements were executed in a timely manner, within stipulated budgets and in accordance with firm's methodologies and professional standards.
- Secured and developed significant relationships with several high-profile clients and enhanced these affiliations by identifying ideas of added value to clients.
- Collaborated with executives on budget development, billing and collection activities to maximize job recoveries.
- Ensured all client deliverables (draft financial statements, management letters, business review memoranda and related client communications) were prepared on a timely basis and with a high degree of accuracy and professionalism.

EDUCATION & PROFESSIONAL DEVELOPMENT

- **Certified Public Accountant Designation**, Delaware, USA (2006)
- B.Comm (Accounting & Auditing Major) Bharathiar University, India (1997)

Professional Development & Training

- Investment Funds Certificate program at Hopewell College (Currently enrolled)
- Registered with the Institute of Canadian Bankers
- Canadian Income Tax Preparation courses (Levels 1 & 2)
- Tax Update training (through FreedomTax Service)
- Certified Information System Auditor (CISA) review course, US
- Advanced Bank Accounting & Auditing (E & Y)
- Auditing & Accounting I – III (E & Y)
- CaseWare & ACL Train-the-Trainer courses (E & Y)
- Registered with the Institute of Canadian Bankers

PROFESSIONAL AFFILIATIONS

- Associate Member, American Institute of Certified Public Accountants (AICPA)
- Member, Information Systems Audit and Control Associations (ISACA)
- Candidate for the Chartered Accountant Designation

ANABELLA DOMINGO

16831 West Lake Road ▪ Miami ▪ Florida 33131
Home: (954) 333-4656 ▪ Cell: (305) 333-4994
anabella@hotmail.com

TRAVEL AGENCY MANAGER

Accomplished travel industry manager with outstanding record of business development and growth. Demonstrated expertise in full range of managerial accountabilities: marketing; strategic planning; sales; finance and human resources. Successfully motivate employees to achieve common goals. Profit-driven and results-focused with strong analytical skills and proven ability to deliver exceptional client services. Key proficiencies include:

- General Management
- Emerging Venture Planning
- Financing-Private and Public
- Office Relocation / Scouting
- Travel Agency Management
- Marketing Campaigns
- Pricing Structures
- Fluency in English and Spanish
- Sales Strategies
- Operations – Continuous Improvement
- Outsourcing Coordination
- Research and Analysis

PROFESSIONAL BACKGROUND

BUSINESS MANAGEMENT

➢ Established two of the leading boutique travel agencies in Chile. Attained 900+ individual clients and 30+ corporate accounts in first five years of operation. Surpassed U.S. $200 million in air fare revenues in 13 years.
➢ Achieved average annual sales growth of 30% while managing all aspects of agencies' operations including sales, purchasing, logistics, and marketing. Focused personal efforts in the area of business client account development and supplier negotiations, significantly driving profitability.
➢ Designed and implemented an integrated management system that optimized timeliness of sensitive business travel data, ultimately increasing efficiency and contributing to enhanced productivity.
➢ Managed human resources functions for the two agencies, including recruitment, training, and appraisals. Implemented weekly performance reporting process to ensure superior customer service and continuing process improvements.
➢ Achieved 100% employee retention for four consecutive years, unprecedented for the travel industry.

MARKETING AND NEGOTIATING

➢ Applied market research tools to identify and open new market segments for the start-up businesses. Created new customer database with over 150 entries in the first three months of operation.
➢ Developed marketing plan. Designed 10 collaterals for mass mailing campaign, which resulted in second year sales increase of over 50%.
➢ Created eight innovative, international tour packages. Developed parallel marketing campaigns and coordinated all tour providers and media communications to ensure consistent message.
➢ Evolved business plan to focus on marketing of travel packages with larger profit margins to high-end clients. Achieved higher productivity and profitability by implementing this strategy.
➢ Built strategic alliances with vendors, including major airlines, cruise ships, and international hotel chains to enhance profitability. Negotiated pricing to achieve the market's most competitive rates.
➢ Invited by major travel / touring entities to attend over 40 international trips geared for elite clientele. Attended over 20, with destinations including Australia and New Zealand; Kenya; the Middle East; Europe; and Alaska.
➢ *Achieved ranking among top five travel agencies in Chile.*

MORTGAGE, REAL ESTATE AND INSURANCE SALES

➢ Achieved, as a loan officer, monthly closing rate of 90%, a full 30% higher than colleagues' rates.
➢ Attained 30% year-over-year increase in residential real estate sales working with a South Florida realtor.

Résumé Continues

Resume Writer: Claudine Vainrub Kupchick

WORK HISTORY

CHASE FUNDING – *Plantation, FL*   *2006 - Present*
Loan Officer

HR REALTY – *Miami, FL*   *2004 - Present*
Licensed Real Estate Salesperson

ACME LIFE & CASUALTY – *Miramar, FL*   *2005 - 2006*
Licensed Life and Health Insurance Consultant

TREX MORTGAGE BANKERS – *Miami, FL*   *2003 - 2005*
Mortgage Broker

ATOMIC VIAJES – *Santiago, Chile*   *1990 - 2003*
Owner / CEO – Boutique Travel Agency

TRAVEL TOURISM – *Santiago, Chile*   *1985 -1990*
Partner / Marketing Manager – Boutique Travel Agency

INSTITUTO ESCUELA – *Santiago, Chile*   *1980 - 1985*
English Teacher – Various Private K-12 Schools

BERLITZ SCHOOL FOR TRANSLATORS – *Santiago, Chile*   *1978 - 1979*
Translators' Teacher – Top International Foreign Languages School

ACADEMIC BACKGROUND

GOLD COAST SCHOOLS – *Miami, FL*   *2004 - 2005*
   Life and Health Insurance - L-215 License (2005)
   Real Estate - Real Estate Salesperson - Realtor (2004)
   Mortgage Brokers' Division - Mortgage Broker (2004)

LUFTHANSA TRAVEL AGENT SCHOOL – *Düsseldorf, Germany*   *1986*
   Fair Calculation Course – Travel Agency Administrator Diploma

BERLITZ SCHOOLS OF LANGUAGES – *Santiago, Chile*   *1978*
   School of Simultaneous and Consecutive Translation - Diploma
   ➤   Emphasis in Simultaneous English-Spanish-English Translation
   ➤   Specialized in translation of medical and psychology texts

PROFESSIONAL AFFILIATIONS

Weston Chamber of Commerce, *Member* 2005 - Present
Realtor Association of Greater Miami and the Beaches, *Member* 2004 - Present
Chilean Association of Travel and Tourism Agencies – A.V.A.V.I.T., *Director* 2001-2003 / Member 1990-2003
International Association of Travel and Tourism Agencies – I.A.T.A., *Member* 1990-2003

PERSONAL

Permanent Resident Alien ~ Eligible to Work for Any Employer
Fluent in English, Spanish, Hebrew and Romanian; Conversational French and German
Excellent knowledge of Microsoft Office Suite (Word, Excel, Access, and Outlook Express) and Internet
MLXChange, Calyx, and DU Mortgage Systems
Co-authored the Spanish translation of five English medical articles on Mio-Functional anomalies, 1982
Interests in History, Classical Music, and Tai-Chi

DAVID ALDINE

10 Azure Court, Rosevale SA 8278
(H) 08 9341 9928 • (M) 0412 040 435 • (E) davidva@hotmail.com

PHARMACEUTICAL SALES PROFESSIONAL

Dedicated, top performing Sales Professional with solid track record of exceeding targets, growing strong territory, and establishing lasting client relationships. Proven ability to drive market penetration through effective analysis, business planning, presentation, and training expertise. A personable high achiever, relocating from South Africa.

SALES CAREER HIGHLIGHTS

Challenge:	Poor regional sales results due to neglect of rural pharmacies.
Action:	Developed aggressive marketing campaign targeting under-served pharmacies. Established and nurtured rapport with other pharmacies passed over by prior company representatives.
Result:	**Increased sales by $65,000 in first two quarters.** Received management recognition award for exceeding sales targets and posting highest sales figures for Free State.
Challenge:	Unfavorable company reputation created by numerous adverse encounters between clients and previous product representatives.
Action:	Approached prospects in friendly manner, demonstrating product knowledge and sincere desire to help. Ensured prompt follow through on commitments. Negotiated discounts and reward system for loyal customers.
Result:	**Revitalized positive company image and established profitable relationships.** Increased sales revenue and created a win-win environment.

RELATED EDUCATION

Pharmaceutical and Medical Representative Training (2007)
PHARMACY REPS PTY LTD – Adelaide, SA
Curriculum overview: Territory Management / Sales Data Analysis / Detailing Doctors / Approaching & Educating Pharmacists / Medical Rep Best Practice / Industry Operations, Standards and Regulations / More

Master Trainer HIV/ AIDS: Disease Prevention (1998)
GENERAL HEALTH SERVICES – Pretoria, South Africa
Curriculum overview: Small group facilitation / Nature / Causes / Prevention

Business Administration: Advancement Course to Rank of Full Officer (1997)
ARMY UNIVERSITY – Pretoria, South Africa

RELEVANT PROFESSIONAL EXPERIENCE

MEDICO PHARMA PTY LTD – Pretoria, South Africa   9/2005 to 3/2006
Pharmaceutical distribution company with 140 employees.
Pharmaceutical Sales Representative
Marketed range of generic analgesics and antihistamines to pharmacies. Initiated cold calls, comprehensively prospected territory; developed new client relationships; enhanced existing accounts and increased sales.
Key Strengths & Achievements:
➢ Surpassed all sales targets by securing 15 new client pharmacies and increasing revenue by $75,000 in two quarters. *Received bonus recognition.*
➢ Overcame unfavorable company reputation and significant client dissatisfaction with predecessors through personable, informed approach. Developed and introduced bulk-buy discounts and loyalty rewards.
➢ Conducted informative product presentations consistently resulting in strong orders. Persuaded buyers to purchase superior products at higher prices to gain reputation for quality with their customers.
➢ Maintained detailed and accurate records, analyzed data, and took appropriate actions to optimize sales.
➢ Maintained current awareness of competitors' products.
➢ Identified compelling selling points for each product to highlight in innovative sales presentations.

Resume Writer: Beverley Neil

DAVID ALDINE

Resume - Page Two

(H) 08 9341 9928 • (M) 0412 040 435 • (E) davida@hotmail.com

RWQ REAL ESTATE – Pretoria, South Africa   1/2003 to 9/2005
Major property sales company, employing 32 estate agents.
Real Estate Sales Agent
Identified motivated sellers and buyers, marketed properties, led negotiations, and finalised sales contracts.

Key Strengths & Achievements:
➢ Networked extensively with current and previous associates, particularly military personnel who were eligible for housing grants and subsidies, resulting in significantly increased revenue.
➢ Presented proposals to groups and individual prospects on location for off-the-plan units. Worked closely with developers to successfully launch townhouse complexes.
➢ Developed and introduced successful strategy of recruiting and employing "spotters" that was later adopted by many other sales agents.

WORK HISTORY

JONES & SONS ENTERPRISES LTD – Rosevale, SA   5/2006 to Present

Despatch Operator
Position undertaken upon arrival in Australia while examining local employment opportunities.
Process orders; package products for shipment; compile production records; organise efficient floor layout; operate and maintain hydraulic lifting equipment; ensure compliance with OH&S procedures.
➢ Promoted quickly to permanent employee status; offered access to unlimited overtime based on reliability.

MEDICO PHARMA PTY LTD – Pretoria, South Africa   9/2005 to 3/2006
Pharmaceutical Sales Representative

RWQ REAL ESTATE – Pretoria, South Africa   1/2003 to 9/2005
Real Estate Agent

TUCKER'S MEN'S CLOTHING – Pretoria, South Africa   1/1999 to 12/2003
Branch Manager
➢ Trained and motivated staff to provide friendlier, more focused level of customer service.
➢ Increased revenue through development and implementation of weekly sales incentive program.
➢ Implemented inventory control system that improved efficiency and reduced shrinkage.

THE SCHOOL OF ARMOUR – South Africa   1990 to 1999
Armoured Corps of the South African Defence Force.
➢ Achieved Rank of Colonel

TECHNOLOGY PROFICIENCIES

Microsoft Office: Word, FrontPage, Excel, PowerPoint, Outlook; Various Internet search engines; Ability to accurately type 70 WPM.

LANGUAGES

➢ Comprehensive fluency in English, German, Dutch, Sotho, Afrikaans.
➢ Read and write Greek and Hebrew.

COMMUNITY INVOLVEMENT

Overseas Service League / P&F Association / Adelaide Collective Baptist Church

OTHER INTERESTS & ACTIVITIES

Golf / National Level Judo / Competition Mountain Biking / Water Skiing / Wake-Boarding

Chapter 11

Resumes for Self-employed Workers

In this chapter, find resumes for people who work for themselves, but now wish to secure jobs as employees. Job targets include:

Business Development / Marketing
Park Manager / Grounds Maintenance
Web Developer / E-Marketing Specialist
Golf Course Superintendent
Retail Management
Pharmaceutical Sales

Being your own boss can be a fantastic experience, but it requires a great deal of discipline and personal sacrifice to be truly successful. Some people try it for a few years and decide it's not right for them. Some entrepreneurs find that running a maturing business isn't as exciting as managing its start-up, and still others face up to the fact that a steady paycheck with someone else's signature on it has some definite advantages. If you've been running the show for a while but now feel that it's time to work for someone else, there are several key things to keep in mind when you prepare your resume and cover letters. Here are just a few tips that you may find helpful:

1. Avoid calling yourself the owner on your resume. Some employers are a bit skittish about hiring someone who's been in business for themselves, worrying that you won't be happy and will succumb to the urge to once again strike out on your own. Because you're the boss, you can choose any job title you wish to use; president or general manager, for

example, will convey the level of accountability you held without tagging you as the owner. Depending on your current target, think about using project manager, Web developer, or director of business development as job titles if they reflect what you do as a business person and, more importantly, what you hope to do for an employer.

2. Emphasize your versatility. If you've been running a small business, you've probably worn many hats, and, in doing so, you've gained a wealth of diverse business skills. Document these different areas of accountability in your summary section. This can work to your advantage if an employer is seeking a generalist who is skilled in many areas and can balance competing priorities.

3. Consider leading with a career highlights section that focuses on four to six success stories from your career, each showcasing a different competency. Perhaps one short paragraph would demonstrate your project management skills; another would talk about your ability to maintain customer loyalty; and yet another would mention process improvements that enhanced operating efficiency. The surveys you completed in Chapter 1 should prove helpful with this.

4. If you're returning to a field in which you have had previous experience before you were self-employed, you might consider creating a "relevant experience" section of your resume. This section should appear just after your summary (assuming you chose not to use the "career highlights" approach) and should include only the work experience directly relevant to the job you're targeting. Then show the rest of your work experience under "additional related experience" after the "relevant experience" section.

On the following pages is an excellent example of a cover letter as well as several resumes for self-employed people seeking to return to more conventional work settings. (Note: Some of the resumes contained in this chapter were written by Canadian or Australian resume professionals for candidates seeking work in those countries. With this in mind, we have left in place the accepted spelling, grammar, and wording used in those countries. Even if you're not looking for work in Canada or Australia, the overall format and structure of these documents may prove helpful to you in preparing your job-search documents.)

MICHAEL JEFFRIES

85 Ariel Lane
Atlanta, GA 08779

(655) 880–9944   Jeffries@msn.com

January 8, 2008

Mr. Fred Simmer
Executive Director
Greater Atlanta Chamber of Commerce
4200 Broad Street
Atlanta, GA 08779

Dear Fred,

As a long-time member of the Greater Atlanta Chamber of Commerce, I was excited to learn about the opportunity for a Membership Development Manager with your organization. As a successful business entrepreneur and manager, I would bring the following qualifications to this critical role:

✓ **Your Need: To Recruit and Retain Members**
Along with my Bachelor's degree in marketing, I offer experience in targeting, prospecting, lead generation, and customer presentations leading to sales results, both as a business owner and in my prior sales career. I have developed a solid network through my community activities and Atlanta Country Club membership. I would enjoy promoting the Chamber and developing new business relationships to continue the Chamber's membership expansion.

✓ **Your Need: To Provide Excellent Customer Service and Follow-up**
Customer satisfaction has always been a key focus throughout my career. Personally handling inquiries and ensuring that customer service issues are effectively resolved is one of my strengths. I possess an innate understanding of human nature and proven effectiveness in relating to / working with others from all levels and backgrounds.

✓ **Your Need: Planning, Organization & Program Administration**
Through my experiences in sales, community relations activities, people management and business operations, I have honed my planning, organizational and administrative skills – which are the critical skills necessary for coordinating and facilitating membership drives, as well as project management, report preparation and other details related to this position.

At the heart of my success is the ability to win the confidence and trust of others, communicate clearly, and cultivate long-term relationships. I would welcome the opportunity to contribute my talents to your organization. May we meet to discuss how I can assist the Chamber in achieving its mission and goals?

Sincerely,

Michael Jeffries

Enclosure

Resume Writer: Louise Garver

MICHAEL JEFFRIES

85 Ariel Lane
Atlanta, GA 08779

(655) 880-9944   Jeffries@msn.com

PROFESSIONAL QUALIFICATIONS

Business Management Professional with achievements in sales, marketing, human resources, purchasing and operations. Track record of consistent contributions to business growth in retail and other industries. Strong organizational leadership and planning skills combine with effective communications, negotiations and customer relations that result in successful operations.

EXPERIENCE & ACCOMPLISHMENTS

GENERAL MANAGER • JEFFRIES MART, ATLANTA, GA • 1985-Present

Operations / Procurement / Inventory – Hands-on business manager with experience in full range of operations, including business planning, personnel, customer service / relations, purchasing and inventory management. Developed and maintain relationships with supplier / broker network.

- Automated all office functions, increasing efficiency and accounting accuracy. Expedited customer processing and service through implementation of an automated register system.
- Financial experience includes budgeting, sales forecasting, oversight of accounts payable, accounts receivable, payroll and payroll tax reporting.

Marketing / Merchandising / Sales – Demonstrated ability to capitalize on economic and consumer trends, exercising responsibility for product planning and selection, merchandising strategies, advertising and e-commerce development.

- Developed and managed 20 wholesale accounts, producing 10% of overall business volume.
- Contributed substantially to building a highly profitable business, including initiating or expanding three successful profit centers, one of which drove sales instantly by 25%.
- Established wholesale outlet for fruit and gift basket business.
- Increased company's market exposure through development of Website.

Human Resources / Training – Manage all aspects of human resource activities for the business, including hiring, scheduling, training, evaluating performance and supervising staff of 25. Proven ability to select and match employee talent with the right positions.

- Effective in team building and creating a motivating environment that results in 98% employee retention, productivity and individual contributions.

MANUFACTURERS' REPRESENTATIVE • ANDERSON ENTERPRISES, ATLANTA, GA • 1980-1985

Recruited to develop and manage new sales territory, encompassing the Eastern seaboard states. Represented and sold 35 consumer product lines.

- Launched and established a profitable new territory that produced $28.5 million in five years in a highly competitive market through prospecting, solutions selling, and relationship-building strengths.

SALES MANAGER • WILTON MARKETING GROUP, ATLANTA, GA • 1981-1984

Initially joined company as a Sales Representative and was promoted to Sales Manager from a group of six reps. Created and implemented sales / marketing strategies for the Southeast territory at a regional company serving the retail food and beverage industry as well as food and beverage wholesalers and manufacturers. Supervised and developed team of sales professionals.

- Penetrated new markets and substantially grew account base, contributing to company's success.

EDUCATION

B.S. in Marketing
Ohio University, Columbus, Ohio

Resume Writer: Louise Garver

Tom Kensington

920 Woodsfield Court
Denver, CO 68971

(548) 777-7474
tomkenny18@hotmail.com

PARK MANAGER

Highly motivated, reliable park manager with more than 10 years of park operations experience, six years of management experience, and lifelong appreciation for camping. Twenty-year business owner – familiar with public relations and customer service. Hired and managed teams of up to nine employees. Excellent communication skills, quick learner, and proven leader who champions honesty and integrity.

"I believe in the campground experience…as a chance for families to escape the stress of daily life and the city."

CAREER HIGHLIGHTS

Self-Starter / Manager

- Maintained five national forest campgrounds, ensuring highest standards of cleanliness and service. Addressed camper concerns, collected fees, performed accounting duties and general maintenance.

- Started and successfully managed freelance photography business for 18 years. Photography and marketing projects included such prestigious clients as: Home Depot; Davis & Associates, Inc.; Carol & Carol; Target, Inc.; Morgan Stanley; University of North Florida Athletic Department; Denver First National Bank, and TSA Incorporated. Broad experience with promotion advertising on the Web and in television, newspaper, annual reports, and other publications.

- Independently contracted to represent aerial photography company. Kept accurate, detailed sales records and met with the public.

Results-Oriented

- Purchased and transformed failing 18-acre, 70-campsite, eight-cabin park into an attractive, profitable campground within three years. Single-handedly conducted spring openings and fall closings. Operated convenience store, managed four employees, and performed all general maintenance, plumbing, electrical repairs, lawn care, landscaping, and carpentry for entire site.

- Increased profitability from $8,000 loss to more than $10,000 in profits in one season by turning around Florida RV Park's failing restaurant / bar. Hired staff, set consistent hours, established reputation for service.

- Started utility / cargo trailer dealership; grew to ninth largest dealer in company in three years.

EDUCATION

Undergraduate coursework in general arts and sciences, University of Denver, Denver, CO
Completed HVAC Theory & Operations Course, Denver Community College, Denver, CO

WORK HISTORY

Independent Contractor, Photos Up There, Inc., Denver, CO, 2004–Present
Park Attendant, Funtimes Recreation, Cascade Mountains, OR, 2004
Campground Owner / Mgr, Georgia Sky Campground, Creekside, GA, 1998–2003
Park Restaurant / Bar Manager, Mobile Makers Campground, Melbourne, FL, 1995–1998
Freelance Photographer, Kensington Photography, Denver, CO, 1977–1995

Resume Writer: Sandy Neumann

BRADLEY BUCKINGHAM

1763 Raleigh Place • Merrick, NY 11566 • O: 516-570-4022 • C: 516-755-8811 • bradley@buck.com

PROFILE

WEB DEVELOPER AND ONLINE BRANDING SPECIALIST

Combining knowledge of online marketing, branding, consumer search patterns, and leading-edge technology with visual and artistic sensibility to deliver web solutions that generate sales leads, measure and increase key sales metrics, and deliver sustainable ROI to shareholders.

- **Ten years of experience in online marketing** including consultative web design sales, site design and development, site analytics, and project and staff management.

- **Knack for quickly diagnosing and solving web marketing problems** as they relate to lead generation, site traffic, click through, and conversion rates.

- **Exceptional technical skills** as evidenced by diversified knowledge of programming languages, desktop publishing tools, and digital photography treatments.

- **Industry "trend watcher"** with reputation for being on top of best-in-breed technology and educating clients on ways to leverage technology to improve site performance.

CORE COMPETENCIES

Design

Website Audits and Re-branding • Website Consulting / Strategic Planning • Web Design Internet and Intranet • Usability Testing • Content Management Systems • Search Engine Optimization • Online Marketing • e-Commerce • Art Direction / Graphic Design • Online Copywriting

Development

HTML• DHTML• JavaScript • Adobe GoLive • Adobe Photoshop • Adobe Image Ready • Adobe Acrobat Quark Express • Macromedia Flash • Macromedia Director • Digital Imaging • Microsoft Office • Microsoft PowerPoint • Perl • CSS • FTP • TCP/IP • Macintosh OS • Windows

CAREER HIGHLIGHTS

Business Development

- **Launched Sweet Scent's first website and grew traffic to over 200,000 visitors in first year** by introducing sweepstakes, building 90,000+ member mailing list, implementing banner campaigns, and creating fragrance blog to announce sponsorship with MR International modeling agency and introduce national cover girl competition. Established web presence for six additional product lines related to the parent company.

- **Boosted number of visitors from 240,000 to 1.3 M in less than one year** for *Hale and Hearty* fast food chain by analyzing pages viewed, monitoring customer base, trending times visitors were most likely to view site, and uncovering key demographics indicators.

- **Accelerated web-based sales leads from virtually zero to over 250 annually** for *JRJ Investigators,* the largest private investigation firm in Long Island, by redesigning copy to incorporate less text and more consumer-centric content.

BRADLEY BUCKINGHAM

- **Captured new multimillion-dollar vertical market and garnered attention on the front page of Newsday** for *Hale and Hearty's Healthy Bites* meals by being first fast food chain to include nutritional values on home page of website.

- **Introduced lucrative new revenue stream** for photography agency by building 2,000-image stock photo search engine.

Process Re-engineering

- **Pitched development of Internet portal projected to shave hundreds of hours off hospital nursing assistant certification program;** portal will allow for transition from classroom to virtual training and exceptional streamlining of administrative back end functions.

- **Reduced shopping cart redundancies by 100%** for *Simple Pleasures* gourmet candy manufacturer by re-engineering check-out features to include customized plug-ins such as a personal address book feature.

- **Significantly improved ability to track advertising dollars** for *Sweet Scent* by implementing unique page addresses to monitor origins of site visits.

- **Eliminated thousands of dollars in consulting fees** for photography agency by customizing site's back end to enable users to update portfolios independent of designer.

- **Recommended strategy to reposition hospice center as industry leader** by re-branding website and text to capitalize on facility's unique attributes and market differentiators.

CHRONOLOGY

Web Developer / CEO, Buck Web Designs, Merrick, NY   **2002 to Present**

Full P&L and management responsibility for boutique web design firm that has designed over 100 websites for major corporations in the consumer goods, food services, and healthcare space as well as sites for entrepreneurs and small businesses. At peak, manage staffs of more than a dozen people.

Freelance Web Developer and Desktop Publisher, Bellmore, NY   **1997 to 2002**

Created web pages with functionality, innovative design, custom forms, and interactive tools for multiple professional and promotional websites and digitally retouched high resolution images. Oversaw full life-cycle of projects and maintained sites after build phase was completed. Managed sub-contracting teams.

Photographer, New York and Los Angeles   **1994 to 1997**

Created photo editorials for magazines including *Vogue, Elle,* and *Mademoiselle.*

EDUCATION AND SKILLS

Self-taught in Website user behavior patterns, website usability, server analytics, click path tracking, and consumer centric design methodology

Apprenticeship in Photography, School of Applied Science, London, England, 1994

JASON VALE, CGCS

567.543.2198   2664 E. Superior St., Grand Falls, MN 56201   jason.vale@gmail.com

CERTIFIED GOLF COURSE SUPERINTENDENT

- ◆ Specialize in constructing and growing in new golf courses, including three 18-hole projects, one 9-hole project and one Reese Jones-designed course voted No. 4 best new course in 2000.
- ◆ Possess 10+ years of expertise in tournament preparation and golf course construction.
- ◆ Specify and purchase maintenance equipment.
- ◆ Maintain course, lawns and plantings by developing and implementing cost-efficient and environmentally responsible agronomic programs.
- ◆ Communicate effectively with board, staff and golf course management team.
- ◆ Coordinate safe and productive staff training and development.
- ◆ Thoroughly understand and enjoy golf.

EXPERIENCE

WATERFALL, INC., Grand Falls, MN   2006 to Present
President, start-up irrigation installation and repair service. Recent projects include:

- Repaired irrigation and wiring at Valley Golf Course, Grand Walk Golf Course and Grand Falls Park District, Grand Falls, MN.
- Designed and installed clubhouse irrigation system at Washington Golf Course, Grand Falls, MN.

VALLEY GOLF COURSE, Grand Falls, MN   2003 to Present
Consultant, part time, 9-hole semi-private golf course expanding to 18

- Plan long-range capital expenses for entire operation.
- Assist with growing in new holes.

GRAND WALK GOLF COURSE, Grand Falls, MN   2001 to 2006
Golf Course Superintendent, 18-hole municipal course, $500K maintenance budget with 20 seasonal staff members

- Created long-range capital investment budget for equipment and course improvements.
- Designed and oversaw $250K construction of cart paths 1-1/2 years after course completion.
- Grew in Arnold Palmer-designed golf course, reseeding 120 acres, rebuilding seven greens and resetting project timeline to accommodate additional work.
- Recruited and developed all personnel.
- Helped design maintenance facilities.

RIVER COURSE, Brewster, IN   2000 to 2001
Golf Course Superintendent, 18-hole public course on and adjacent to existing ski resort, eight in-house and 15 seasonal staff.

- Supervised in-house construction of greens, tees, bunkers and fairways and installation of irrigation system.
- Specified and recommended equipment purchases.
- Developed and implemented agronomic programs, including pesticide and fertility.

Resume Writer: Jeri Dutcher

JASON VALE, CGCS

EXPERIENCE (continued)

BIG OAKS GOLF COURSE, Otter Rapids, OH   1997 to 1999
Golf Course Superintendent, 18-hole Reese Jones-designed public course voted No. 4 best new course, 2000

- Oversaw construction of entire golf course, including extensive erosion control measures.
- Designed and built cart paths for course.
- Specified and recommended equipment purchases.
- Hired and trained entire staff.
- Developed and implemented agronomic programs, including pesticide and fertility.
- Assisted in designing maintenance facilities.

THOUSAND LAKES GOLF COURSE, Calethea, MI   1994 to 1997
Golf Course Superintendent, (1995 to 1997) 27-hole public golf complex, $650K maintenance budget, 35K rounds, staff of 25

- Returned declining course to No. 3 position from No. 6 between 1995 and 1997.
- Hosted numerous state tournaments and Independent Insurance Agents Junior Classic.
- Managed all aspects of course maintenance.
- Reduced chemical usage 25%.

Assistant Golf Course Superintendent (1994 to 1995)

- Promoted to Golf Course Superintendent for successfully managing construction of and growing in additional nine holes.
- Recommended equipment purchases for new nine.

Prior positions: Assistant Golf Course Superintendent at Deer Run Golf Course, Deerfield, MN; Spray Technician at Hazelwood National Golf Club, Clarion, MN; Irrigation Technician at Taylorville Country Club, Taylorville, MN.

AFFILIATIONS

GOLF COURSE SUPERINTENDENTS ASSOCIATION OF AMERICA, Class A Certified Member.
MINNESOTA GOLF COURSE SUPERINTENDENTS' ASSOCIATION, Class A Member.
NORTH CENTRAL TURFGRASS ASSOCIATION, Member.
UNIVERSITY OF MINNESOTA GOLF SYSTEMS ADVISORY COMMITTEE, member.

EDUCATION

UNIVERSITY OF MINNESOTA, Taylorville, MN
AAS, Nursery and Turfgrass Technology

PESTICIDE APPLICATOR'S LICENSE, State of Minnesota

Gabe Connor

19 Lawnside Drive
Leichhardt NSW 2041

Home: (02) 9876 5432
Mobile: 0414 981 062
Email: gabec@optusnet.com.au

Retail Manager / General Manager

Turning under-performing businesses into profitable performers with sustainable market share

Take charge leader who embraces challenges and achieves business objectives. Proven strengths in building sustainable market share and achieving high levels of customer satisfaction through unparalleled service have been the foundation of career successes. An ideas person who assesses personnel and situations, streamlines operations, drives cost reduction actions and uncovers new business opportunities through logical thinking, brainstorming fresh ideas, hands-on leadership and a participative management style that successfully mitigates risk, drives market share, revenue and profit growth.

"Gabe's flair & talent for retail saw him open his Petersham store & within 11 months of trading, elevated the profile of the business to the level where he won our prestigious 'Store of the Year' group award."

Gregory Passemonte, General Manager – Leading Edge Video

Areas of Expertise

- Project Management
- Business Development
- Market & Segment Expansion

- Communication
- Issues Management
- Contract Negotiations

- Customer Retention
- Campaign Management
- Team Development / Leadership

Professional Experience

TOP VIDEO (ORIGINALLY JACOB'S VIDEO) – *Balmain, NSW*   1995 to Present

General Manager - Owner/Operator

Transformed an under-performing store into a proven performer that increased turnover 250% within first two years of operation.

With no prior experience within the industry, led the business in defining strategies for development, growth, expansion and profitable financial performance through the implementation of corrective actions, marketing initiatives and appropriate administrative tools.

Overcame challenges by researching the industry, comparing costs with industry standards, researching customer demographics, identifying and driving cost reductions, brainstorming ideas for business growth, developing lucrative relationships, implementing aggressive marketing campaigns, increasing the standard of customer service and improving staff morale.

RESULTS / ACCOMPLISHMENTS:

- Led company to a functionally streamlined **cost-effective business with measurable results** through practical planning, an improved managerial approach, researching industry and customer demographics and improved leadership practices that motivated high staff morale. Results were impressive:
  - → Reduced overheads by 34%.
  - → Increased profits margins from -5% to 38%.
- **Developed lucrative relationship** by joining buying group Top Video, which played an active role in achieving sustainable market share. Ranked as one of Top Videos best performing members/stores within a relatively short timeframe, with this ranking still held today.
- **Recaptured a lost market** through the implementation of aggressive monthly marketing campaigns in Balmain and surrounding suburbs, resulting in nearest competitor closing their doors. Key outcomes included:
  - → Increased average customer spend by 50%.
  - → Expanded new business by approximately 40% within 18 months.

Resume Writer: Jennifer Rushton

Professional Experience Continued...

- **Improved staff performance and productivity by 100%** by identifying productivity roadblocks, implementing customer service training and allowing staff issue/opportunity ownership. Key outcomes included:
  - → Reduced shrinkage by 65%.
  - → Increased employee retention by 100%.
  - → Elevated customer satisfaction by 85% by reinforcing team focus towards core fundamentals of customer service.

BROTHERS VIDEO ENTERPRISES – *Leichhardt, NSW*   2001 to 2005

Owner/Operator

Transformed a relatively small video wholesaler into a profitable business with an annual turnover in excess of $2.1 million within 12 months.

Project was run concurrently while managing existing Balmain store and involved learning a new skill set and adapting to a completely new industry. Within 12 months exceeded ROI and increased staff levels by 150% by implementing best business practices and improving operating areas.

RESULTS / ACCOMPLISHMENTS:

- **Increased annual turnover by over 200%** within 12 months through the negotiation of contract partnerships and the implementation of new ideas and initiatives.

- Negotiated to become **Leading Edge Video Group's preferred supplier** for all video / DVD accessories and corporate materials. Contract provided access to 420 potential new customers and resulted in the expansion to supply and design of corporate uniforms for the 3 Groups operating under the Leading Edge banner.

TOP VIDEO– *Petersham, NSW*   1999 to 2001

Owner / Operator

Rapidly grew a start-up into a successful business through a hands-on leadership and management approach that achieved measurable results and a 60% ROI.

Analysed and interpreted a wide variety of demographic, geographic and marketing data to conclude that the area could sustain a second video store. Negotiated attractive lease terms and submitted design layouts and DA for council approval.

Transitioned venture from a concept to a proven performer by implementing new ideas and a strong management approach. Aggressive marketing strategies established a competitive market position further strengthened by negotiation of favourable contract partnerships.

RESULTS / ACCOMPLISHMENTS:

- Led successful start-up that was sold 11 months after opening, **achieving a 60% ROI.**
- **Increased market share** within the first six months of opening through the implementation of an aggressive marketing campaign, which ultimately led to closure of the nearest competitor within the year. Key outcomes included:
  - → Rapidly increased annual turnover, achieving a 62% growth on the first six months.
  - → Achieved a 43% growth in customer membership on the previous six months.
  - → Grew market share by approximately 29%.

- **Awarded Top Videos "Store of the Year"** within 11 months of opening in recognition of a rapid growth curve that exceeded expectations and gaining market share within a relatively short period of time.

REFERENCES AVAILABLE UPON REQUEST

Marlene Antonucci, D.C.

1100 Webster Avenue   (314) 555-1111
St. Louis, MO 63155   m.antonucci@totalwellcare.com

Objective   To transfer skills developed as a chiropractic physician to a medical / surgical sales position.

Summary of Qualifications

Highly energetic, entrepreneurial professional with 18 years of business experience in the medical services field. Excellent communication and motivational skills based on enthusiastic belief in a product. Able to gain people's trust and discover their true wants and needs, using a knowledgeable and caring approach. Successful in establishing longstanding personal and professional relationships throughout the area. Expertise also includes:

- Health care consulting
- Public relations
- Group presentations

- Program development
- Training and education
- Time and resource management

Education   PALMER UNIVERSITY OF CHIROPRACTIC, DAVENPORT, IA

Doctor of Chiropractic, *cum laude*, 1989

Studies included:

Anatomy (osteology, myology, embryology, splanchnology, arthrology, and neuroanatomy) physiology, chemistry, biochemistry, pathology, physical diagnosis, radiology, and related labs.

Postgraduate courses through accredited chiropractic colleges:

Therapeutic techniques, sports injuries, advanced radiology, functional medicine, CPR, AIDS, and risk management.

Member, Diplomate of National Chiropractic Board of Examiners

Professional Experience

TOTAL WELLCARE CENTER, ST. LOUIS, MO   1989–Present

President   *(Sale of business in process)*

A high-volume, multi-disciplinary holistic health center, treating patients of all ages with a variety of musculoskeletal, neurological, or digestive disorders. Perform all chiropractic services and employ a massage therapist, acupuncturist, and nutritionist.

- Built a successful practice from zero to 200 client visits per week, generating 75% of business through referrals.
- Actively marketed the benefits of holistic wellness programs within the community through educational lectures to civic organizations.
- Promoted long-term therapeutic regimens by convincing numerous clients of the value of continuing a full course of treatment and follow-up care despite limits on their insurance coverage.
- Conferred frequently with orthopedic surgeons and neurologists about certain cases requiring medical intervention.
- Managed the business functions of budgeting and forecasting while maintaining total quality control.

Resume Writer: Melanie Noonan

Chapter 12
Resumes for Career Changers

In this chapter, find resumes for people who are making a major career change.

Transitioning	
From	*To*
Medical Technician	Medical Sales
Human Services	Customer Service
Waitress	Health Care Aide
Clothing Designer	Landscape Designer
Field Service Engineer	Industrial Arts Teacher
Elected Official	Paid Town Manager
School Custodian	Medical Assistant

Transitioning from one career to another has become so common that it's almost not unconventional anymore. The average worker has three or four distinctly different careers over the course of the 40 years or so spent in the workforce. Even though it's becoming more commonplace, however, making the big switch still presents certain challenges when developing a resume. Here are just a few tips that you may find helpful:

1. Lead with your strengths. You must have something in your background that leads you to believe that you can be successful in the new career. Whatever that something is, that's what you need to emphasize on

your resume. It may be education, either recently completed or from years ago; it might be volunteer experience that has convinced you that you've found your calling; or it could be technical expertise that has prepared you for your next endeavor. Keep in mind the advice from Chapters 2 and 3 about expressing it forward and highlighting the skills most relevant to your new career target.

2. Use your cover letter to make your case. Even with a compelling resume that is "front-end-loaded" with all of your relevant skills, employers may not immediately grasp how you can be an asset or why you are making the transition. Your cover letter is your chance to be passionate about your new career choice. Maybe there's a compelling story about an incident in your life that convinced you to enter the healthcare field. Perhaps your engaging personality causes your friends to keep saying, "You should be in sales." Whatever your reasons for making the change, use your cover letter to sell a prospective employer on your enthusiasm for the new opportunity.

3. Express your competencies in language that is rich in the keywords of your career target. If you're transitioning from healthcare to the private sector, "patient care" becomes "customer service." If you're moving into sales from some other field, emphasize "time management" and "meeting goals and objectives." The prospective new employer will appreciate your use of keywords they are familiar with.

4. If you're returning to a field in which you have had previous experience, place this in a section called "relevant experience." This section should appear immediately after your summary and should include just the work experience that is similar to the job you're targeting. Then show the rest of your work experience under "additional related experience," which comes after "relevant experience," or maybe even after your education.

On the following pages is an excellent example of a cover letter as well as several resumes for candidates changing from one career path to another.

LYNDA C. MORGAN

1777 Manual Street • Baltimore, Maryland 21201
lcmorgan@verizon.net • 410.837.5555 (Home) • 410.837.5554 (Cell)

February 1, 2008

Lance Trebuchet, Director
Medical Sales Administration
United Medical of Maryland
6890 Oak Street
Baltimore, MD 21209

Dear Mr. Trebuchet:

Initiative, intelligence, and a personality that is conducive to a successful career in sales are among the qualifications I enthusiastically offer United Medical of Maryland. Although my career path has been focused in nuclear medicine, I am well-prepared to excel in an opportunity in Medical Sales that includes room for merit advancement based on personal performance and contributions to exceeding sales goals and company revenues.

The enclosed resume outlines my skills, education, and experience, which include:

- ◆ **Academic Preparation:** B.H.S. in Nuclear Medicine Technology from University of Maryland; graduated *cum laude* with a 3.9 / 4.0 G.P.A.

- ◆ **Healthcare Experience:** Ten years of experience in a variety of medical settings; possess technical knowledge, patient relations skills, and administrative support abilities.

- ◆ **Personal Strengths:** Solid track record of successfully fostering relationships, especially with physicians; equally effective establishing positive rapport with administrators, employees, and other members of the medical community; extensive experience in addressing sensitive patient-related matters.

Should your organization need an individual with my strengths and potential, I would welcome the opportunity to meet with you. I recognize that tangible achievements require commitment, intelligence, and hard work. I believe the skills that contributed to my achievement thus far in the medical field would transfer well to a successful career in medical sales.

Your schedule is undoubtedly busy; I can be available for an interview at your convenience. I am eager for the opportunity to meet and explore how my capabilities can contribute to generating bottom-line profitability for United Medical of Maryland. Thank you for your time and consideration.

Sincerely,

Lynda C. Morgan

Enclosure

Resume Writer: Deanne Arnath

LYNDA C. MORGAN

1777 Manual Street • Baltimore, MD 21201
lcmorgan@verizon.net • 410.837.5555 (Home) • 410.837.5554 (Cell)

QUALIFICATIONS PROFILE

Medical technologist poised to leverage dynamic communication and relationship management expertise into successful **Medical Sales** career with a company seeking a driven, people-oriented team player committed to supporting company objectives.

♦ **Communication / Presentation:** Ten years of medical science experience working closely with doctors, patients, and other members of the healthcare team to identify abnormalities and administer treatment plans within nuclear medicine departments. Skilled in medical terminology with the ability to present test results in a clear and concise manner.

♦ **Administration / Productivity:** Valuable experience and training in medical technology and administration. Able to maintain an exceptional rate of productivity, accuracy, and efficiency through attention to detail and continuous training regarding new healthcare initiatives and leading-edge technology.

♦ **Technical Skills:** Proficiencies include Windows OS; Microsoft Word, Works, and Outlook. Knowledgeable working with radiology and healthcare information systems including Medical Manager, Micro MD, Nu Quest, and Wackers Lieu. Familiar with medical billing and collection operations.

♦ **Key Strengths:** Customer service oriented. Skilled in time management. Able to handle numerous tasks simultaneously while maintaining strict quality standards. Demonstrate professionalism with patients, physicians, coworkers, and other staff.

PROFESSIONAL EXPERIENCE

CARDIOVASCULAR CENTER OF MARYLAND – Baltimore, MD   2002 to Present

Nuclear Medicine Technologist

Local practice offering a complete range of cardiology services, including echocardiography, halter monitor, nuclear stress testing, and scope for pacemaker and defibrillator clinics.

Complete diagnostic nuclear stress imaging to determine the presence or absence of coronary artery disease. Calculate, measure, and record radiation dosage or radiopharmaceuticals received, used and disposed, following physician's prescriptions. Interpret data and provide recommendations for optimal patient care. Maintain RAM Licensure and diagnostic clinical protocols.

- Manage 12 to 15 procedures per shift, while maintaining high quality patient care.
- Mastered medical billing and collection systems.

BALTIMORE CITY CARDIOLOGY – Baltimore, MD   1999 to 2002

Nuclear Medicine Technologist

Independent clinic specializing in examination, prevention, diagnosis, and treatment of heart disease.

Explained test procedures and safety precautions to patients and provided assistance during procedures. Administered radiopharmaceuticals or radiation to detect or treat diseases, using radioisotope equipment. Processed automated cardiac function studies and produced computer generated or film images for physician interpretation.

- Maintained and calibrated radioisotope and laboratory equipment.
- Disposed of radioactive materials and stored radiopharmaceuticals, following radiation safety procedures.

continued...

LYNDA C. MORGAN

- Page Two -

MARYLAND HOSPITAL & HEALTH SERVICES – Baltimore, MD   1996 to 1999
Nuclear Medicine Technologist
Regional healthcare network that includes 70 healthcare facilities and 1,900 patient beds in the Baltimore-Washington metropolitan area.
Provided technical expertise, patient care, and administrative support in the daily operation of the nuclear medicine department. Detected and mapped radiopharmaceuticals in patients' bodies, using a camera to perform body function and organ imaging. Analyzed biologic specimens and presented findings to physicians.

- Served a diverse caseload consisting of adult and geriatric patients.
- Adhered to safety standards to minimize radiation exposure to workers and patients.

EDUCATION & HONORS

Certified Nuclear Medicine Technologist (1996)
NUCLEAR MEDICINE TECHNOLOGY CERTIFICATION BOARD

Bachelor of Health Sciences in Nuclear Medicine Technology (1996); G.P.A. 3.9 / 4.0; *Cum Laude*
UNIVERSITY OF MARYLAND – College Park, MD

Phi Eta Sigma Honor Society ~ Golden Key Honor Society ~ Mallinckrodt Award of Excellence

JOANNE BRIGHTON
65 Connelly Drive
Port Hampton, New Hampshire 03586
603.505.2987

PATIENT CARE SPECIALIST

CAREER GOAL: To provide caring and supportive services to patients and staff at a healthcare facility where my combination of training and experience will contribute to superior patient care.

RELEVANT TRAINING AND EXPERIENCE

PHLEOBOTOMY
Phlebotomy Certificate, New Hampshire Technical Academy, Port Hampton, NH (2007)
- Learned and practiced safe clinical techniques for obtaining blood samples in compliance with CDC and OSHA guidelines
- Developed familiarity with medical terminology as well as basic anatomy and physiology
- Practiced quality control techniques

COMPUTER SKILLS
Introduction to Computers Course, NH Technical Academy, Port Hampton, NH (2007)
- Proficient in Microsoft Word; Excel; PowerPoint and Access
- Learned effective Internet research approaches and E-mail skills
- Earned 4.0 / 4.0 GPA

CUSTOMER SERVICE and CLERICAL EXPERIENCE
- Greeted guests and answered phones in professional and friendly manner
- Processed orders; conducted inventory; organized and updated files
- Recorded and transmitted messages promptly and accurately

WORK HISTORY

Server, Golden Egg Catering, Port Hampton, NH   (1998 – Present)
Serve a wide range of gourmet specialties at a variety of venues and special events for this renowned, upscale caterer.

Clerk, Starlight Merchandising, Dougherty, NH (1996 – 1998)
Performed clerical functions at busy headquarters office for this large distribution facility.

Waitress, Oasis Bar & Grill, Port Hampton, NH (1993 – 1996)

REFERENCES AVAILABLE UPON REQUEST

Resume Writer: Heather Carson

Rodney Fowler

39 Longmeadow Road, Unit 4
Riverbrook, NH 03055

(603) 683-9234
rfowler@hotmail.com

RESULTS-ORIENTED CUSTOMER SERVICE REPRESENTATIVE

Background in healthcare and human services industries. Excellent telephone skills. Work well with others, as well as independently, to achieve organization goals. Recognized for initiative and ability to solve problems creatively.

EXPERIENCE

Working Futures, Riverbrook, NH
A Second Start community work experience program.

Community Resources Coordinator   2006–2007

- Contacted and scheduled guest speakers from various community organizations. Result: participants gained new information in an engaging format.
- Maintained and updated resources. Result: obtained current publications for program use.
- Designed products for fundraising purposes. Result: contributed to increases in funds raised through sale of products.

Plus Company, Riverbrook, NH
Statewide job-readiness program for clients with developmental disabilities.

Community Integration Specialist   2006

- Trained clients with behavioral problems to significantly improve behavior in the community and work site. Result: 50% of the clients moved on to advanced jobs.
- Taught client with attention deficit to use learning program on the computer. Result: client improved ability to focus and increased attention span six-fold.
- Addressed issue concerning client who was unwilling to participate in exercise program. Result: client willingly joined in exercise program.

Maxim Healthcare, Marshfield, NH
Nationwide home healthcare company.

Home Health Aide   2004–2005

- Identified potential health crisis exhibited by client and sought emergency aid. Result: patient received immediate care and recovered within two days.
- Bathed immobilized client utilizing wheel chair lift. Result: client was able to maintain skin integrity.

Resume Writer: Barbara Warren

Rodney Fowler

St. Joseph Hospital, Riverbrook, NH
A Southern New Hampshire acute care hospital and trauma center.

Licensed Nursing Assistant   2002–2004

- Measured and recorded vital signs, enabling nurses to recognize changes in patients' condition.
- Responded to call lights within an average of less than five minutes, promptly addressing client needs.

United Parcel Service, Calumet, NH
A worldwide courier company.

Overnight Delivery Center Auditor   2000–2002

- Verified insurance on high value packages.
- Identified and pulled all questionable overseas packages for return.
- Scanned packages at the end of each shift.

Blue Mountain Rehabilitation Center, Marshfield, NH
Residential school and rehabilitation hospital

Life Skills Trainer – Brain Injury Unit   1994–1999

- Instructed and supervised residents in activities of daily living.
- Monitored medical needs of residents according to their individual care plan.
- Employed motivational techniques to encourage residents to comply with required exercises.

EDUCATION

New England Med Pro

Medical Coding   Anticipated Completion, 2008

(603) 683-9234   rfowler@hotmail.com

Andrea Keyes

1232 Lynwood Place
Los Angeles, CA 90010

Cell: 310/781-0032
andreakeyes@yahoo.com

LANDSCAPE DESIGN

Creative, enthusiastic, and innovative Landscape Designer with an extensive background of abilities, skills, knowledge, and experience. Exceeded employers' goals and customers' expectations by planning, conceptualizing, presenting, and implementing unique, artistic designs that are technically accurate and aesthetically pleasing. Collaborate with clients and team members to set priorities, resolve problems, and complete projects on time and within budget. Very organized, detail-oriented and work well under pressure. Develop loyalty in staff as a productive, approachable leader. Areas of expertise include:

Landscape Design/Installations	**Upgrade Fixtures**	**Project Management**
Lighting Systems	**Staff Management**	**Supervise Work**
Soil Composition	**Planning & Scheduling**	**Sprinkler Systems**
Visual Merchandising	**Vendor Relations**	**Recommend/Plant**
	Tradeshow Booths	**New Gardens**

KEY ACCOMPLISHMENTS

- Designed landscape, sprinkler systems, walkways, and patios for residential properties.
- Directed and supervised gardeners in landscaping design and grounds maintenance.
- Coordinated jobs with homeowners, vendors, and clients during the construction process.
- Created unique backyard retreats filled with good energy, plants that please the senses and outdoor environments that are lush and low maintenance.

CAREER HISTORY

Designer: Sportswear & Loungewear, RHONDA INTIMATES, Torrance, CA   2004 – Present

Creative Director: Contemporary Loungewear, B.J. SAVAGE, Orange, CA   2000 – 2004

Designer: Contemporary Sportswear, FRANKLIN FITWEAR, Philadelphia, PA 1998 – 2000

Designer: Young Men's & Women's Sportswear, SKATEBOARD & SNOWBOARD APPAREL, San Diego, CA   1995 – 1998

EDUCATION

Horticulture & Landscape Design Certificate/AA degree, Spring 2007
Mission Viejo College, Mission Viejo, CA
<u>Relevant Coursework:</u>
Plant Materials – Groundcovers; Plant Materials - Trees/Shrubs; Plant Propagation; Soils & Fertilizers; Horticultural Science; Landscape Design; Landscape CAD; Planting Design; Irrigation Systems; Hardscape and Construction Materials.

Bachelor of Arts, Fashion and Textile Design, 1990
California State University, Santa Ana, CA

TECHNICAL SKILLS

Proficient with Microsoft Office, Photoshop, Illustrator, and CAD

PROFESSIONAL AFFILIATIONS

- Torrance Garden Club / Los Angeles County Arboretum & Botanical Gardens

Resume Writer: Pearl White

WALTER MARKOVICZ

385 Cornfield Terrace ◆ Flemington, NJ 08822 ◆ 908-237-0604 ◆ mark@aol.com

Dynamic Teacher / Trainer with strong instructional presence and a talent for creating stimulating classroom environments that foster learning and growth

SUMMARY OF QUALIFICATIONS

- Certified teacher with a background that includes five years of classroom experience, as well as extensive corporate training expertise.
- Organized and effective with strong planning skills. Creative in developing lessons and activities that engage students and reinforce learning. Flexible in adapting lessons to meet specific needs.
- Polished public speaker with demonstrated ability to engage an audience. Excellent relationship-building skills. Able to establish instant rapport with students, quickly earning trust and respect.
- Energetic leader with strong record of service.
- Solid foundations in electronics, as well as the industrial and graphic arts.

SELECT ACCOMPLISHMENTS

Classroom Experience

- Accumulated five years of high school teaching experience, building solid reputation based on strong lesson planning skills, creativity in developing engaging learning activities, and commitment to program goals.
- Revitalized and reorganized Industrial Arts program, substantially increasing enrollment in classes while building industrial arts program into largest elective area in school.
- Rebuilt shop facilities into state-of-the-art wood-based operation. Introduced new equipment and new processes that enhanced offerings, presenting new opportunities that ignited interest among students.
- Played key role in development of first-in-state computer center that featured central networking system. Touted as showcase for the district, earned kudos from superintendent for outstanding contributions.
- Developed and updated curriculum, challenging students to harness undiscovered capabilities. Led students in creating items such as grandfather clocks, bookcases, and wine racks that awed parents and students alike.
- Proposed plan for new electronics program, presenting recommendations that were well-received by board.

Training Expertise

- As field service engineer in the printing and electronics industries, gained considerable expertise in training customers in the intricacies of new products.
- Led training classes for as many as 40 people; created blend of formal instruction and hands-on training, presented in easy, engaging style, that was consistently well-received by clients.
- Effectively adapted training programs, creating application-based training to meet specific customer needs.
- Earned recognition as the most frequently requested corporate trainer among all field service engineers.

Leadership & Service

- Served as assistant coach for varsity football and baseball teams at two high schools.
- Currently serving as assistant coach for community baseball and soccer teams.
- Actively support other community youth activities; for example, built stage for local youth club.
- Earned selection to Aviation Officer Candidate School. Served as Squad Leader prior to receiving Honorable Discharge.

Resume Writer: Carol Altomare

PROFESSIONAL TEACHING EXPERIENCE

LAKEWOOD HIGH SCHOOL, Lakewood, NJ, 1982 to 1985
Industrial Arts Instructor
Instructed and supervised students (7th through 12th grade) in woodworking and mechanical drawing. Developed and updated courses. Purchased and maintained equipment and supplies.

BERNARDS HIGH SCHOOL, Bernards, NJ, 1980 to 1982
Teacher, Industrial and Graphic Arts
Taught industrial and graphic arts courses to high school students.

OTHER PROFESSIONAL EXPERIENCE

B&B GRAPHIC PRODUCTS, Newark, NJ, 1987 to present
Field Service Engineer
Provide field service support for leading manufacturer of auxiliary equipment associated with high-volume offset printing presses. Coordinate all aspects of installation and start-up. Troubleshoot problems. Conduct extensive product training.

ADVANCED PRINTING. CORPORATION, East Rutherford, NJ, 1986 to 1987
Field Service Engineer
Provided installation and troubleshooting support for advanced, multi-color offset web printing presses across the US and Canada.

SECURITY RESEARCH CORPORATION, Washington, D.C., 1985 to 1986
Electronics Technician
Provided on-call installation and troubleshooting support for digitally-controlled x-ray security inspection equipment and metal detectors. Assisted in editing and updating technical manuals.

EDUCATION & CERTIFICATION

MONTCLAIR STATE COLLEGE, Upper Montclair, NJ
Bachelor of Science Degree in Industrial Education
  New Jersey State Teacher Certification

Computer Processing Institute, Paramus, NJ
Electronics Technology Diploma

SHAWNA NICKELS

789 Angel Lane   St. Petersburg, Florida 33733   (727) 555-1212

PROFESSIONAL OBJECTIVE

Seeking a position as a *Medical Assistant* for a Family or Geriatric medical practice
that values compassion, dedication, integrity and results.

EDUCATION

ST. PETERSBURG UNIVERSITY, ST. PETERSBURG, FLORIDA (2007)
DIPLOMA- Medical Assisting

❖ **EXTERNSHIP, Central Florida Palms Family & Geriatric Practice, St. Petersburg, Florida (2007)**
❖ Perfect attendance record: never missed a day of class or of my Externship.
❖ Recognized by Externship Physician for thoughtful, effective patient interaction and quick mastery of clinical skills.
❖ Received positive feedback from Externship staff and patients for providing compassionate, quality patient care.

COURSE HIGHLIGHTS

Anatomy & Physiology ~ Clinical Procedures ~ Medical Office Procedures
Practical Procedures ~ Health Care Automation

NORTH EAST HIGH SCHOOL, ST. PETERSBURG, FLORIDA (1996)
DIPLOMA- General Studies

❖ Volunteered at *St. Theresa's Hospital;* worked primarily with geriatric patients after school and during summer recess.
❖ Received commendations for my excellent communication skills, compassion and self-motivation.
❖ Perfect attendance record throughout high school and hospital volunteer career.

EMPLOYMENT EXPERIENCE

PINELLAS COUNTY SCHOOL SYSTEM, HURRICANE HIGH SCHOOL, ST. PETERSBURG, FLORIDA
School Janitor (1996 To Present)

❖ Thoroughly clean fifteen classrooms each with 32 seats daily.
❖ Effectively utilize variety of cleaning equipment and tools to efficiently prepare rooms for next day's use.
❖ Manage time well and effectively prioritize tasks; work independently without direct supervision.
❖ Perfect attendance record for nearly 12 consecutive years of employment with Hurricane High School.

COMPUTER SKILLS

Proprietary Medical Practice Management Software
Microsoft Office (Excel & Word)
Windows 95, 98 & 2000
Microsoft Outlook   Internet Research

REFERENCES AVAILABLE UPON REQUEST

Resume Writer: Sharon McCormick

Chapter 13

Resumes for Managers Without College Degrees

In this chapter, find resumes for managers in the following fields:

Hospitality / Food & Beverage
Education Services
Business Office Operations
Product Support / Engineering Operations
Business-to-Business Sales

If you've risen to the top through diligence, hard work, your innate ability to lead people, and your grassroots knowledge of your industry, you should be proud of your accomplishments. However, if the time has come to switch companies and you lack that college diploma, it may take a bit of extra convincing for a prospective new employer to consider your candidacy. Again, the primary purpose of your resume is to get you in the door so that you can sell yourself in a job interview. If you're a manager without a college degree, there are several key things to keep in mind when you prepare your resume and cover letters. Here are just a few tips that you may find helpful:

1. Because you don't have the diploma, it's all about experience. Make sure that your resume is "front-end loaded" with a strong summary section touting your knowledge and expertise. Focus on what you can do and have already done that is most relevant to your target job.

2. Consider leading with a career highlights section that focuses on four to six success stories from your career, each showcasing a different

competency that is highly relevant to your target job. Perhaps one short paragraph demonstrates your project management skills; another may talk about your ability to maintain customer loyalty; and yet another mentions process improvements that enhanced operating efficiency.

3. Be sure to include any professional development or training that you've completed. Depending on the size and philosophy of your current and past employers, you may have been selected to attend an extended leadership development program at a prestigious business school. Perhaps you've completed numerous workshops on employee relations or received technical training in a specific area. Have you been exposed to Six Sigma, lean manufacturing, or ISO training? All of these can strengthen your resume.

4. If you have some college but did not earn a degree, consider how best to portray your education on your resume. *Never* fabricate a college degree or lie about attending college. As many recent examples in the media have demonstrated, it's too easy to get caught; most importantly, it's simply dishonest. If your college experience is recent, consider listing the degree, followed by "in process" (see Example 1). This works if you have significant coursework under your belt and there is a legitimate possibility that you might continue or go back and complete your degree.

5. Another scenario: perhaps you have attended two or three different universities and accumulated more than enough credit hours to equal a degree but haven't met the specific requirements to actually receive a diploma. List the colleges you have attended and the total credit hours completed (see Example 2).

If you have absolutely no college experience or very minimal coursework, it may be best to leave education off the resume completely; that includes leaving off high school, as well. When a mid- to senior-level manager lists his or her high school graduation, it merely draws attention to the fact that the person did not attend college. However, there is an exception to this rule: If you attended a prestigious prep school or highly regarded parochial high school, mentioning it on your resume may lead to networking opportunities you might otherwise miss (see Example 3).

Example 1
Bachelor of Science, Accounting (In Process)
State University of New York at New Paltz; New Paltz, NY

Example 2

    Harvard University; Cambridge, MA

    University of Massachusetts at Amherst; Amherst, MA

    Completed a total of 136 credit hours in Marketing and Business Management

Example 3

    Graduate of Springfield Day School; Springfield, IL

    Class of 1983; Varsity Tennis; Varsity Crew; Glee Club

On the following pages is an excellent example of a cover letter as well as several resumes for candidates seeking management positions without the benefit of a college degree. (Note: Some of the resumes contained in this chapter were written by Canadian or Australian resume professionals for candidates seeking work in those countries. With this in mind, we have left in place the accepted spelling, grammar, and wording used in those countries. Even if you're not looking for work in Canada or Australia, the overall format and structure of these documents may prove helpful to you in preparing your job search documents.)

Bill Lowery

785 Glendale Street
Indianapolis, IN 46204

Residence: (317) 554-1111
Mobile: (317) 414-3025
Email: lowerybill@msn.com

January 3, 2008

Alfred Periwinkle
Periwinkle Designs
5232 Highway 31 South
Carmel, IN 46032

Dear Mr. Periwinkle:

As an experienced sales executive, I have a strong interest in the National Sales Manager opportunity with Periwinkle, Inc. My credentials include successful experience in acquiring and managing key account relationships as well as recruiting, training, and directing a field sales force. Complementing my sales background is my involvement in sourcing, product development, and marketing activities, providing me with the skills to excel in this role.

At Allmentigen, I assembled a national sales force of independent, commissioned representatives. My duties involve educating them on product lines and merchandising programs, providing sales tools, defining target markets, and accompanying them on sales calls. Our accounts are comprised of independent dealers primarily on the east coast as well as national online retailers, such as furniture.com.

Over 10 years of my career was spent as the managing principal of Bill Lowery & Associates. I led the company's sales efforts, directing sales representatives, calling on furniture manufacturers, cultivating relationships, and responding quickly to customers' material and component needs. My business supplied woodworking components to furniture manufacturers; as a result, I have strong working knowledge of this industry and requirements relating to product design, styling, and specifications.

I would like to discuss how my capabilities can meet or exceed your needs, and will contact you early next week to arrange a mutually convenient time for an initial conversation. In the meantime, feel free to call or e-mail me if you have any questions.

Thank you for your time and consideration. I hope to speak with you soon.

Sincerely,

Bill Lowery

Enclosure

Bill Lowery

Residence: (317) 554-1111
Mobile: (317) 414-3025
Email: lowerybill@msn.com

785 Glendale Street
Indianapolis, IN 46204

Summary of Qualifications

Finished-Goods Executive with 20+ years of furniture industry experience and strong knowledge of design, manufacturing, and quality processes, both domestic and international. Expertise includes:

- Sales and Sales Management
- Merchandising Management
- Line and Product Development
- Sourcing
- Program Design and Execution
- Vendor Performance Management

Professional Experience

ALLMENTIGEN FURNITURE, *division of Allmentigen Group, a global trading company specializing in timber and wood products, headquartered in Spain.*

Manager of Furniture Imports   Indianapolis, IN, March 2003-Present

- Direct all aspects of a finished-goods / furniture-import business to include sourcing, merchandising, product development, marketing, and sales.
- Devise sourcing strategies to leverage the company's existing country and vendor relationships. Travel to vendor sites (Brazil and Vietnam) for the purpose of providing design consultations, reviewing quality, and monitoring production status. Maintain compliance with all regulations including legal and environmental requirements.
- Establish merchandising direction based on knowledge of market trends and niche opportunities as well as vendor capabilities and customers' specific needs.
- Oversee line-development and product-development activities through communication with vendors on design, product specifications, quality standards, and cost targets.
- Create sales forecasts and merchandising plans that include floor-plan and product-mix packages as well as promotional activities to support inventory sell-through.
- Direct marketing and sales to casual / outdoor furniture dealers and online retailers: manage showrooms; organize participation in trade shows; supervise development of ads and marketing materials; and lead independent sales force to include making joint sales calls.
- Conduct sales meetings, emphasizing product features and benefits, competitive positioning, quality, utility, and other strengths of the product line and merchandising programs.
- Manage financial performance, and conduct monthly reviews of sales and expenses.

Accomplishments:

- Managed business start-up and growth; achieved annual sales of $138,000 generated from 21 items in its first year; expanded line to 80+ items and generated annual sales of $1.1 million in 2004 and $2.3 million in 2005.
- Established "All Outdoors" brand name from inception to well-recognized resource in the casual-furniture industry through advertising, direct-mail, and promotional campaigns; press releases; and trade shows for furniture and casual living.
- Developed sales aids including catalogs, catalogs on CD, and materials with technical descriptions, style features, and multifunctional applications.
- Negotiated an agreement with Shalloteam® to serve as the exclusive distributor of its outdoor furniture line in the US and established a relationship with Bingor Company for a complementary line of rockers, deep seating, bar stools, and modular groups.
- Collaborated with a cushion manufacturer in creating a cushion/fabric program for presentation with the furniture lines, generating incremental sales with no investment.
- Developed and sourced a new program in Vietnam with Mexinon, Inc., meeting the design specifications and price-point targets of a U.S. retailer.

Resume Writer: Julie Rains

Bill Lowery

Manager of Furniture Imports – *Accomplishments* - continued
- Established distribution capabilities by sourcing a third-party vendor and negotiating an agreement for warehousing and order-fulfillment services.
- Secured coverage in trade publications such as *Casual Home, Furniture Now, Garden Today*, and *Outdoor Living.*
- Streamlined process for meeting the documentation requirements of leading online retailers, reducing lead times for approval from three to four months to approximately three days.

BILL LOWERY & ASSOCIATES, *sourcing / purchasing business servicing furniture manufacturers*

Managing Principal   Carmel, IN, 1990-2003
- Managed all business operations and supervised up to four employees consisting of sales and administrative staff.
- Communicated extensively with furniture manufacturers' buyers and specification staff; identified specific needs for hardwood lumber, cuttings, and value-added items.
- Worked with vendor sources consisting of sawmills, lumber companies, and value-added manufacturers that produced items such as legs, table tops, panels, cabinet doors, rails, turnings, and carvings.
- Evaluated vendors for production capabilities, capacities, quality, compliance with specifications, timeliness of shipments, and pricing.
- Developed markets and customers for vendors' product lines.
- Advised vendors regarding material needs, negotiated pricing, made purchases, arranged transportation with carriers, and monitored orders through all phases of order fulfillment to ensure adherence with customers' product specifications and order requirements.

Accomplishments:
- Managed business start-up and grew annual sales to $4 million.
- Established relationships with all major furniture companies in Michigan, Illinois, Indiana, and Wisconsin.
- Developed sources of high-quality products among approximately 50 vendors throughout the Midwest.

PRIOR EXPERIENCE – FURNITURE INDUSTRY
- Positions held include sales representative for a brokerage services firm, commissioned sales representative for furniture manufacturers, and sales associate for a furniture dealer.

Education

INDIANA UNIVERSITY-BLOOMINGTON   Bloomington, IN
- English Major; completed six semesters.

Military

UNITED STATES MARINE CORPS
- Served four years; honorably discharged.

Professional Associations

American Furniture Manufacturers Association (AFMA)
Summer and Casual Furniture Manufacturers Association (SCFMA)

SHIRLEY A. EDWARDS

H. (416) 519-7775 ❖ tnt_hr@rogers.com ❖ C. (416) 647-7775
❖ 415 Willowdale Avenue Unit 807 ❖ Toronto ON M2N 5B4 ❖

INNOVATIVE QUALITY ASSURANCE MANAGER

LEADERSHIP PROFILE

Dedicated Quality Assurance Professional with nearly 10 years of successful career progression in quality optimization and operations management. Proven performer who transitions easily from vision and strategy to implementation and follow-through. Focused on adhering to organizational missions and philosophy while positively impacting bottom line and daily performance. Recipient of multiple company awards for superior leadership, technical expertise and innovative contributions.

❖ **Quality Control** ❖ **Product Development** ❖ **Vendor Relations** ❖
❖ **Technical Analysis** ❖ **Internal Auditing** ❖ **Project Management** ❖
❖ **Performance Testing** ❖ **Budget Planning** ❖ **Process Improvement** ❖
❖ **Problem Resolution** ❖ **Cost Control** ❖ **Team Building** ❖

KEY PERFORMANCE INDICATORS

- Spearheaded ISO-9001 certification project; certification granted on first attempt.

- Stabilized vendor relations smoothing product flow; increased revenue by 7%.

- Implemented process refinement, improving discard rate from 18% to 2%.

- Instituted team concept work philosophy, doubling staff performance efficiency.

- Elevated total product quality by 10% through strict adherence to methodologies.

- Increased customer satisfaction by 20% by implementing timely delivery process.

- Authored standard operating procedures manual for 100% training consistency.

- Conducted plant visits and tours for customers, elevating company credibility.

- Initiated installation of computerized audit stations reducing test time by 24%.

- Interfaced with senior managers successfully attaining highest profits in five years.

Shirley A. Edwards
H. (416) 519-7775 ❖ tnt_hr@rogers.com ❖ C. (416) 647-7775

Resume Writer: Tanya Taylor

SHIRLEY A. EDWARDS

H. (416) 519-7775 ❖ tnt_hr@rogers.com ❖ C. (416) 647-7775

CAREER DIGEST

ABC METALS, Concord ON   **1998 – Present**

North American manufacturer of thermoplastic injection moulded components and assemblies specifically for the automotive industry offering 30 leading product lines. Annual revenues in excess of $180 Million. A division of the worldwide Fortune 200 Company, ABC Tool Works.

Quality Control Supervisor   2005 – Present

Selected to lead a 23-person team of Technicians and Assemblers responsible for quality assurance and acceptance testing for the various lines of products. Act as a hands-on leader and mentor to staff while maintaining positive relationships with vendors and customers.
Career Advancement:
- Identified as the leading successor for the Quality Control Manager role.

Quality Technician   2000 – 2005

Appointed to perform a variety of inspection related duties and testing on incoming materials and outgoing products to ensure compliance with quality assurance system requirements. Analyze and compile data for the preparation of statistical reports.
Career Advancement:
- Promoted to Quality Control Supervisor through outstanding performance.

Machine Operator   1998 – 2000

Hired to operate and maintain conventional, special purpose and injection-moulding machinery. Responsible for setting up all machines to produce quality products.
Career Advancement:
- Appointed as Quality Technician. Recognized for dedication and taking iniative.

EDUCATION

Certificate - *Certified ISO-9001 Auditor,* *York University*   2006
- Achieved honourable standing while working on a full time basis.

Certificate - *Business and Commerce,* *Durham School of Business*   2000
- Awarded Durham Leaders Bursary for outstanding academic achievement.

COMPUTER SKILLS

Expert computer proficiency in MS Office programs and quality control systems.

Nancy A. Monroe

670 E. Higgins Road • Naperville, IL 60563

630.983.7544
namonroe@hotmail.com

VALUE OFFERED AS DIRECTOR OF EDUCATION DELIVERY

Demonstrated track record of improving and directing global education services programs that maximize instructor effectiveness, curriculum quality, revenue growth and profitability at technology organizations.

- **Provide the vision, innovation and leadership to improve internal processes in Education Services** with a talent for identifying and resolving operational challenges to enhance revenues / profits.
- **Effective in assessing and driving instructor skill set development, budget and resource management** as well as partnering with internal departments to meet education needs for a diverse customer base.
- **Experienced in the design and delivery of curriculum programs** that support and achieve business objectives.
- **Repeatedly built and empowered cohesive teams that achieved high standards** of quality and productivity in competitive markets.

PROFESSIONAL EXPERIENCE

SIMTECH CORPORATION, CHICAGO, IL   1996 to Present
Promoted through series of high-profile management positions in global Education Services and Customer Support: Global Support Programs Manager (2003 to 2005), Best Practices Manager (2000 to 2003) and Education Services Manager (1996 to 2000).

➤ **As Education Services Manager, repositioned, upgraded and transformed Education Services Department from an underperforming training function to a profit-generating global organization. P&L management accountability for 12 global Customer Education Centers, team of 17 instructors, curriculum design, facilities management / leasing negotiations and budget growth to $4MM.**

- Introduced and educated team on concepts of adult learning theory to better serve students. Improved team morale from a low of 2 to an average high of 4 (on scale of 5) as indicated by survey results.
- Determined core product offering, set revenue mix and gross profit margin, and developed knowledge transfer process in collaboration with Product Management and Customer Support departments.
- Established a consistent learning environment for all students, globally, that eliminated revenue delays and led unit's revenue growth from $4MM to $10MM in billable customer education during 12-month tenure.
- Implemented ASP model for online registration and payment. Produced $600K in additional revenue in first three months; achieved double annual quota in first 6 months; doubled revenues in six months.
- Succeeded in creating additional revenue stream with multimillion-dollar potential by implementing complex software package that represented a $250K capital investment by the company.
- Created multi-level certification programs with validation protocol for customers, partners and employees using ASP model for less than $50K. The certification program revenue potential is millions of dollars annually.
- Took charge of and delivered new education class for applications product line in just three months despite failure of consulting team to produce program after nine months of effort.
- Enhanced company's ability to launch new product lines by designing and ensuring curriculum availability on all product lines by the rollout date. Created incremental education product updates for existing customers.

WORLDWIDE SOLUTIONS, NEW YORK, NY   1990 to 1996

➤ **As Operations Manager of Education Services, provided strategic planning and leadership effectiveness that drove Education Services revenue growth by 150% ($5MM to $7MM). Directed 12 instructors globally. Supervised curriculum development with team in Germany.**

- Managed the training channel, created certification program, conducted Partner Certification programs and ensured accreditation of internal resources and third party delivery resources (partners and subcontractors).
- Automated Education Services function and enrollment process using Access database, enhanced employee morale and improved customer satisfaction, reducing customer calls from 500 a week down to just 25.

EDUCATION: Tapped for and completed Leadership Development Program for High Potentials at SimTech.

Resume Writer: Louise Garver

Tondra Magretta

21211 Ten Gallon Hat Drive • Richardson, TX 75080 • 972.993.5226 • lmagretta@yahoo.com

OPERATIONS MANAGER / BUSINESS ADMINISTRATOR

— Instrumental in creating the office systems that facilitated the growth of a tractor equipment company from a $1 million to an $8 million enterprise —

Loyal and accomplished professional experienced in setting up and managing office operations that include staff hiring, training and supervision, payroll, accounts receivable and payable, financial reporting, data management, inventory, equipment, and office systems. Exceptional leadership, organizational and problem-solving skills. Recognized by staff as a fair but flexible manager – consistently maintained low turnover. Strong computer and software proficiencies. Additional capabilities in:

New Business Development…Benefits Administration…Regulatory Compliance…
Event Planning & Management…Banking Relations…Lease & Fleet Operations

EXPERIENCE & ACHIEVEMENTS

ARMADILLO PARTS & SERVICE INC., Richardson, TX   1990–Present
Operations Manager (1996–Present)

Oversee all daily operations that include administrative, financial, and equipment inventory of up to $1.5 million and employee training in a company that has grown to 64 employees. Act as plan administrator for a $2.3M 401(k) plan, and manage all benefit and insurance plans. Simultaneously serve as software administrator. Supervise a staff of four assistants, and work with other department managers to meet company objectives.

✓ Improved financial, management and customer reporting capabilities by co-leading implementation of an open data base connectivity (ODBC) system that facilitated use of Microsoft software. Saved $20,000 by hiring consultant to help with installation and provide administrator training.

✓ Planned and coordinated a golf outing and an awards ceremony for employees and 200+ customers to celebrate award for top sales by an equipment dealer and to show customer appreciation.

✓ Helped to open two satellite offices in NY, provided training on computer system and inventory functions.

Operations Manager / Business Partner (2000–2002)

Concurrently helped owner diversify business and helped to convert a convenience store into a new liquor store (Cool Cactus Wine & Spirits). Acted as full partner in new business venture.

✓ Set up new QuickBooks system, point of sale (POS) system and inventory management controls.

✓ Organized marketing and advertising promotions, and established a discount program for customers.

Office Manager (1993–1996)

Promoted to take on increasingly progressive responsibilities as company underwent a growth phase. Hired and trained new office staff, and delegated administrative duties.

✓ Fully automated office operations. Researched computer systems and worked with an external consultant to implement a fully networked UNIX system. Trained for six months and became company systems manager.

✓ Developed new inter-departmental policies and procedures that ensured seamless operations, reduced inefficiencies and improved productivity.

Administrative Assistant (1990–1993)

Recruited by former manager at Southwest Tractor to set up and handle administrative functions for a three-month old company with six employees.

✓ Created policies and procedures for all office and inventory functions, introduced filing system, tracked customer orders and implemented a multi-line phone system.

Earlier Experience: Southwest Tractor Corp. (Assistant to Branch Manager)

PROFESSIONAL DEVELOPMENT

RICHARDSON COMMUNITY COLLEGE – School of Business Learning, Richardson, TX
Courses in MS Excel, Word, Access and Outlook, QuickBooks and UNIX systems

Resume Writer: Jill Grindle

CLINT BISHOP

P.O. Box 34097, Somerville, MA 02155
Phone: 909-234-7786 • Email: bishop@gmail.com

PROFESSIONAL PROFILE

Motivated, accomplished ***Product Support Engineer*** focused on providing thorough, ongoing support from initial client evaluation through sale, installation, customer training, maintenance, and subsequent upgrades.

- Eight-plus years' experience in Product Support role as both employee and consultant for Olsen Company.
- Three-plus years' experience working overseas to support clients in Korea, Singapore, Taiwan, and Japan.
- Three-plus years' experience managing product support teams ranging in size from 2-12 staff members.
- Expertise in carrying a workload of short- and long-term assignments including NPIs and enhancements.
- Knowledge of U.S. government contracting regulations, bidding procedures, and terminology.
- Background in testing, troubleshooting, and providing quality assurance (QA) on hardware and robotics.

EMPLOYMENT RECORD

WACHTEL, INC., Faluja, Iraq   **December 2006 – December 2007**

Director of Services
Accepted a one-year contract from a construction engineering company, as a hiatus to Product Support career, in order to learn the intricacies of government contracting, including federal acquisition regulations (FAR).

- Streamlined operations for U.S. military dining, laundry, and recreation facilities, securing a record-high customer satisfaction rate of 98.77% (2006).
- Saved company over $300K/year in bulk purchases and $140M through vendor contract resolicitation.
- Passed all quarterly government-sanctioned audits as well as Wachtel's internal audits.

HEARTLAND MANUFACTURING, INC., Watertown, MA   **March 2005 – October 2006**

Customer Support & Operations Manager
Recruited by former manager at Olsen & Company to streamline and oversee RMA, DMR, and other manufacturing procedures for this producer of robotics, RF, and microwave components.

- Led support services and field operations for Olsen & Company, accounting for 80% of business.
- Project-managed major relocation of corporate facilities to new 10,000 sq. ft. location.

OLSEN & COMPANY, Boston, MA   **March 1993 – January 2005**
Provided full-scale product support on pneumatic, electronic, mechanical, gas, and RF products for clients in Korea, Japan, and Taiwan from sales demos through maintenance and enhancement. Originally hired into QA and testing role; promoted in 1995 to client-facing Product Support position due to relationship-building and diplomacy skills.

Senior Product Support Engineer (June 2000 – January 2005)
Served as lead integrator of the Integrated Platform Product Group (automation technology / robotics), leading three full-time support engineers as well as six to eight ad hoc staff to execute both internal and external projects.

- Balanced a dynamic task list of short- and long-term projects including at least three annual new product introductions (NPIs) plus up to six smaller product enhancement / maintenance projects.
- Traveled to Japan and Taiwan six times per year for up to 60 days at a time to ameliorate client concerns, install new products, and / or rectify malfunctioning product module(s).
- Identified and addressed all hardware and system-related issues, including software integration, calibration, quality control, and testing. Directed and mentored junior product support staff on best practices.
- Accurately compiled, maintained, and disseminated project requirements and documentation, positioning team to complete projects ahead of schedule 90% of the time.
- Resolved escalated issues from within Olsen & Company's 300-person internal engineering organization.

Resume Writer: Cliff Flamer

CLINT BISHOP

Phone: 909-234-7786 • Email: bishop@gmail.com
Page 2 of 2

OLSEN & COMPANY (continued)

Global Product Support Engineer (June 1995 - September 1999)
Placed in charge of South Korean client base, handling six concurrent projects as a member of the Firmware Product Business Group. Managed client relationships and provided support services from inception through production and upgrades, maintaining 100% client retention rate and earning numerous contract extensions.

- Resided in Korea for a total of two years (out of four) in five- to nine-month stretches in order to offer immediate support for alpha and beta versions of cutting-edge products valued upwards of $100M.
- Served as onsite "go-to" person and technical liaison for sales and marketing teams, as well as field engineers, during product demonstrations, source inspections, installations, and retrofits.
- Interfaced extensively with Korean clients to gather pertinent feedback for eventual (re)implementation, address time-sensitive concerns, and provide formal training on product features and enhancements.
- Reduced consumables cost considerably by sourcing and qualifying new manufacturing vendors.
- Expedited production output by 5-10% by revamping calibration procedures.
- Created and managed variable installation and warranty budgets ranging from 8-12% of total product cost.
- Compiled and presented product division plans detailing client performance in cost of consumables, cost of ownership, and technical improvements in hardware, software, and process (chemical) technology.

Quality Engineer, Firmware Product Business Group (March 1994 - June 1995)
Leveraged sponsored and unsponsored training in electronics engineering to ensure new and existing products met defined engineering specifications, workmanship, and quality standards in addition to satisfying customer-specified requirements. Led QA teams in improving engineering, manufacturing, and shipping processes.

- Collected non-conformance data and performance indicator charts to generate comprehensive reports.
- Conducted regular global field visits to respond to quality, shipment, and customer satisfaction issues.

Engineering Technician, ECB & Firmware Technologies Division (March 1993 - March 1994)
Recruited out of Apex Tech's 4-year BSEE program to administer final testing, troubleshooting, and repair of complex semiconductor equipment consisting of pneumatic, electronic, mechanical, gas, and RF control systems.

OTHER EXPERIENCE

General Contractor / Subcontractor   *June 2003 – March 2005*
Accessed knowledge of mechanics, electronics, and robotics to build and repair solar panels for residential and commercial clients as well as remodel homes. Took leave from product support to achieve personal goal of earning general contractor's license which requires four years of experience prior to passing a written exam.

EDUCATION & PROFESSIONAL TRAINING

Olsen & Company Global University, Boston, MA
Completed 40+ hours of technical, product, safety, and career development training.

Apex Technology Institute, Chicago, IL
Completed 95% of BSEE degree. (Recruited out of school by Olsen & Company.)

State of Massachusetts, Licensed General Contractor
Passed exam after meeting requirement of gathering four years of related experience.

CANDACE B. REYNOLDS

2217 Nottingham Drive
Mentor, OH 44456

Home: 330-521-3456   cbreynolds@abcdocuments.com   Mobile: 330-652-3456

PROJECT MANAGEMENT / ACCOUNT MANAGEMENT

Sales / Merchandising / Training

Dynamically motivated, results-driven professional with more than four years of success in both project management and key account management. Dedicated team leader with compelling client/vendor rapport building skills and a high degree of integrity. Equipped to use visionary, nonconforming, innovative talents to break new ground and encourage employees to flourish. Employ diversified sales and marketing expertise to enhance sales and profitability. Combine a positive attitude with innovative intellect to motivate teams to peak performance. Consistently promoted to positions of increased responsibility.

Core Qualifications

- Cold Call Sales
- Personalized Service
- Educating Consumers
- Attending Client Functions

- Trade Shows
- Creative Presentations
- Team Building & Leadership
- Fostering Client Relationships

PROFESSIONAL EXPERIENCE

TechNetwork, Cleveland, OH   12/97–Present
National retail technology merchandising and training company providing both dedicated and syndicated programs as a full one-stop solution for merchandising, training and selling services.

DIRECTOR OF PROJECT MANAGEMENT (2004–Present)
Manage, direct and approve all activities for eight project managers and six account managers including yearly reviews, and overseeing management of their accounts. Primary contact for departmental communications. Establish budget goals and forecast potential company revenue. Direct and oversee merchandising work for all field representatives.

Selected Accomplishments:

- Increased by millions client's ROI and market share for their products by effectively aligning them with Sony, Microsoft, and Panasonic.

- Catapulted Panasonic Plasma TVs market share from #8 to # 1 through innovative team leadership and implementation of resourceful demonstration and training teams.

- Sold and managed successfully the huge launch of PlayStation 3 on-time in all national Best Buy and Circuit City locations despite delays and obstacles.

- Garnered high praise and generated a guarantee from Sony to launch next big promotion by initiating a successfully impressive launch of PlayStation 3.

continued

Resume Writer: Barbara Kanney

CANDACE B. REYNOLDS   Page 2

PROFESSIONAL EXPERIENCE

- Secured over 50 accounts to continually sign annual contracts due to personalized service and training efforts, including videos and comprehensive in-store training.

- Decreased employee turnover approximately 50% by maintaining an opendoor policy, setting accomplishable goals, and empowering employees to make daily decisions which boosted employee confidence and motivated teams to peak performance.

OPERATIONS MANAGER (1999–2004)
Managed 4 in-house divisional managers, 15 regional field managers, and 3000 field employees. Communicated changes, new jobs, terminations, salary increases and packages, and coordinated assigned locations for field managers and full-time field employees.

Selected Accomplishments:

- Reduced by 100% travel costs for 30 sales representatives in one year by executing a key initiative to extend local sales representative coverage nationwide.

- Expanded account base from one to 85 accounts in a five-year period.

- Created the position of operations manager and resourcefully set forth new processes to manage the field and introduce proper training tools.

- Established quality control department and generated yearly review process which increased employee morale.

REGIONAL FIELD MANAGER (1997–1999)
Traveled to ensure full coverage of territories; interviewed and trained new candidates. Performed merchandising where needed, including store set ups, plan-o-grams, audits, secret shopping, display assembly, product training, and demonstrations.

Selected Accomplishments:

- Hired and trained sales representatives for store coverage in six-state area including Ohio, Pennsylvania, Michigan, Indiana, West Virginia, and New York.

- Trimmed turnover rate by 30% due to strong management and training expertise.

EDUCATION AND TECHNICAL SKILLS

Santa Barbara City College, Santa Barbara, CA

Software Skills: Windows 95, 98 and XP, Excel, Access, Word, Crystal Reporting

Chapter 14

Resumes for Members of the Military Transitioning to Civilian Careers

In this chapter, find resumes for:

Medical Laboratory Supervisor
Power Plant/Utility Supervisor
Truck Driver / Equipment Operator
Systems Engineer
Marketing Manager
Chief Financial Officer

You've served your country proudly, protecting and defending the American way of life. Now your duty is done and you're ready to take that big step back into civilian life. Perhaps you had a career before your service which you hope to return to; maybe you're counting on your military training to provide you with marketable skills. Whichever the case, if you are a member of the military about to move back into the civilian world, there are several key things to remember as you prepare your resume and cover letters. Here are just a few tips that you may find helpful:

1. Think of your skills and experiences in civilian terms. Much of the jargon that is commonly used in everyday military operations has little meaning for a civilian audience. Some of the acronyms familiar to military people are positively cryptic to a civilian audience. Whenever possible, use terms in your resume that relate to the civilian world. For example, if your skills include driving tanks or repairing half-tracks, your resume should say something similar to, "operated heavy equipment" or "maintained large diesel engines."

187

2. Use civilian job titles instead of military ranks or designations. As an example, a colonel in the Army whose responsibilities encompassed budgeting and financial management for a military base can legitimately use the job title "controller" or "chief financial officer" on his or her resume, which is indicative of his or her civilian career objective. Instead of "sergeant" or "E-5," use the term "supervisor," "warehouse manager" or "logistics coordinator," as the case may be.

3. Use your cover letter to describe how your military experience has prepared you for your next career. If you have completed training that prepares you for a particular career field, be sure to mention it prominently in your cover letter. If the discipline of the military environment has taught you how to set priorities, meet goals, and exercise sound judgment under pressure, be sure to highlight these abilities as well. Civilians often speak of grace under fire in figurative terms, but you may have exhibited such qualities in literal terms on the battlefield, as part of a flight crew, or aboard a warship.

4. Be quantitative in talking about your responsibilities. The hiring manager who is interviewing you may have no idea how many infantrymen there are in a platoon, how many sailors are aboard a destroyer, or the volume of equipment and supplies a typical Marine division may inventory. If your areas of accountability include such things, be sure to explicitly spell out how many or how much when you write your resume and cover letters.

On the following pages is an excellent example of a cover letter as well as several resumes for candidates leaving the military and seeking positions in the civilian world. (Note: Some of the resumes contained in this chapter were written by Canadian or Australian resume professionals for candidates seeking work in those countries. With this in mind, we have left in place the accepted spelling, grammar, and wording used in those countries. Even if you're not looking for work in Canada or Australia, the overall format and structure of these documents may prove helpful to you in preparing your job search documents.)

Stephanie A. Johnson
203 Marler Boulevard • San Diego, CA 92100 • (619) 514-5569 • sajohnson@net.com

January 31, 2008

Dr. Sangre Sample
Director of Laboratory Operations
General Hospital
123 Doctors Drive
Pittsburgh, PA 15299

Dear Dr. Sample:

Your requirements for a **Medical Laboratory Supervisor** are a perfect match with my background. As a medical laboratory management professional with a 10-year record of success, I offer the following qualifications:

- **B.S. degree in laboratory science combined with advanced training in laboratory procedures, techniques and operations.**

- **Well-rounded hands-on and management experience in all aspects of medical laboratory operations in major medical centers in the U.S. and overseas.**

- **Certification as a Laboratory Technician.**

Throughout my career, I have achieved recognition for my expertise, leadership, team-building strengths, and focus on quality standards. Recent examples of my accomplishments include:

- **Managing the launch of multiple medical laboratory operations, including coordination of personnel recruitment, staff training, and equipment implementation.**

- **Developing and implementing consistent policies and procedures, as well as staff training on best practices, which resulted in efficient operations and a 100% safety record.**

- **Planning and coordinating educational programs adopted organization-wide that have been recognized for excellence.**

I will be completing my service with the United States Navy next month and would welcome the opportunity to discuss the contributions I would make to your medical lab operations. Please contact me by phone or e-mail to arrange a mutually convenient time for an initial conversation.

Thank you,

Stephanie A. Johnson

Enclosure

Resume Writer: Louise Garver

Stephanie A. Johnson

203 Marler Boulevard • San Diego, CA 92100 • (619) 514-5569 • sajohnson@net.com

Medical Laboratory Management

Certified Medical Laboratory professional with 10 years of progressive team leadership, policy development, and management experience in a major medical center, clinic, and field environments. Solid background in staffing, training, developing and supervising emergency and lab personnel. Budget planning and administrative expertise includes successes in cost reductions while maintaining highest quality standards. Proven analytical, problem solving and organizational abilities resulting in effective approaches to operations and administration.

Career Milestones

- Selected to establish, staff, and manage medical lab operations at an overseas clinic. Developed policies/procedures and led operations to attain licensure and certification in only 14 months.
- Chosen to lead the start-up of medical laboratory functions at naval hospitals in two states, coordinated staffing and procurement of state-of-the-art equipment.
- Achieved and maintained 100% safety record in laboratory operations through effective staff training, team building, and supervision in all clinical areas.
- Initiated the first blood DNA collection program for the Naval Academy and Department of the Navy to be launched organization-wide. Credited by senior management for "phenomenal planning, meticulous attention to detail and flawless program execution."
- Annually awarded and achieved five promotions for superior performance record and initiative in the development of staff educational and other programs.

Experience & Accomplishments

UNITED STATES NAVY (1988–present)
Assistant Medical Laboratory Supervisor, Naval Hospital, San Diego (1999–present)
Sr. Medical Laboratory Technician, Clinic & Naval Hospital, New Mexico (1993–1999)

Lab Operations & Management

- Supervise medical laboratory operations and staff of 24 technicians in performing over 2,000 procedures weekly, utilizing state-of-the-art equipment.
- Plan and administer $150,000 annual budget for laboratory operations. Successfully reduce year-over-year costs by 20% through staff training and accountability.
- Play a key role in managing administrative functions, including medical billing, patient records maintenance, purchasing, and inventory/stock control.
- Coordinate and prepare all documentation required by JCAHO and OSHA regulatory agencies.
- Develop, implement, and monitor compliance with department policies and procedures.
- Ensure stringent compliance with standards on quality control, infection control, safety, and disposal of hazardous materials.

Staff Training, Development & Supervision

- Supervise and develop teams of up to 45 staff members, setting goals, motivating teams, and evaluating performance to maximize efficiency and productivity.
- Train staff on laboratory equipment procedures and protocols to improve productivity while maximizing safety.
- Develop and conduct training programs for new recruits on infectious diseases and preventive medicine.
- Implement training curriculum for health science students on nursing, laboratory policies, procedures and operations.

continued...

Resume Writer: Louise Garver

Stephanie A. Johnson   Page 2

Experience & Accomplishments continued...

Patient Technician, Naval Medical Center, Germany (1991–1993)
Emergency Medical Technician, Naval Hospital, Persian Gulf (1988–1991)

Lab Procedures/Emergency Medicine

- Performed hematology, blood banking, chemistry, microbiology, urinalysis, phlebotomy, serology, specimen collection and other lab procedures.
- Diagnosed and provided routine/emergency medical care to broad range of patients (ICU, CCU, neuro ICU, geriatric, and pediatric) in emergency/trauma, home care and acute care environments.
- Prescribed medications and performed thorough patient assessments and medical procedures: taking vital signs, audiograms, IV and oxygen therapy, suturing, casting, venipuncture, starting arterial lines, EKGs and tracheotomies.
- Advocated for patients, effectively resolving issues to ensure quality care and excellent patient relations.

Education / Certifications

Bachelor of Science, Laboratory Science, 2000
University of California, San Diego, CA

Additional Training

UNITED STATES NAVY: **Advanced Laboratory School,** 1994; **Basic Laboratory School,** 1992; **Emergency Medical Technician School,** 1990; **Hospital Corpsman School,** 1988

Seminars

Leadership Development, Critical Care, Field Emergency Medicine, Bacteriology

Certifications

Laboratory Technician, Emergency Medical Technician, Phlebotomy, CPR/First Aid, Health Educator

William Daniels

billdaniels12@aaatargeted.com

5415 N. Clark Street
Chicago, Illinois 60640

H: (773) 907-8660
C: (312) 555-8660

POWER PLANT SUPERVISION / PLANT ENGINEERING & OPERATION
Gas Turbines • Diesel Engines • Electric Power Generation

PROFILE:

EXPERIENCE: Dedicated professional who earned positions of increased responsibility in 20 years of service with the U.S. Navy.

TECHNICAL SKILLS: Hands-on problem solver who has extensive understanding of the operation, calibration, repair, and maintenance of complicated gas turbine and electrical power generation systems.

LEADERSHIP: Results-oriented manager who has supervised, trained and motivated staff to follow strict guidelines and work calmly during emergencies.

EDUCATION:

AURORA UNIVERSITY
B.S., Work Force Education, Training & Development   2007
Relevant studies include:
• Training Needs Assessment (TNA)   • Human Resources Management

RELEVANT EXPERIENCE:

UNITED STATES NAVY   1983-2006
[Accountable for two LM 2500 GE gas turbine engines, three 2,000 kW generators, and related equipment]

OPERATOR & TRAINER (1998-2002)
Served as primary decision-maker in the operation of power plant consoles and engine operations. Supervised crews of 6-15 in 24/7 operation of a war ship at sea. Trained engineers and non-engineering staff to operate equipment in normal and emergency situations. Evaluated progress and reported to superiors.
• Qualified 25 sailors in engineering related skills with special expertise in turbine and electrical systems.
• Qualified 75 sailors in engineering duties in casualty/emergency situations.

POWER PLANT SUPERVISOR (1994-1998)
Ensured that engine systems were maintained and ready to operate on short notice. Supervised a staff of 40 technicians trained in electrical and mechanical operations. Monitored systems and controls in regular duties as watch officer.
• Cross-trained 11 junior officers to understand engineering operations and to be able to communicate procedures to subordinates.
• Designated "Special Evolution Engineering Officer," assuming control of the power plant in emergency situations and battle, including fueling operations which involve the safe handling of 250,000-500,000 gallons of volatile fuel.

[Supervised operation of four LM 2500 GE gas turbine engines, three 2,000 kW generators, and related equipment]

ELECTRICAL/MECHANICAL SUPERVISOR (1989-1994)
Supervised 8 electrical technicians and 14 mechanical technicians. Ensured that calibration and repairs were executed to standards. Scheduled and directed regular maintenance.

Resume Writer: Clay Cerny

William Daniels

(Page Two)

**RELATED
EXPERIENCE:**

MAINTENANCE CHIEF (2002-2008)
Managed operations with an annual budget of $2 million. Supervised staff of eight to ensure that outsourced contractors maintained 41 buildings. Reviewed billing and inspected properties as part of quality assurance.
- Saved $500,000 in repair costs by implementing a tracking system to hold contractors accountable and measure project goals.
- Reduced costs for maintenance and operations by streamlining procurement procedures and initiating tracking programs.

**PROFESSIONAL
TRAINING:**

U.S. NAVY

- Power plant supervision
- Electricity & electronics
- Gas, steam, and diesel engines
- Fueling operations

**COMPUTER
SKILLS:**

Software to control power plant/fueling operations, Excel, Word

References available upon request.

Resume

WAYNE JORDAN

Telephone: 293 Eden Road
Home: 08 8278 9999   jordanw@outback.com.au   BLACKWOOD SA 5051

OBJECTIVE

Truck Driving
• Mine Site   • General Haulage   • Remote Area Work

QUALIFIED BY

Licensed to drive a range of vehicles, including Heavy Combination (prime mover), Medium Rigid Truck, and Medium Bus, with metropolitan and remote area experience. Quick and productive worker with experience with a floor installation Company including driving heavy delivery vehicles. Fork lift licence to 10 tonnes. Background as a general hand on a number of remote area sheep and cattle stations with duties ranging from mustering to fencing, welding, and tank/trough erection. High level of physical fitness combined with the ability to make quick and confident decisions and to work as part of a team, reinforced by recent military service. Strong customer service skills developed through experience in the hospitality industry and as a console operator / driveway attendant.

KEY SKILLS

• Driving   • Customer service   • Manual skills   • Team work
• Problem solving   • Welding   • Fork lift operating

AREAS OF EFFECTIVENESS

• Licensed to drive a range of medium to heavy rigid and articulated vehicles

• Remote area driving and living experience

• Proven ability to handle hard work by working as a labourer for a floor installation company

• Experienced in working with a range of hand and power tools and other equipment

• Relating to customers in commercial, retail, service or domestic situations

• Experienced in cash handling, banking, stocktaking, and ordering

ACHIEVEMENTS

• Followed agriculturally-focused education with full-time employment on two remote area mixed sheep and cattle stations in the Flinders Ranges of South Australia, developing a wide range of farming skills including animal husbandry, fencing, water tank and trough installation, and cattle yard construction, as well as developing outback living and survival skills.

• Maintained contact with the commercial area through casual weekend employment as a driver and floor installer during period of full-time military service in Adelaide, and separately as a hospitality worker during earlier service in Sydney.

Resume Writer: Brian Leeson

WAYNE JORDAN _____ **2**

EMPLOYMENT HISTORY

Detachment Commander
Artillery Testing Range, Port Wakefield SA   2000-2008

Artillery Gunner
8/12 Artillery Regiment, Holdsworthy, Sydney   1998-2000

Installer / Driver (casual weekends)
Floating Floor Company, Adelaide   2004-2005

General Station Duties
Balcanoona Sheep and Cattle Station   1998

General Station Duties
Wertaloona Cattle Station   1997

EDUCATION AND TRAINING

On-the-job civil construction and haulage training
Civil Training Services, Adelaide   2008

Haul Truck Operators Course
Mining Training Services, Adelaide   2007

Heavy Combination Driver Training
Transport Training Centre, Adelaide   2007

Certificate in Agriculture (Year 12)
Urrbrae Agricultural High School, Adelaide   1996

CIVILIAN LICENCES

Heavy Combination (prime mover) with 500 hours of experience
Medium Rigid Truck
Fork-lift (10 tonne)
Front end loader,
14 tonne tipper
Medium Bus (22 seater)

REFEREES

Warrant Officer Paul Ericsson   08 8867 0326
Artillery Testing Range
Port Wakefield, South Australia

Vince Strauss   08 8278 5153
Floating Floor Company
Blackwood SA 5051

TUCKER FORD

2404 Dunbar Road • Mynfee, Oklahoma 74126 • (918) 631-5968

SYSTEMS ENGINEERING AND INTEGRATION

Talented young professional with 18 years of experience pioneering efforts in process, productivity, efficiency, and quality improvement. Provided the strategy and implemented plans that delivered **over $10 million dollars in cost savings** to the US Air Force. Strong qualifications in team building and team leadership.

➢ Expert in large-scale information systems; i.e. **BMC4I Systems** (Battle Management, Command, Control, Communications, Computers, and Intelligence) and **imagery systems**. Effective combination of technical / engineering and business communication skills.
➢ Outstanding communication and interpersonal skills; persuasive speaker.
➢ Acted as liaison between various intelligence communities within Department of Defense and U.S. Government, including **NSA** (National Security Agency), **CIA** (Central Intelligence Agency), and **NRO** (National Reconnaissance Organization).
➢ Strong background in military and commercial satellite systems. 18 years of military work ethic.
➢ All projects completed **on time** and **within budget**.
➢ Computer literate (Windows, Word, PowerPoint, Presentations).

SECURITY CLEARANCE

Top Secret Special Security Background Investigation
Awarded December 1993

PROFESSIONAL EXPERIENCE

UNITED STATES AIR FORCE
Systems Engineer for Worldwide Telecast Service, Rosamond AFB, CA   1997 - Present

• Fielded the world's **first Global Broadcast Service imagery transmission satellite system** ($500 Million effort) in the Pacific region. Integrated a diverse group of contractors and government agencies into one team. Handled project planning; followed detailed engineering, job safety, and cost control procedures. Directed integration of **fiber** and **SATCOM systems**. Performed site inspections and controlled material flow. Coordinated, oversaw, and directly supervised 12 field technicians. Project served as a model for worldwide implementation. Reported directly to senior military leadership in Washington, D.C.

Airborne Collection Systems Engineer, Ft. Sam Houston, TX   1995 - 1997

• Coordinated **first-of-its-kind** integration of strategic and tactical assets in direct support of **NRO**, reducing targeting time lines for **Time Critical Mobile Targets** by over 50%.

• Integrated **first-ever** special collection payload into **T1 Ku SATCOM Imagery Transmission System** on unmanned airborne platform in direct support of European Command, managing cross-cultural relationships among four different major contractors.

• Performed **first-ever** controlled test of a special collection payload on high-altitude reconnaissance aircraft, delivering a 100% increase in mission readiness to European Command. Led a cross-functional team of 35 members (e.g. program management, marketing, and engineering) to develop and implement this capability.

Resume Writer: Myriam-Rose Kohn

TUCKER FORD   Page 2

MILSATCOM Systems Engineer (Military Satellite Communications), Buckley AFB, NY   1994

- Spearheaded the development team of the **first-ever MILSATCOM** Tactical Requirements Document for Air Force Space Command and Air Combat Command (ACC). Designed the initial **imagery** and data transmission systems; integrated radio and **SATCOM** communications between airborne command and control platforms (**AWACS, Joint STARS**) and ground command and control and targeting nodes.

BMD Systems Engineer (Ballistic Missile Defense), Buckley AFB, NY   1990 - 1993

- Led the **BMDO** (Ballistic Missile Defense Office) BMC3 team that recommended **STAR WARS** be replaced by a limited strike missile defense, **NMD** (National Missile Defense), working closely with US Space Command.

- Directed the initial **ABL** (Airborne Laser) BMC3 team in direct support of Air Combat Command.

- Laid the foundation for the Air Force's **first-ever TMD** (Theater Missile Defense) Program by working **requirements-definition** and **imagery** transmission issues with Air Combat Command.

- Directed three-year effort to incorporate **TMD** capabilities onto the **AWACS** aircraft to track ballistic missiles in flight with laser ranger radar, working closely with Air Combat Command and Boeing Aircraft.

- Managed the **first-ever** effort to incorporate off-platform missile defense imagery capabilities onto the **Joint STARS** aircraft, working closely with Air Combat Command and the U.S. Army to translate lessons learned from the Persian Gulf War into vastly improved combat capabilities.

EDUCATION

Completed four courses toward a Master in Liberal Arts at Yale University, New Haven, CT.

Bachelor of Science, **Physics** with concentrations in **Electrical Engineering** and **Applied Mathematics**, California Polytechnic University, Santa Maria, CA, 1989.

Squadron Officer School, Maxwell Air Force Base, Alabama, 1995.

TRAINING

ACQ 101	Systems Acquisition Fundamentals, 2004
ACQ 201	Systems Acquisition Intermediate, 1999
SYS 201	Systems Engineering Intermediate, 1998

Jeremy Rivera

1000 Sweetwater • Huber Heights, Ohio 45424 • jriver@mail.com
H: (937) 543-2109 • C: (937) 567-8901

SUMMARY OF QUALIFICATIONS

Intelligent and success-driven professional offering a strong project management background and higher education in marketing and business administration to excel in an **Advertising or Marketing role.**

➢ **Marketing:** Leverage academic knowledge assisting organizations in developing strategic marketing and advertising plans that establish and maintain brand recognition and consumer loyalty. Well-grounded in marketing theory and the power of influencing the awareness, perceptions, attitudes, and behaviors of targeted audiences. Imaginative, intuitive, and original thinker.

➢ **Business Administration:** Completed capstones which examined business successes and failures while analyzing complex issues involving the impact of competing interests. Acquired key value propositions in functional business disciplines including economics, finance, marketing, operations, and business management. Combined exposure to quantitative and qualitative elements with a solid foundation in reasoning and thinking.

➢ **Project Management:** Define and manage project resource needs and implement, track/report progress, and revise project plans as necessary. Serve as integral project team member capable of meeting expected timelines and goals that contribute to organizational growth and profitability. Resourceful and detail-orientated with the ability to maintain high energy and positive attitude in the face of constantly changing priorities.

➢ **Key Strengths:** Superior technical and quantitative knowledge. Natural communicator capable of performing in challenging environments requiring focused decision-making and the ability to execute strategic and long-term goals. *Fluent in English, Portuguese, and Spanish.* Proficient utilizing MS Office Suite; MS Project; QuickBooks; and major online browsing tools.

EDUCATION

UNIVERSITY OF DAYTON, Dayton, Ohio
Master of Business Administration, Marketing, 01/2007
Bachelor of Arts, Project Management (Minor in Linguistics), 2003

CAREER HIGHLIGHTS

UNITED STATES AIR FORCE, Wright Patterson A.F.B. – Dayton, Ohio
Analyst, 2004-2008
Responsible for transmitting thousands of classified historical recordings into a leading-edge digital database system; effectively collaborate with some of the most influential and prominent individuals within the private and public sectors. Work with project managers in coordinating the implementation of digital files with the media department. Utilize innovative technologies, graphic processors, and computer applications in transferring 16mm film into digital files. Manage extensive documentation and reporting functions. Hold top-secret security clearance. Military service will conclude in June 2008.

• Partnered with four team members in creating a flawless system that transformed 1800+ hours of film recordings into digital format.
• Saved hundreds of man-hours by executing key projects ahead of schedule in the most efficient manner.

continued . . .

Resume Writer: Susan Barens

Jeremy Rivera • **Page Two**

Career Highlights Continued . . .

Instructor, Cryptology Operations, 1999-2004
Served as a leading member of an elite training facility team responsible for training hundreds of students. Accountable for $40M in operations including all administrative and operational procedures essential for smooth functioning of Voice Processing Training System (VPTS). Created all lesson plans, edited curriculum, and facilitated classroom instruction. Supervised a six-member team and maintained entire student database.

- Successfully graduated 400+ students and improved training methodology resulting in more efficient training and a 20% reduction in the dropout rate.
- Selected and highly recommended to become an instructor due to unusual natural ability / knowledge normally afforded to individuals only after several years of on-the-job training.

PROFESSIONAL DEVELOPMENT

Non-Commissioned Officer (NCO) Leadership School • System Development & Database Maintenance (Classified System) Management Course • Technical Training Instructor Course • Cryptologic Linguist Course (Spanish)

~ **Excellent Professional & Character References Furnished Upon Request** ~

GRIFFIN M. HANKERD

1732 Resort Rd.   gmhankerd1@aol.com   313-732-5302
Utica, MI 48233   787-443-8100

CHIEF FINANCIAL OFFICER

Chief Financial Officer with over 20 years of experience managing U.S. Army's fiscal operations. Offer a unique blend of business, financial and military experience, backed up by practical actions and programs that have been a vanguard for change management. Expertise in strategic planning, project management, department / organization re-engineering, and staff development. Exceptional financial analysis, planning and accounting skills with a track record of success working at the top levels of a global organization down to niche operating units. Additional qualifications include:

- Financial Analysis/Reporting
- Financial Controls
- Operational Budgets
- Strategic Planning
- Project Accounting
- Treasury

PROFESSIONAL EXPERIENCE

UNITED STATES ARMY, Active Duty, Baghdad, Iraq   1994 to 2008
Chief Financial Officer, Colonel (2003 to 2008)
Transferred to Joint Task Force headquarters to take over more than $180 million in base operations, joint military intelligence, and various other operations, maintenance funding and resources for over 2,000 personnel. Primary Financial Advisor to Joint Task Force Commanding General. Supervised daily operations and a staff of 11. Managed strategic planning, programming, and budgeting to meet the demands of the ever-changing resource requirements. Governed payroll and travel reimbursement for U.S. Army personnel and Joint Task Force.

- Hand-selected by the Assistant Secretary of the Army (Financial Management & Comptroller) to receive the prestigious "Annual Resource Management Award" for FY 2003, in the Comptroller/Deputy Comptroller MAJCOM category.
- Led the team that completed in just six months a project slated for one year, reducing human resource expenses by 43%.

US ARMY RESERVES HEADQUARTERS, Boulder, CO
Chief Financial Officer, Colonel (2002 to 2003)
Managed the financial activities of the medical brigade including 22 units, six hospitals and support units of logistics, chaplain, public affairs, medical evacuation, dental services, veterinary services, surgery and sanitation/entomology.

- Created the financial management course, "Resource Management for AMEDD Officers," utilized by over 10,000 officers to balance finances.

US ARMY RESERVES, FORT CUSTER, Olympia, WA
Hospital Administrator/Executive Officer (2000 to 2001)
Brought onboard to direct the daily operations of 600 personnel, 21-vehicle medical facility with over $12 million in equipment and 340 beds. Interpreted and ensured compliance with active duty / reserve regulations and Army Headquarters policies. Defined administrative requirements / procedures for managing a multi-component unit.

- Governed strategic planning, performance measurements, and established goals, objectives and long-range plans for a newly activated unit.
- Created and implemented "Best Practice" local policies and procedures.
- Principal Advisor to Commander for administrative personnel, manpower, training, logistics, operations, patient administration, regulatory compliance resource utilization, and financial stewardship.

Resume Writer: Erin Kennedy

GRIFFIN M. HANKERD

Page Two

JEFFERSON AIR FORCE BASE, San Antonio, TX
Chief Systems Accountant (1994 to 2000)
Managed e-senior system accountants and e-senior computer specialists. Served as Contracting Officer's technical representative for worldwide information technology projects. Drafted statements of work for proposals and determined project training requirements. Budgeted worldwide implementation projects and Agency. ADPE acquisitions.

- Analyzed and instituted improvements to Air Force services financial systems.
- Successfully performed global implementation for Air Force: $6 million dollar 'Time Management System' in 1,600 activities; $1.6 million for "Advance" at 100 bases; $10 million for "American Food and Beverage" point of sale system (POS) and Lunchies, $10 million; $5 million dollar internet-based purchasing system (IBPS); and over $5 million for "Oasis", a hotel property management system.
- Played a key role in the development, testing and evaluation of automated systems for Air Force Services activities globally.
- Spearheaded effective and economical ways to use automation to process data and prepare comprehensive management reports.
- Launched a $7.5 million worldwide Air Force Services Core Management Information System (MIS).
- Served as Project Manager for $4.5 million Jones Hardware Replacement, completing project $500,000 under budget and on schedule.

EARLY MILITARY CAREER (1975 to 1994)

Began military career in roles as Chief of Health Care Operations, Supervisory Systems Accountant, and Computer Specialist. Gained valuable experience in all aspects of finance departments, payroll, budgeting, and accounting.

EDUCATION, TRAINING & CERTIFICATIONS

MBA, Emphasis in Accounting, MICHIGAN STATE UNIVERSITY, Lansing, MI
BS, Accounting, MICHIGAN STATE UNIVERSITY, Lansing, MI

Trained in:

→**Project Management** (Fundamentals, Initiation and Startup, Scope, Communications, Control, Estimating, Human Resources, Procurement, Quality, Risk, Scheduling and Cost Control)
→**Project Management for IT**
→**Professionals Managing Multiple Projects**; Managing Project Teams, Planning, Programming
→**Budgeting System Command and General Staff College**

Certified Public Accountant   **Certified Systems Professional**
Certified Data Processor   **Certified Computer Professional**
     Commercial Pilot with commercial, instrument, multi-engine ratings.

AWARDS & AFFILIATIONS

· U.S. Army's "Comptroller of the Year" under MACOM for FY02
· Comptroller's "Comptroller of the Year, 2002"

Chapter 15
Resumes for Personal Assistants and Domestic Workers

In this chapter, find resumes for people seeking positions serving the needs of people in their homes and other settings. Targeted jobs include:

Personal Assistant
Nanny
Elder Care Specialist
Housekeeper
Estate Manager

One of the more interesting, highly challenging, and potentially most fulfilling career paths one can choose is working directly with people to address their day-to-day needs in their homes or other unconventional settings (for example, hotel suites, tour buses, movie sets, corporate suites, and so on) . This could mean acting as the personal assistant for a celebrity, managing a large estate for a wealthy family, or providing care and companionship for an elderly person no longer able to manage on his or her own. Because you're working in someone's home, and, thus, will have access to a great deal of sensitive information about your employer, the element of trust figures largely in hiring decisions for such positions. If you plan to pursue employment in this arena, there are several key things to remember about preparing your resume and cover letters and conducting a job search. Here are just a few tips that you may find helpful:

1. Emphasize your versatility and resourcefulness. One day you may be picking up dry cleaning and walking the dog; the next day you may be

planning a dinner party for 20 or more guests; and on the next you may be asked to select the perfect birthday gift for a relative living abroad and ensure it arrives on time for the celebration. Your resume needs to demonstrate your problem-solving skills and ability to address such diverse demands in an effective manner.

2. Do your research. Because your prospective employer is likely to be an extremely busy, high-profile person—and possibly one with little patience—you need to do your homework to understand who he or she is, what motivates him or her, and, most importantly, what he or she expects from employees. You probably had to network to learn about this opening in the first place, so use your networking contacts to gather as much information as you can about the position and the employer. Tailor your cover letter specifically to them, and develop answers to anticipated interview questions that will strike just the right chord with the potential new boss.

3. Network, network, network! These opportunities aren't likely to be advertised in the Sunday classifieds or on *Monster.com*. The employers we're talking about are typically very private and guarded about the details of their personal lives and probably wish to be as discreet as possible. There are some agencies in larger metropolitan areas that specialize in placing people in these types of positions. Seek them out and learn what they are looking for in candidates. If you have friends in this line of work, find out if they or their employers know of any opportunities. Do the people you plan to use for references have friends or acquaintances in the market for personal assistants? One of your job requirements will be ingenuity and resourcefulness, so use these abilities to find the job opportunities!

4. Include your references. Most resumes these days do not include references directly on the resume, and even the old standby, "References Available Upon Request" is quickly going out of style. However, in this category it's all about trust, so you should include your references on a separate page that is paper-clipped to the resume (no staples!). Include the references' names, professional affiliations, daytime phone numbers, and e-mail addresses. These people should be former employers, former coworkers, or other professional acquaintances who can genuinely speak to your work-related qualifications. If you know a high-profile public official, celebrity, or person of substance who is willing to serve as your reference, by all means consider going for it. Always ask permission

of all your references before listing their names on your reference sheet. (See an example of a reference sheet accompanying Serena Montoya's resume, which appears first among the resume samples that follow.)

On the following pages is an excellent example of a cover letter as well as several resumes for candidates seeking opportunities to work for people in their homes or other personal settings. (Note: Some of the resumes contained in this chapter were written by Canadian or Australian resume professionals for candidates seeking work in those countries. With this in mind, we have left in place the accepted spelling, grammar, and wording used in those countries. Even if you're not looking for work in Canada or Australia, the overall format and structure of these documents may prove helpful to you in preparing your job search documents.)

Serena L. Montoya

732 Lafayette Circle ◆ Ithaca, New York 14850 ◆ 607.596.7363
E-mail: Serena.Montoya@Earthnet.net

January 14, 2008

Anna Maria Pavarotti, EdD
3487 Devonshire Boulevard
Ithaca, New York 14850

Dear Dr. Pavarotti:

Eva SanAngelo, one of your colleagues at Ithaca College and long-time family friend, recommended that I contact you regarding your search for an Executive Assistant for your husband, Dr. Laurence. Although not actively engaged in a job search at this time, Dr. Laurence's many philanthropic pursuits and related activities sound intriguing, and I am writing to express my enthusiastic interest in the position.

Enclosed is a summary of my experience for your review. Particularly in my current position, as well as several others, my role is primarily behind-the-scenes. It seems that much of my activity is truly "invisible" — yet, largely due to my efforts, operations run smoothly; highly sophisticated major (and minor) events come off as planned; and even the most complex special requests are handled by me efficiently, quietly, and with minimal supervision on the part of my superiors.

As I am comfortable in my current position, I trust that our communication will be held in strict confidence.

Since the enclosed résumé only begins to convey the value that I bring to any endeavor, please contact me at your convenience to arrange a time to meet. I look forward to the opportunity to meet you and Dr. Laurence, to hear firsthand about the position, and to discuss how I can fulfill — and exceed your expectations.

Sincerely,

Serena L. Montoya

Enclosures: Resume and References

"...Serena has an uncanny ability to manage a tremendous volume of complex, simultaneous activities, and make it look effortless...her thoughtfulness and attention to detail are extraordinary... I'd hire her back in a minute..."
~ Former Employer

Resume Writer: Gail Smith Boldt

Serena L. Montoya

732 Lafayette Circle ♦ Ithaca, New York 14850 ♦ 607.596.7363 ♦ E-mail: Serena.Montoya@Earthnet.net

PERSONAL EXECUTIVE ASSISTANT

Versatile and accomplished individual with diverse capabilities in several key areas:

- **Extraordinary people skills:** tact, diplomacy and discretion. Ability to comfortably interact with individuals at all levels, of all ages and backgrounds. Gifted public speaker.
- **Excellent project management skills:** planning, organization, team leadership, and budget accountability.
- **Innovative problem-solver** with ability to develop unique solutions to complex problems.
- **Motivated self-starter** with proven success both as independent contributor and team member.
- **Superior verbal and written communication skills,** with successful experience writing press releases, preparing marketing collaterals, and dealing with print and electronic media representatives.
- **Strong computer expertise,** including word processing, spreadsheets, desktop and Web publishing.
- **Foreign languages: Fluent in Spanish; Proficient in Portuguese, French and Italian.**

RELEVANT EXPERIENCE

Management & Administrative Functions:

Selected Personal Executive Assistant / Managerial Experience:

- Facilitated high-profile, dynamic executive's participation in a wide variety of community activities, including youth soccer coaching as well as numerous major regional philanthropic projects; managed personal schedule and correspondence; and accountable for two personal checking accounts (including monthly reconciliation).
- Planned and managed numerous major special events for children and/or adults including a variety of unique occasions requiring detailed planning and last-minute organization.
- Researched and recommended payroll service, and coordinated implementation; investigated and implemented automated accounting and data management systems for private sector and not-for-profit entities.

As Executive Director of American Red Cross of the Panorama Valley:

- Supervised program and clerical staff for this agency, which focused on educational initiatives.
- Managed the activities of Development Director and coordinated over 175 volunteers in a variety of program and fund-raising events.
- Assisted Advisory Board in developing strategic vision, mission and setting agency goals.
- Prepared and administered annual budgets, and complied with a range of stringent reporting requirements from funding sources and affiliated agencies.
- Organized annual black-tie dinner auction; raised $200,000, majority of yearly operating budget.
- Planned and managed logistics for professional conferences with several hundred attendees.

Supported Vice President of regional healthcare collaborative encompassing twelve hospitals:

- Managed the activities of computer hardware and software vendors interacting with 12 hospitals in the development of community-wide hospital data system on a voluntary, cooperative basis.
- Interviewed, hired, trained, and supervised IT Manager, Executive Secretaries, and Receptionist.

As Assistant to Executive Director of Tompkins County Library System:

- Coordinate logistics and communication among senior management team; two government-appointed boards of trustees; and three affiliated volunteer advisory boards.
- Manage appointment schedule and screen incoming calls and visitors.
- Address customers' issues and concerns, as well as high-level requests for information.
- Participate as active member of system-wide Public Relations Team.

Resume Writer: Gail Smith Boldt

Serena L. Montoya
Résumé - Page Two

EMPLOYMENT HISTORY

2000 - Present Administrative Assistant to the Executive Director
Panorama Valley County Library System; Panorama Valley, NY
Provide administrative support to the Director accountable for managing a library system with 16 urban branches and over 375 employees, as well as a collaborative with 30 member libraries county-wide.

1997 - 2000   **Office Manager / Customer Service Representative,** Laptop Systems; Ithaca, NY
Organized and managed office operations, including payroll processing, order tracking, and shipping / receiving for this repair center servicing domestically built laptop PCs.

1994 - 1997   **Executive Director,** American Red Cross of the Panorama Valley; Ithaca, NY
Managed staff and administered annual budget. Oversaw program and development activities for this not-for-profit agency.

1992 - 1994   **Operations Manager,** Italian Invasion Cycles, Unlimited; Ithaca, NY
Integral member of team that launched domestic operations for Italian bicycle manufacturing consortiums. Established procedures and policies, implemented accounting and payroll systems, and coordinated inventory storage at remote warehouse locations.

1988 - 1992   **Assistant to the General Manager,** ExtraOrdinary Financial Services; Ithaca, NY
Addressed professional and personal needs of General Manager of this top-producing financial planning agency. Maintained personal schedule, coordinated client correspondence, and played a key role in supporting this executive's participation in a wide variety of philanthropic projects and ongoing affiliations.

1986 - 1988   **Assistant Vice President,** Ithaca Regional Hospitals' Cooperative; Ithaca, NY
Supported Vice President in developing and implementing innovative programs to foster cooperation and achieve overall operating efficiencies through sharing of information and collaborative management among twelve regional hospitals.

EDUCATION

1986   **Bachelor of Arts, Romance Languages**
                         Minors: Fine Arts; Economics; Business Administration
Ithaca College; Ithaca, New York
GPA: 3.98 / 4.00

1984   William Smith College; Geneva, New York
Completed two years of study before matriculating to Ithaca College.
GPA: 4.00 / 4.00

PROFESSIONAL DEVELOPMENT & OTHER SKILLS

Total Quality Management Training (Tompkins County).
Microsoft Office – extensive training & experience.
"Innovative Special Events: Developing the Perfect Idea and Planning the Perfect Event" (Association of Fundraising Professionals, previously National Society of Fund Raising Executives)
Knowledge of HTML, FrontPage and DreamWeaver.
Interviewing Skills & Strategies (Ithaca Chamber of Commerce).
Developing Mission & Vision (Institute for Non-Profit Organization Management).
Extensive expertise in a wide range of arts and crafts including painting; knitting; various techniques in rubber stamping; weaving; calligraphy; doll-making; basket weaving; and creative cake-decorating.

Serena L. Montoya

732 Lafayette Circle ♦ Ithaca, New York 14850 ♦ 607.596.7363 ♦

E-mail: Serena.Montoya@Earthnet.net

Personal and Professional References

Rebecca J. Travanti
President, Advisory Board
American Red Cross of the Panorama Valley
617.823.4069
Becky@aol.com

Jared VandenBruhl
Manager, Retired
ExtraOrdinary Financial Services
617.216.5518
JVB@cs.com

Alexander H. Patrick
IT Consultant
(Former Owner, Laptop Systems)
716.518.2918
AHPatrick@buffalo.rr.com

Resume Writer: Gail Smith Boldt

Will Jackson

532 West 30th Street, New York, NY 10017
212-123-2458 (home)
917-345-6778 (cell)
willjackson@gmail.net

Clients & Key Associates
· Laurence Olivier, *Actor*
· Jack Welch, *CEO*
· George Lucas, *Director*
· Stephen Sondheim, *Composer*
· Dan Akroyd, *Actor*

◙

"Will is intelligent and gracious. If he were willing to relocate to San Francisco, I would hire him in an instant."
George Lucas
Film Director
San Francisco, California

◙

"Among the most industrious and capable employees we have ever had."
Jack Welch, CEO, Retired
General Electric
Fairfield, Connecticut

◙

Wrote article published in *Gentleman's Quarterly* (June 2004) entitled, "All About Olivier"

◙

Technical Proficiencies
· Type 65+ wpm
· Microsoft Word
· Microsoft Outlook
· PC / Mac
· Dictation
· Bookkeeping

PERSONAL EXECUTIVE ASSISTANT • ADMINISTRATIVE MANAGER

Accomplished administrative professional with outstanding record of contributing to productive and efficient management of dynamic and high-profile individuals. Dedicated to translating individual values into deliverable objectives for over 20 years.

PROFESSIONAL SUMMARY

Administration & Planning
- Plan international and domestic travel and meetings arrangements including hotel, air / ground travel, and meal reservations.
- Provide personal assistant services to visiting guests (clients and colleagues).
- Arrange for complimentary theater, ballet, and opera tickets.
- Organize dinner parties, receptions and other special events. Oversee caterers, florists, musicians, security, and limousine services.

Operations & Finances
- Manage corporate office and subsidiary real estate holdings.
- Administer deposits and reconciliations for multiple corporate accounts.
- Coordinate day-to-day operations; manage office scouting / relocations.
- Oversee care and upkeep of personal residences.

Communications / Correspondence
- Draft and revise business agreements and contracts.
- Compose letters on behalf of executives and celebrities.
- Manage calendar; field phone calls; take dictation; select gifts.

Business Development & Client Relations
- Managed all aspects of client accounts; prospected new business.
- Polished and pitched six successful proposals on behalf of advertising design firm to Los Angeles-based studios. *Resulted in six design contracts for movies including Terminator I and II, Pumpkin, and Aussies Down Under.*

WORK HISTORY

Advertising Sales, Freestyle Communications; New York, NY	2004 - 2007
Personal Assistant, Charlotte Rampling; New York, NY	2002 - 2004
Executive Assistant to CEO, Sam Advertising; New York, NY	1987 - 2002
Personal Assistant to Jack Welch, GE; Fairfield, CT	1984 - 1987
Actor, *As the World Turns,* CBS; New York, NY	1982 - 1984
Personal Assistant, Sir Laurence Olivier; Los Angeles, CA	1975 - 1979

EDUCATION

Bachelor of Arts, English, 1984
State University of New York (SUNY), Stony Brook, New York

Resume Writer: Jared Redick

AMY ATKINS

Dynamic childcare provider with a wealth of experience, a creative, engaging style, and a passion for making a difference in the growth and development of children.

SUMMARY OF QUALIFICATIONS

- Accomplished nanny with more than 20 years of experience caring for children.
- Distinctive background that includes comprehensive two-year training program in England.
- Solid foundation in all aspects of infant and toddler care.
- Practiced in recognizing childhood ailments. Trained in first aid and CPR.
- Highly organized. Easily able to meet the multifaceted needs of multiple-child families.
- Creative in planning and coordinating age-appropriate activities that capture the imagination of children and maintain their interest. Abundantly patient and caring. Dedicated to the needs of the whole family.
- Flexible and accommodating. Easily able to adjust to a variety of family dynamics.
- Appreciated for ability to fulfill children's needs while bringing a sense of organization to the entire household.

CAREER HIGHLIGHTS

Basic Care

- Accumulated extensive experience as a nanny for four different families, establishing reputation for exceptional care and service. Known for going "above and beyond" to meet family needs.
- Entrusted with the care of children of all ages – from infants to preteens. Consistently provide stimulating environment, engaging children in age-appropriate activities that foster growth and development.
- Effectively coordinate busy schedules, chauffeuring children to various activities, while planning and preparing home-cooked meals. Established strong record in making mealtime a pleasure by involving children in kitchen activities.
- Systematically chart infant activity to provide a record of information and progress to parents. Potty-trained babies. Resolved colic problems for one child by varying formula until stomach distress disappeared.
- Always instill strong values and good manners in children. Use trips and activities, such as eating at family restaurants, as opportunities to reinforce proper behavior.

Beyond the Basics

- Traveled with family on extended car trip, managing all details related to children's needs. Organized loading and unloading to maximize time for enjoyment. Kept twin infants entertained and quiet, while finding time to play with three-year old.
- Flexible and accommodating, staying over with children during parent vacations. While in charge, dealt with all issues including emergency doctor visits due to illness.
- Highly-regarded and asked to relocate to remain with children; moved to provide continuity of care services.
- Step in for traveling mom as needed, creating Halloween costumes, baking cupcakes for school parties, organizing play groups and classes.
- Researched nursery schools for parents, identifying one that met the specific needs of family.
- Explored surrounding areas to find activities and play opportunities for child when no neighborhood opportunities were available.

Activities Planning & Coordination

- Introduced fun, new activities to draw on children's individual interest. For example, organized fossil-making activity; sewed clothes for dress-up play; planned nature walks to encourage learning.
- Drawing on creativity and resourcefulness, guided children in making stained-glass ornaments from crayons and wax paper.
- Planned exciting day trips to the zoo, museums, or places of special interest to nuture each individual child's particular love.
- Arranged full schedule of summer activities for children, precluding the need to send them to camp.

33 VILLAGE SQUARE   ◆   FRENCHTOWN, NJ 08825
(908) 537-3355 HOME   ◆   (908) 642-1883 CELL   ◆   AATKINS@AOL.COM

Resume Writer: Carol Altomare

Special Projects for Special Interests

- For a "Thomas-the-Tank-Engine" enthusiast, created train track layout from cardboard box, painting tracks and scenery, and adding tube tunnels. Layout became a valued, frequently played-with treasure.
- For American Girl doll lover, fashioned four-poster bed out of wood, making pillows and covers that proved more precious than expensive, commercial beds.
- For colonial days enthusiast, obtained loom in order to learn weaving. Also led colonial peg doll projects.
- For the fashion conscious, spent two days carefully braiding hair with beads, creating a special, stylish look.

EXPERIENCE

DODD FAMILY, Rocky Hill, New Jersey   Apr 2004 to Present
Nanny
Provide daytime care for three children: three-year-old twins and a five-year old. Prepare lunch and dinner. Travel with family as requested.
- Oversee many arts and crafts projects, effectively channeling energy of older child.
- Traveled with family on month-long car trip. Organized packing and kept children entertained during drives.

WESTON FAMILY, Princeton, New Jersey   May 2000 to Mar 2004
Nanny
Cared for two girls through their early childhood years. Handled all meals, organized activities, helped with schoolwork, and coordinated busy schedules.
- Filled in as needed for mom who frequently traveled. Put together last-minute Halloween costumes, made cupcakes for birthday parties at school, found recreational classes for girls, organized play group.
- Researched nursery schools, identifying one that met the needs of the family.

PUCCI FAMILY, Frenchtown, New Jersey   Nov 1996 to May 2000
Nanny
Attended to two children from infancy through preschool years. Handled meals and organized activities.
- Provided for all needs of infants, charting activity as reference for parents. Potty-trained older child.
- Drawing on his love of dinosaurs, planned trips to the museum and library to expand the curiosity and knowledge of the older child.

TENNYSON FAMILY, High Bridge, New Jersey   Apr 1987 to Oct 1996
Nanny
Cared for two children from infancy through preteen years. Planned and prepared all meals, organized activities, helped with schoolwork, coordinated busy schedules.
- Arranged full schedule of summer activities as an alternative to camp.
- Organized age-appropriate trips and activities that often including the children's friends.
- Stayed with children during parent vacations, effectively handling all issues including illness and other health problems.

EDUCATION

NEWBURGH COMMUNITY COLLEGE, Newburgh, England
Completed two-year Nursery Training Program.

Completed 60 credits of coursework toward Bachelor of Science degree in Psychology.

SPECIAL SKILLS

Infant care, Potty training, Cooking, Knitting, Sewing, Painting, Arts & crafts, Travel planning and preparations.

Georgia Harkness-Smith

87 Raintree Avenue, Apt. 112   Toronto, Ontario M2M 6X9   (416) 268-9121

A nurturing and compassionate healthcare professional
dedicated to improving the quality of life for the elderly.

SUMMARY

- ❖ Excellent people skills: easily develop positive relationships; nurturing and kind
- ❖ Promote safety, cleanliness, and independence with special patient groups
- ❖ Innovative problem-solver; proficient in resolving conflicts
- ❖ Proven ability to work cooperatively within inter-disciplinary teams
- ❖ *Recognized by employer with Friend of Seniors award for dedicated service*

EXPERIENCE

MYRTLE PARK Home Care Agency, *Toronto, Ontario, Canada   Jan. 2003 to Present*
- ❖ Assist clients (elderly and recuperating) with daily living activities including hygiene and nutrition
- ❖ Provide engaging companionship
- ❖ Ensure clean, safe and comfortable environment
- ❖ Teach basic mobility, exercise and strengthening techniques

CLINICAL PRACTICE

- ❖ **Community Seniors Home**, *Toronto, Ontario, Canada* (180 hours pre-graduate experience)
- ❖ **Blessed Hearts Lodge**, *Toronto, Ontario, Canada* (200-hour Supervised Practicum)

EDUCATION & TRAINING

- ❖ **PSW Certificate**, *Seneca College, Yorkgate Campus, May 2002*
- ❖ **Supporting the Geriatric Patient** (10-day Refresher Course)
- ❖ Current CPR & First Aid Certification
- ❖ Knowledge of American Sign Language

VOLUNTEER ACTIVITIES

- ❖ Meals-on-Wheels Team Toronto, serving 80+ shut-ins per week *2005 – Present*
- ❖ East Side Seniors' Advisory Council   *2000 – 2007*

Resume Writer: Daisy Wright

Sheren Hendersen
22 Dakota Street
Wellington, WA 98333-2222
(306) 289-4104
E-mail: Sheren@gmail.net

HOUSEKEEPER

"...an absolute model of calm efficiency, adaptability, general competence..." - Private Employer, Washington

"...remarkable job managing an extremely high-pressure job with a limited budget and staff...quite conscientious and demonstrates personal pride in her work...a self-starter...very good at dealing with conflicting demands of the job...."   - Operations Manager, Bay Resort

PROFILE

Professional housekeeper with well-established reputation for reliability, follow-through, and commitment to providing excellent service. High-energy worker; hands-on management style with proven ability to organize, delegate and direct the work of others as appropriate. Creative problem-solver who consistently exercises good judgment and keeps a clear head in times of crisis. Easily establish rapport and cooperative, productive working relationships with employers, colleagues and guests of all ages. Traveled extensively throughout United States.

AREAS OF EXPERTISE

✓ Housekeeping: State-of-the-art cleaning procedures with experience in hotels, motels, lodges, private homes, and medical offices
✓ Staff Supervision: Interview, hire, motivate, organize, schedule, train, and evaluate housekeeping staff
✓ Crisis Management: Fully trained in emergency procedures (fire, flood, blood-borne pathogens, etc.)
✓ CPR / First Aid Certification
✓ Inventory Management: Stock and order linens, cleaning supplies and equipment as appropriate
✓ Budget Management: Develop accurate projections and work within established guidelines

SUMMARY OF EXPERIENCE

Executive Housekeeper, Bay Village, Inc., Okay, Washington   1995 – Present
• Oversee daily cleaning and maintenance of 38 cabins, four public areas including restrooms and shower houses, and guest kitchen.
• Interview, hire, train, schedule, motivate and supervise housekeeping staff.
• Inspect all cabins and public areas twice daily — before and after cleaning.
• Manage linen supply (wash, dry, fold, and restock); ensure continuous, adequate supply of hot tub towels; bundle for delivery to outside laundry; monitor quality.
• Select and order cleaning supplies.
• Administer departmental budget; review monthly expense reports and plan accordingly to continue to meet budget targets

Assistant Manager, Hoot Owl Lodge, Gato, Alaska   Winter 1994 – 1995
Oversaw housekeeping for this busy, well-attended lodge in remote area of Alaska: log cabin with bar, restaurant, game area, and six guest cabins. Tended bar and cooked meals on as-needed basis. Managed inventory (limited supply deliveries). Operated snowmobile.

Executive Housekeeper, Bellingham Travel Lodge, Wellington, Washington   1992 –1993
Managed daily housekeeping-related assignments, including cleaning, inspection, and laundry for 115 guest rooms. Substituted for front desk clerk as necessary.

EDUCATION

Valley College—Business Machines
Wellington County Vocation School—Word Processing / Secretarial coursework

Resume Writer: Janice Sheperd

Rodney Jessup

P.O. Box 950, Beverly Hills, CA 90213 ■ Voice Mail: (1-800) 998-6482 Ext. 6348

Estate Manager

Versatile professional with excellent track record of coordinating and overseeing domestic requirements and amenities for elite households. Areas of effectiveness include:

- Roof-to-basement repair work including carpentry, electrical, plumbing / heating / air conditioning systems, and small appliances.
- Maintenance of automobiles, yard, pool, and other recreational facilities.
- Horticulture: indoor and outdoor plant care.
- Full range of animal care from house pets to horses.
- Planning and organizing comprehensive project details for dinner parties and other social events for adults, adolescents and young children.
- Interior design: knowledge of fabrics, furnishings and decorating accessories; especially familiar with contemporary and French country styles as well as English antiques.
- Highly proficient in Microsoft Office Suite; Internet; Various proprietary PDAs including Blackberry and Bluetooth.
- Exercise the utmost tact, discretion and respect for clients' privacy.

Related Experience

2006–Present **Estate Manager** for properties of an Academy Award-winning actor.
(Interim substitute while permanent incumbent recovers from serious accident)

- Maintain two houses on five acres of land with a 60,000-sq. ft. lawn.
- Vigorously protect privacy of well-known actor, securing property to discourage paparazzi and other intruders.
- Perform all housekeeping and maintenance duties, including caring for guard dogs and maintaining automobiles.
- Manage employer's schedules, routines, and a variety of personal services.
- Hire, fire, and direct activities of other domestic staff and occasional maintenance workers according to employer's exacting preferences.
- During employer's absences, apprise him of important mail and phone messages.
- Manage household bank account (deposits, bill paying, and reconciliation).
- Designed and supervised construction of a 1,500-sq. ft. dog kennel and adjoining shed.

2005–2006 **Domestic Caretaker** at residence of Mr. and Mrs. Ashley Bertrand, a socially prominent couple in Charleston, SC
(8 month-assignment, until Charleston property was sold and family relocated to Cuernavaca, Mexico)

- Enhanced value of property by completing numerous repairs and maintenance projects within the home and elaborate gardens this on three-acre property to increase its market value prior to listing for sale.
- Carried out daily feeding and grooming of family's prize racehorses.

Resume Writer: Melanie Noonan

- Assisted with kitchen activities, which included organizing and serving formal dinner parties for up to 36 guests.

2000-2005   **Detail Carpenter** for Prestige Development Corporation, Charleston, SC
(General contracting firm specializing in custom restorations of antebellum mansions)
- Learned high quality woodworking techniques from expert craftsmen, primarily constructing built-in cabinets.
- Honed home repair skills while working after hours and on weekends at the request of homeowners.
- Recruited to join household of the Bertrands, carpentry clients who were favorably impressed with my work.

Education

2000   Honors graduate of Charleston Vocational-Technical Institute
Building trades curriculum

Excellent references will be provided, attesting to highest standards of conduct and integrity.

Appendix A

Resume Writing Worksheet

You can use this handy worksheet as a guide to gathering the critical information you will need to develop your resume. If you wish, you may copy these sheets to capture more of your work history:

NAME _____

ADDRESS _____

CITY_____STATE_____ZIP_____

PHONE (Home): _____(Cell): _____

E-mail Address:_____

CAREER OBJECTIVE(S): 1) _____
                              2)_____

EMPLOYMENT HISTORY:

FROM: ____/___ TO: ____/___ JOB TITLE: _____

COMPANY:_____CITY:_____STATE:_____

KEY DUTIES: _____

_____

_____

_____

_____

ACCOMPLISHMENTS:

_____

_____

_____

_____

_____

MILITARY SERVICE: FROM: ____/___ TO: ____/___

BRANCH: _____ RANK: _____

SPECIALTY (MOS):_____UNIT: _____

COMMENDATIONS: _____

_____

_____

EDUCATION:

SCHOOL: _____ GRAD. (SEP.) ___ / ___

DEGREE: _____ MAJOR: _____

LOCATION: _____

SIGNIFICANT COURSE WORK:

_____

HONORS/CLUBS: _____

(Use additional sheets to capture other degrees, diplomas, etc.)

PROFESSIONAL LICENSES / CERTIFICATIONS:

_____

PROFESSIONAL SEMINARS:

_____

_____

_____

COMPUTER SKILLS: TECHNICAL SKILLS:

_____   _____

_____   _____

_____   _____

FOREIGN LANGUAGES:

_____

MEMBERSHIPS / AFFILIATIONS:

_____

_____

_____

VOLUNTEER WORK / COMMUNITY INVOLVEMENT:

_____

PUBLICATIONS / PUBLIC SPEAKING:

_____

_____

_____

OTHER HONORS & AWARDS:

_____

This worksheet is only intended to be used as a guide. After reading Chapters 2 and 3, you may think of other sections to add that will be important for you to include, or you may decide that some sections are not relevant to your situation.

Appendix B
Keywords—Keying in on Your Strengths

Entire volumes have been written on the importance of keywords and keyword phrases in developing a powerful resume. Caution: Although it is vital that your resume contain keywords which demonstrate your value to the targeted prospective employer, as with so many good things, it's quite possible—and easy—to overdo it. Take care that you avoid littering your job search documents with keywords merely for the sake of including them; you must demonstrate that you have the "steak" to justify the "sizzle." The truth is that these industry-specific buzzwords are only truly effective if they reflect actual skills and abilities that you bring to the table, which, in turn, are supported by the training and/or experience shown on your resume. That's why the best approach here is for you to discover your own keywords; plucking them from a list risks their not being current and/or truly relevant to your target field. This is especially true for the job seekers this book is intended to help—those pursuing unique career paths or with unconventional employment histories.

The very best source for keywords that will truly resonate with your targeted prospective employer is the job posting itself. Carefully examine the employer's requirements in each of several postings for positions that appeal to you. You should soon detect a recurring pattern in the terms those employers choose to describe the ideal candidate. Look for the terms that also reflect your own strengths—these will become your keywords. The newspaper classifieds, the Internet, or your networking contacts (who may have connections to positions similar to your job target) are all good sources for this information.

Additional quality sources for current and relevant keywords include professional associations and other organizations in your target industry. Chambers of commerce, colleges, universities, technical training facilities with related programs, and public libraries can be valuable resources in your quest for keywords. Search the Internet for current articles and other postings related to your target industry, and identify keywords most relevant to your skills and abilities. These will be the field-specific words and phrases that reappear consistently throughout these documents. Integrate these keywords into your resume.

Typically, most keywords are nouns and noun phrases. As mentioned in Chapter 2, however, it's also vital to use the appropriate action verbs properly in order to portray yourself as a dynamic, capable individual who is prepared for the challenges of the target job. Be sure to lead with positive, targeted action verbs without repeating yourself. For example, notice how "took over failing territory and turned around the department that was losing money" becomes so much more compelling when expressed as "revitalized sales territory and ignited revenue growth; drove profitability from -5% to 18% in first 10 months."

Following are just a few examples of other resources for developing your own unique list of keywords:

- *www.jobweb.com* offers a variety of other job search resources. *www.jobweb.com/Career_Development/prof_assoc.htm* takes you directly to their list of professional associations.
- The Occupational Outlook Handbook, *www.bls.gov/oco* lists hundreds of different occupations by job title. With complete job descriptions, this is a tremendous resource for keywords, as well as a valuable tool for researching whether you are interested in a certain field or profession.

For senior level candidates, these sites can prove most helpful in both researching opportunities and discovering the right keywords:

- *www.kennedyinfo.com*
- *www.execunet.com*
- *www.RiteSite.com*

Appendix C
List of Contributors

The following professional resume writers have contributed their best resumes to this publication. All have years of experience in professional resume writing, and many have earned distinguishing professional credentials, including:

CARW	Certified Advanced Resume Writer
CCM	Credentialed Career Master
CCMC	Certified Career Management Coach
CCTJ	Certified Career Transition Jumpmaster
CDFT	Career Development Facilitator Training
CEIP	Certified Employment Interview Professional
CERW	Certified Expert Resume Writer
CHRP	Certified Human Resources Professional
CIS	Certified Interview Strategist
CLBF	Certified Life Blueprint Facilitator
CMF	Certified Fellow Practitioner
CMP	Certified Management Professional
CPBS	Certified Personal Brand Strategist
CPC	Certified Personnel Consultant
CPRW	Certified Professional Resume Writer
CRS	Certified Resume Strategist
CTMS	Certified Transition Management Seminars
CTSB	Certified Targeted Small Business

CWDP	Certified Workforce Development Professional
FIRO-BR	Fundamental Interpersonal Relations Orientation—Behavior Assessments
FRWCC	Federal Resume Writer and Career Coach
GCDF	Global Career Development Facilitator
IJCTC	International Job and Career Transition Coach
JCTC	Job and Career Transition Coach
MBTI	Myers-Briggs Temperament Instrument (certification)
MCC	Master Career Counselor
MCDP	Master Career Development Professional
NCC	Nationally Certified Counselor
NCCC	Nationally Certified Career Coach
NCRW	Nationally Certified Resume Writer
PHR	Professional in Human Resources
RPR	Registered Professional Recruiter

Tom Albano, CARW
All Star Career Services
Lake Hiawatha, NJ
Tom@allstarcareer.com
973-387-0134
www.AllStarCareer.com

Carol Altomare, CPRW
World Class Résumés
Flemington, NJ
carol@worldclassresumes.com
www.worldclassresumes.com
908-237-1883

Deanne Arnath, CPRW
A Résumé Wizard & Services
Arlington, TX
deanne@aresumewizard.com
www.aresumewizard.com
866-422-0800

Susan Barens, CPRW, IJCTC
Career Dynamics
Olmsted Falls, OH
Careerdynamics1@aol.com
440-610-4361

Karen Bartell, CPRW
Best-in-Class Résumés
Massapequa Park, NY
Kbarteil@bestclassresumes.com
www.bestclassresumes.com
631-704-3220
800-234-3569

Laurie Berenson, CPRW
Sterling Career Concepts, LLC
Park Ridge, NJ
laurie@sterlingcareerconcepts.com
www.sterlingcareerconcepts.com
201-573-8282

Shannon D. Branson, CPRW, CEIP
El Paso, TX
sgriffin24@hotmail.com
678-643-2627

Dawn S. Bugni, CPRW
The Write Solution
Atkinson, NC
dawnbugni@thewritesolution.info
www.thewritesolution.info
910-540-0544

Heather Carson, CPRW, GCDF, JCTC, CWDP
Second Start
Rochester, NH
hcarson@second-start.org
www.second-start.org
603-344-8076

Clay Cerny, PhD
AAA Targeted Writing & Coaching Services
Chicago, IL
info@aaatargeted.com
www.aaatargeted.com
773-907-8660

Nicole Darby, PHR, MBTI, FIRO-BR
Career CAFE (Career Alterations For Everyone)
Decatur, GA
darby-n@bellsouth.net
www.yourcareercafe.com
404-219-1639

Eileen M. Davis
Assistant Director of Career Development
College of Business
University of Louisville
Louisville, KY
eileen.davis@louisville.edu
www.business.louisville.edu/careers
502-852-7756

Jeri Hird Dutcher, CPRW
Workwrite
East Grand Forks, MN
jeri@workwrite.biz
www.workwrite.biz
218-791-4045

Robyn L. Feldberg, CCMC
Abundant Success Career Services
Frisco, TX
Robyn@AbundantSuccessCareerServices.com
www.AbundantSuccessCareerServices.com
866-WIN-AJOB (946-2562)

Cliff Flamer, CPRW, NCRW, NCC
BrightSide Résumés
Oakland, CA
writers@brightsideresumes.com
www.brightsideresumes.com
877-668-9767
510-444-1724

Louise Garver, CPRW, MCDP, JCTC, CLBF, CPBS, CEIP, CMP
Career Directions, LLC
Broad Brook, CT
LouiseGarver@cox.net
www.CareerDirectionsLLC.com
860-623-9476

Jill Grindle, CPRW
A Step Ahead Résumé
Agawam, MA
jill@astepaheadresume.com
www.astepaheadresume.com
413-789-6046

Sheri S. Hawes, CPRW
Clarksville, MD
Sherihawes@hotmail.com
410-707-7323

Andrea Howard
New York State Department of Labor
Albany, NY
USAAH3@labor.state.ny.us
www.labor.state.ny.us
518-462-7600 x 124

Billie P. Jordan
Advantage Résumés and Career Services
Maysville, NC
bjordan1@ec.rr.com
www.advantageresumes4you.com
910-743-3641

Barbara D. Kanney
ABC Distinguished Documents
Massillon, OH
bkanney@abcdocuments.com
www.abcdocuments.com
330-834-0182

Erin Kennedy, CPRW
Professional Résumé Services
Lapeer, MI
ekennedy@proreswriters.com
www.proreswriters.com
866-793-9224

Myriam-Rose Kohn, CPRW, CEIP, IJCTC,
CCM, CCMC, CPBS
JEDA Enterprises
Valencia, CA
myriam-rose@jedaenterprises.com
www.jedaenterprises.com
661-253-0801

Brian Leeson
Vector Consultants Pty Ltd
Echunga, South Australia
Australia
brian@vectorconsultants.com.au
+61 8 8388 8183

Sharon McCormick, CPRW, MCC, NCC
Career & Vocational Counseling Services
Durham, NC
careertreasure@gmail.com
www.careertreasureonline.com
919-424-1244

Beverley Neil, CRW, CERW
d'Scriptive Words
Queensland, Australia
beverley@d-scriptivewords.com
www.onlineresumewriterscourse.com
+61 7 3820 8051

Sandy Neumann
Best Résumés Win
Fernandina Beach, FL
sandy@bestresumeswin.com
www.bestresumeswin.com
904-509-2253

Melanie Noonan
Peripheral Pro, LLC
West Paterson, NJ
PeriPro1@aol.com
973-785-3011

David G. Phreaner, DMin
Working Futures
Rochester, NH
dphreaner@second-start.org
www.second-start.org
603-335-6847

Kris Plantrich, CPRW, CEIP
RésuméWonders
Ortonville, MI
support@resumewonders.com
www.resumewonders.com
248-627-2624
888-789-2081

Julie Rains, CPRW
Executive Correspondents
Clemmons, NC
jsrains@gmail.com
www.WorkingToLive.com
336-712-2390

Jared Redick
The Résumé Studio
San Francisco, CA
jredick@theresumestudio.com
www.TheResumeStudio.com
415-846-6640

Jane Roqueplot, CPBA, CWDP, CECC
JaneCo's Sensible Solutions
Sharon, PA
jane@janecos.com
www.janecos.com
888-JANECOS (888-526-3267)
724-342-0100

Jennifer Rushton, CARW, CEIC
Keraijen Certified Résumé Writer
Sydney, Australia
info@keraijen.com.au
www.keraijen.com.au
+61 2 9994 8050

Barbara Safani, CPRW, NCRW, CERW, CCM
Career Solvers
New York, NY
info@careersolvers.com
www.careersolvers.com
866-333-1800

Kimberly Schneiderman, NCRW, CEIC
City Career Services
New York, NY
kimberly@citycareerservices.com
www.citycareerservices.com
917-584-3022

Janice M. Shepherd, CPRW, JCTC, CEIP
Write On Career Keys
Bellingham, WA
Janice@writeoncareerkeys.com
www.writeoncareerkeys.com
360-738-7958

Joanne Fasolo Shugrue, CPRW, GCDF
Hartford CT Works
Connecticut Department of Labor
Hartford, CT
joanne.shugrue@ct.gov
www.ctdol.state.ct.us
860-256-3688

Bob Simmons
Career Transition Associates (CTA)
Plainview, NY
Bob@ctajobsearch.com
www.ctajobsearch.com
516-501-0717

Denise Sleeper, GCDF, NAWDP
Working Futures
Laconia, NH
dsleeper@second-start.org
www.second-start.org
603-228-1341

Gail Smith Boldt
Arnold-Smith Associates
Gail@ResumeSOS.com
www.ResumeSOS.com
585-383-0350

Tanya Taylor, CRS, CHRP
TNT Human Resources Management
Toronto, Ontario, Canada
info@tntresumewriter.com
www.tntresumewriter.com
416-887-5819

Claudine Vainrub, CPRW, CPBS
EduPlan, LLC
Aventura, FL
info@eduplan.us
www.eduplanweb.com
888-661-8234
786-547-9339

Nancy Walkup, CPRW, CCMC
Walkup Career Management, LLC
Fenton, MI
info@walkupcareermanagement.com
www.walkupcareermanagement.com
810-252-9907

Barbara L. Warren, CPRW, CDFT, CWDP
Second Start
Concord, NH
bwarren@second-start.org
www.second-start.org
603-882-9080 Ext. 240

Pearl White, CPRW, JCTC, CEIP
A 1st Impression Résumé Service
Irvine, CA
pearlwhite1@cox.net
www.a1stimpression.com
949-651-1068

Beth Woodworth, CWDP, JCTC
Career Innovations
Redding, CA
bethwoodworth@sbcglobal.net
www.career-innovations.org
530-604-4347

Daisy Wright, CDP
The Wright Career Solution
Brampton, Ontario, Canada
careercoach@thewrightcareer.com
www.thewrightcareer.com
www.nocanadianexperience-eh.com
905-840-7039

Index

About the Author

Arnie Boldt could easily fit into several of the categories covered in this book. He is self-employed, has changed careers a couple of times, and, yes, has a few career gaps thrown in for good measure. After experiencing his own downsizing in 1994, he explored a number of options before partnering with his wife, Gail Smith Boldt, to form Arnold-Smith Associates, which has helped thousands of job seekers in transition. Since then, he has honed his skills to become recognized as one of the premier resume writers in the country. Coauthor of *No-Nonsense Resumes* and *No-Nonsense Cover Letters* (both published by Career Press), he has also contributed to more than 40 books on resume writing and job-search topics.

He is a five-time TORI (Toast of the Resume Industry) Awards nominee in the categories of best creative resume (twice), best cover letter (twice), and best return-to-work resume. He has spoken on resume-related topics to groups in the healthcare and manufacturing fields, and delivered presentations developed for older workers and for executives in transition.

Mr. Boldt holds a bachelor's degree in technical communications from Clarkson University and is a certified professional resume writer and job and career transition coach. He prides himself on his experience working with the broadest array of clients, ranging from trades people and new graduates to seasoned corporate executives. A life-long resident of Upstate New York, he makes his home with his wife and two Chihuahuas in a suburb of Rochester.